MONEY INTO LIGHT

MONEY INTO LIGHT

THE EMERALD FOREST

A DIARY
JOHN BOORMAN

FOREWORD BY PHILIP FRENCH

faber and faber
LONDON · BOSTON

First published in 1985
by Faber and Faber Limited
3 Queen Square London WC1N 3AU

Printed in Great Britain by
Butler & Tanner Ltd, Frome and London
Designed by The Small Back Room

British Library Cataloguing in Publication Data
Boorman, John, *1933*–
    Money into light: a diary.
    1. Boorman, John, *1933*–   2. Moving-picture
    producers and directors—Biography
    I. Title
    791.43'0233'0924   PN1998.A3B6

ISBN 0-571-13731-8

For TAKUMA
Shaman of the KAMAIRA

CONTENTS

FOREWORD

PHILIP FRENCH

The Magic Circle, I believe, swears its members to secrecy. No such restraints have ever been imposed upon their fellow illusionists and conjurors in the cinema. Film-makers have always been ready to share the tricks of their trade by way of interviews, books, documentaries and films. Even before the arrogant young Scott Fitzgerald informed the middle-aged D. W. Griffith in 1920 that the most interesting subject for the movies was the movie business itself, directors had started making pictures on the film-making process. Few have completely resisted the temptation. John Boorman, for instance, in his feature film début, *Catch Us If You Can*, chose to transform the Dave Clark Five into a team of stuntmen, though this may have been because he despaired of making them plausible as musicians.

Certainly since *Cleopatra* in the early 1960s, but possibly as early as Griffith's *Intolerance*, there has been the phenomenon of a film's production with its attendant *Sturm und Drang* being of greater significance than the final outcome. *Apocalypse Now!* and *Heaven's Gate* went some way towards institutionalizing this. The definitive state was reached when Werner Herzog visited the Amazon a couple of years ahead of John Boorman to make *Fitzcarraldo*. The journeys that avant-garde artists like Richard Long and Hamish Fulton take are the works of art; the photographs, maps and rocks they subsequently exhibit in galleries are merely a colourful form of evidence. By the same token, Les Blank's documentary, *The Burden of Dreams*, is far more valuable as a record of the true art-work – i.e. Herzog's heroic struggles filming along the Amazon – than the final muffled feature film. Appropriately *The Burden of Dreams* and *Fitzcarraldo* were unveiled on the same day at the 1982 Cannes Festival, and the former judged the more authentic. Unquestionably, making pictures is a great adventure for John Boorman too; but I am happy to say that interesting as it is, his diary remains an appendage to the completed film.

I am not sure who was the first director to write a book on the making of a film. Robert Flaherty's *My Eskimo Friends*, published shortly after the successful launching of *Nanook of the North* in 1923, is certainly one of the earliest and revealed how he had faked various scenes. Since the Second World War we have had Jean Cocteau's *Journal d'un film* on the creation of *La Belle et la bête*; Vilgot Sjöman's *L136: a Diary with Bergman* (on making his first film *The Mistress* and assisting Ingmar Bergman on *Winter Light*); and the journal François Truffaut kept while shooting *Fahrenheit 451* (published in magazines but never collected), whose ranks Boorman's book joins.

These day-by-day accounts – life caught on the wing or the hoof – are of greater value than those more familiar retrospective ones where the memory has re-edited the experience and added additional dialogue. They are also, perhaps, more advisable than giving journalists, however sympathetic, the free run of the set for the duration of the film. These observers invariably prove to be Jonahs – Lindsay Anderson's *Making a Film* chronicled the production at Ealing of *The Secret People*, which proved to be Thorold Dickinson's forgettable final feature; Lillian Ross's *Picture* charted the disastrous course of John Huston's misadventure with MGM, *The Red Badge of Courage*; and, with rather lower initial expectations, Edward Buscombe's *Making Legend of the Werewolf* traced the dispiriting progress of a horror flick Freddie Francis directed for Tyburn Productions.

There are catastrophes, crises, heroes and villains in Boorman's *Emerald Forest* diary to compare with anything in those just mentioned, as well as hints of sexual activities that in the hands of Harold Robbins or Jackie Collins would be the stuff of a raunchy Hollywood novel. Gentlemanly British backers pull the plug at the last moment; tough American businessmen step in to save the day. A trusted friend threatens to scuttle the whole project. The director is forced to ask himself whether a crucial casting decision is wholly objective or influenced by nepotism. All the while he is planning and leading a cultural and economic expedition to Latin America on a scale comparable with, possibly greater than, those undertaken 500 years before him by Cortés and Pizarro, neither of whom had to make daily reports home, consider the delicate sensibilities and complicated laws of the natives, or answer the questions put by his own nagging liberal conscience.

So this is an exciting story, and for anyone remotely interested in the business of movie-making today, a revealing and informative one. Boorman is not a naïve artist venturing into a Hollywood wonderland. He entered the movies after some years spent working within the complex bureaucracy of the BBC. And he has not only made nine feature films, but has also devoted a great deal of time to creating a film industry in Ireland and producing the films of two gifted protégés: *Angel*, directed by the Irish novelist Neil Jordan; and *Nemo*, directed by the young Frenchman, Arnaud Selignac. He understands the film industry and its relationship to the art of the cinema. When Cecilia Brady, the narrator of Fitzgerald's *The Last Tycoon*, claimed that 'Not half a dozen men have ever been able to keep the whole equation of pictures in their heads,' she was perhaps exaggerating the fewness of such people. But Boorman belongs to this small group.

He is, however, also a major cinéaste, an *auteur* who expresses a personal vision and view of the world through the detailed *mise-en-scène* and the totality of his movies. I became aware of this on seeing his second film, *Point Blank*, for it was clearly the work of the man who'd made *Catch Us If You Can* (though a considerable advance on that modest début) and announced certain themes, preoccupations and motifs that have recurred in the subsequent films. In my review of *Point Blank* (*Sight and Sound*, Spring 1968) I noted 'the underlying theme of a disillusioning quest where nothing turns out to be as it seems – and even the conclusion on a deserted island with an ambiguous meeting between pursuer and pursued'. Although I evoked the concept of the knight errant in negatively defining the character played by Lee Marvin, I was unaware at the time of Boorman's obsession with the Grail legend, and I had not noticed that he and his screenwriter, Peter Nichols, had drawn on Malory, if only parodically, for *Catch Us If You Can*. One can see now a clear line of development from these first two pictures through *Hell in the Pacific*, *Leo the Last*, *Deliverance* and *Zardoz* up to *Excalibur* in 1980.

The Emerald Forest is a film that brings him back into the twentieth century and takes him on from *Excalibur*, with a romantic story of the clash between so-called primitive and civilized worlds, of ritual and myth, sympathetic magic, ecological balance, and the conflicting demands of reason and emotion. Once again there is a quest where the seeker becomes the quarry, and in the course of his mission undergoes a transformation. Appropriately, the director's son Charley Boorman, who played the young Mordred, illegitimate son of King Arthur, raised outside Camelot in *Excalibur*, should now be the abducted son of the American engineer brought up by Amazonian Indians in *The Emerald Forest*.

One of the threads running through this diary is of the director holding on to his initial vision while shaping the movie with his scriptwriter, producers, backers, and the team he put together to make it in Brazil. Another is of the co-existence within Boorman of, on the one hand, the instinctive artist with a belief in the revivifying powers of mythology who sympathizes with the Indians and their culture, and, on the other, the level-headed executive, administrator and leader, responsible for a complex operation costing millions of dollars and involving hundreds of people. The investors evidently recognized in Boorman a man they could trust, just as Takuma, the Shaman of the Kamaira tribe, acknowledged an affinity with Boorman the artist – 'You make visions, magic. You are a *paje* like me.'

This visit to Takuma is the most moving section of the book, and for students of Boorman's *oeuvre* it is the most illuminating. Particularly important is the memory the visit triggers, something of which he has not spoken publicly before, of a journey by kayak down the Thames at the age of sixteen. After camping overnight at Runnymede Island, he apparently awoke to find himself in some sort of spiritual communion with the distant past, with the spirit of the numinous place where Magna Carta was signed. I would suppose, though he does not say it, that in Boorman's mind the reign of King John and Magna Carta are subsumed within the romantic vision of medieval life shaped by *Le Morte D'Arthur*. The experience at Runnymede, he says, 'sent me searching for images, through cinema, to try and recapture what I knew that day'. This is as eloquent a description as I know of an epiphany that revealed to someone his or her vocation, and has the mood of an incident in a John Boorman film.

MONEY INTO LIGHT

A DIARY

---

1 JUNE 1982 *EN ROUTE: LONDON-LOS ANGELES*

This is the commuter route of British film-makers: London–LA. We go there cap in hand, scripts in briefcase, hearts on sleeve.

My first time there was in 1965. I had made my first feature film, *Catch Us If You Can*, on leave of absence from the BBC and had then gone back to do my last documentary, which was about D. W. Griffith. The research took me to LA. I rented a car at the airport and drove all the way down Sunset Boulevard, some twenty miles, to the Pacific Ocean. The sun was sinking into the sea through a haze of smog. It looked as phoney as hell. So did the streets. The buildings looked so fake I was amazed to see that the façades had backs to them. I stayed in the Robin Hood Motel in Santa Monica. Opposite was a restaurant with a neon sign proclaiming, THE BROKEN DRUM – YOU CAN'T BEAT IT. It is a silly city.

Twilight is best in LA: magic hour, they call it, and so it is. Is there anything so fine as that coloured neon moving against a garish orange sky as the car glides along with the stereo FM car radio (unknown in Europe then) underscoring it all?

Then there are the grey days. 'There's a fog upon LA,' sang the Beatles. And there is. Most of the time. It seems insubstantial in this light. Streets, people, sky melt into one another. We have all seen the special-effects shot of the Bomb's final arrival: everything frazzles and shimmers and disintegrates. LA, on these grey days, is perpetually caught in the first frame of that shot.

Those perfect California days that are said to follow each other in endless succession actually occur about as frequently as a perfect summer's day in England, that is to say, perhaps fifteen a year. LA weather is a sham, like most things there. The Ocean is always cold. In summer the sun only burns

1

through the mist by 1 pm and is gone again by 4. But I love
the light.

It is so easy to find your way in LA that no one should get
lost, but on that first visit I did all the time. I stumbled upon
gaunt and desolate places. I returned a year later to make
Point Blank. Many of those places found their way into the
film, which is very much a response to the experience of getting lost in LA. *Point Blank* is about betrayal. And LA, for all
its fleshy delights and hedonistic pleasures, is a place that has
betrayed the human spirit, for here one's grip on reality, identity, is subtly loosened. Here one feels what Milan Kundera
calls 'the unbearable lightness of being'. The back lots of the
studios with their Western streets, New York brownstones,
Middle America main streets, seem more solid than the suburbs surrounding them. As reality slips away, and unbearable
lightness takes hold, you must hurry into a movie theatre and
connect with a film. In LA the shadows are more real than
the substance.

We have passed over the desert and the plane is crossing
the San Bernardino mountains. I watch out the window to
catch that wondrous sight of LA stretched out below, the
100-mile city. A plague of smog hangs over it, but it does not
prevent a hundred thousand swimming pools from winking a
welcome. This is the view that finished Khruschev. There
were just too many pools, far too many to belong to the ruling
capitalists who oppress the millions. Clearly the oppressed
millions had them too.

My last film, *Excalibur*, took me three years and more to
make. Since then I have written a script with a young Irish
writer, Neil Jordan, *Broken Dreams*, a strange and beautiful
vision of the end of the world. I have sent it around. No one
will finance it.

I have some other ideas and projects and am here to tour
the Hollywood studios, test the mood, sell my wares.

---

2 JUNE 1982 *LOS ANGELES*

Rospo Pallenberg wrote *Excalibur* with me, and last night he fished out a cutting from the *Los Angeles Times*. He had showed it to me some years back when it first appeared. It was appealing, but other projects intervened. It concerned an actual account of a 7-year-old boy snatched by Indians in Brazil.

I was intrigued that his father, an engineer, would spend every vacation for ten years searching the rain forest for his abducted son. But even more extraordinary, when he found him, an integrated member of an Indian tribe, he elected to leave him there. What had each of them, father and son, become in those ten years? Ten thousand years of human progress divided them. Does blood, kin, reach across that divide?

Between projects, all things are possible. I survey, consider. Once the choice is made I am in harness, chains I would say, for two or three years ... whatever it takes. Rospo can see that I am drawn, tempted. He sits with hands folded across his large middle, a knowing smile on his face; he is waiting as I speculate on the possibilities of the story.

His name is Robert. Rospo was a corruption by a mad aunt on the Roman side of his family. It means 'toad' in Italian. A manic insight – for so he looks. We call the story *The Emerald Forest*.

---

4 JUNE 1982

The idea haunts me. Rospo called. I prevaricated. Edgar Gross, my friend and business partner, and I are touring the studios, touting my ideas. Every two or three years I make this trip, meeting the heads of studios. It is a ritual, and therefore certain forms must be observed. It also has substance, but it takes skill and experience to know what that is at a given moment. For instance, no one ever says 'no'. 'Pass' is the strongest term, but is usually conveyed by a minion, seldom mouthed by the man himself, who is in the business of keeping all his options open. If there are no 'no's, there are many degrees of 'yes'. One must learn to interpret them.

Lunch today at MGM with David Begelman. The guard on the gate still greets me warmly. In 1967 I made *Point Blank* in this studio. Hollywood studios are debilitating, bland, numbing, factory buildings, walled-in, grey and dreary. MGM is the only one with glamour. 'Tara' still stands on the back lot. We enter the Irving Thalberg Building; where Louis B. Mayer once held sway, now sit Freddie Fields and David Begelman. When they were partners in the agency business, they represented me for a time. David is charming, sincere, aloof. He has just moved into the job, the first since being fired from Columbia. The office is blue, cool and very expensive. His domain spans an amalgamated United Artists and MGM. From these Olympian heights he is loath to discuss particular projects. He recommends that I talk to Freddie. There is no hint, no clue, in his manner that this same man forged cheques, lied, wept, in the Columbia saga cruelly documented in the book *Indecent Exposure*.

I reminded Begelman of how he helped me finance *Zardoz*. We were turned down by Warners, for whom I had just made *Deliverance*, and by several other studios. A new management had taken over at Fox, Gordon Stulberg was the boss, with Jere Henshaw as his number two. David chose them because they were hungry for product, and would want the prestige of signing a 'name' director. He stage-managed it beautifully: John will take no fee; Fox will guarantee to buy the finished picture for $1 million; they will have no approvals. Jere Henshaw must fly to London where he will be given the script at International Creative Management's (ICM) office in Grafton Street, will have exactly two hours to read it and make an immediate decision.

Jere flew in, was duly installed in an empty office in which a copy of the script lay on the desk. After two hours he emerged, sweating and shaking. David was as cool and relaxed as ever. When Jere came in, the script dangling in his hands and obviously very undecided, David simply began speaking as though it were all settled. He congratulated Jere and me, his dignified benevolence embracing us both like glue. The moment when Jere could have said 'no' had simply passed.

We walked down the hall from Begelman's to Freddie Field's suite of offices. It had an air of confusion as lovely, perplexed girls, black, blonde, Chinese, crossed and recrossed the reception area, puzzled perhaps at finding themselves peopling Freddie's fantasy world. I told him the story of *The Double*, which is the story of a man whose life is taken over by his *Doppelgänger*. I had sent him my story treatment, but most heads of studio stop reading scripts when they get their jobs and become hostage to the reports of low-paid readers, who are usually young, frustrated film-makers. I began the story, but after two minutes his attention began to wander. He made no effort to conceal this and began shuffling through papers on his desk. I finished the story off with a few quick, broad strokes, and launched into Rospo's story. It met the same fate, although there was a flicker of interest when I touched on the Indians' use of hallucinogens. In a flat, disinterested voice, Freddie said both ideas were terrific and very excit ... (fading away like the last word spoken before falling under an anaesthetic).

John Foreman, an old, dear friend, and a colleague of Freddie's at MGM, had given me a script called *Millennium*, a sci-fi story they wanted to make. I had turned it down. Freddie begged me to reconsider. I said there was a fundamental structural flaw in the story in that it depended on duping the audience into believing that what seemed like the present was, in fact, taking place in the far past. Freddie was affronted. 'Duping the audience, I would never do that.' I said, 'Freddie, what is the "now" of the story?' Magnified by huge lenses, panic rattled his eyes. '*Now* is the *now*,' he said, emphatically. 'It isn't, Freddie. That's what the audience is invited to believe. What seems like "now" is really "then".' Freddie had been in tighter corners than this. He got to his feet. 'For Chrissake, haven't you heard of relativity?' Edgar and I were taken aback, to say the least. 'Time ain't straight, it's curved.' He made an arc in the air and glared at us, trying to shame our ignorance, but we sat firm. He cast about him until his eye caught a chunky ashtray on his desk. 'OK, this ashtray is "now", right?' He seized a paperweight inscribed by a fawning client from the agency days. 'This is the future, right? But when you get there, it's *now*, right? My wife's 10-year-old kid knows that! Einstein!' Edgar has a wonderful line in puzzled innocence. Freddie had made no concrete references to the story, and I began to wonder if he had actually read it, or perhaps forgotten its salient points. He just kept describing it as a $100-million grosser. 'I'm talking rentals,' he said, earnestly, as though he had just been studying the returns. 'Explain it to Edgar,' I said. 'He hasn't read the script.' Got him now, I thought. Freddie was trapped. Edgar looked at him with his special brand of mock innocence. (In fact, he had read the script, but would not let on.) Freddie was shaken, but with a sudden, angry gesture he snarled at us, 'If I had a blackboard I could explain it in a minute', grabbed a piece of imaginary chalk, swung around and drew a curve in the air. 'It's bent! Time is bent! You better believe it! I'm talking a $100 million!'

---

12 JUNE 1982

Rospo has made a 'one liner' – a sequential list of events and scenes in pencil on a sheet of yellow-lined legal paper, an attempt to summarize our rambling talks on *The Emerald Forest*. We go over it and decide to test the story on a couple of studios to see if we can get some money for Rospo to do the research and start on a script. Will it be seen as a concealed Western – anathema at the moment? I can also hear them saying nobody's interested in South America.

---

16 JUNE 1982

We try it on Mike Medavoy at Orion. He financed *Excalibur* and did well by it. They have had a lean time since and are now concentrating on low-budget comedies and the youth market – like most everybody in Hollywood. Medavoy is abrasive and cynical. I knew him as a young ambitious agent. I have always liked him for his brutal honesty. He looks tired and worn, having held the job longer than most incumbents. Studio heads seldom last more than three years, when their failures become apparent. Mike is the best of them. He will back adventurous projects, take chances. I shall always be grateful for his courage in making *Excalibur*.

Rospo tells the story while I interject dramatic descriptions, acting out the scenes. Ten minutes in, Mike starts taking calls and moving around the office. He breaks in: 'I've just had a great idea. One of the Rothschilds – Michael – left the bank and went to Borneo and disappeared. Remember that story? I'm interested in a guy, very successful, finds he's jaded with his work, family; his life is all fouled up with women, wives, analysis – goes off to the rain forest and disappears.'

I said: 'Mike, that's not our story.' I then told him about *The Double*. He was intrigued, but cautious. He was not willing to spend money on developing either piece.

We have tried Fox, the Ladd Company, Columbia – no takers. Lunch with Bob Shapiro of Warners. He likes my story of *The Double* and we agree to develop it together. But he will not go for *The Emerald Forest*. He's not keen on Rospo as a writer. All this lack of enthusiasm from Hollywood encourages me that we are on to something good.

---

20 JUNE 1982

A good day on the story with Rospo thumbing through his library of ethnographic and anthropological research. He is wonderfully sceptical about these experts. He is able to suck it all in and sift it through a fine net of imaginative cynicism. One hopes that a patina of what is poetically true of tribal life will begin to emerge. When I made *Hell in the Pacific*, in the Palauan Archipelago in the South Pacific, I came into contact with tribal life and those experiences have haunted me ever since. So, the argument develops between my limited, but direct, experience of tribal life and Rospo's magisterial *Welt-blick*. I remember the old men in Palau laughing about the outrageous stories they invented to shock visiting anthropologists. Were they spinning fictions or simply enlarging their myth? Fiction is, after all, merely the truth liberated from facts. If a story finds a deep-lasting resonance, then it is probably true, mythologically. Our story must be true and real, moment to moment, but its value must be in expanding our own myth to include our tribal past – the past we left behind without a backward glance. It can have no possible importance to people still living tribal life, except to amuse them.

For all my fascination with Palauan life, the real revelations were to do with our world viewed from their perspective. For them, personal freedom came from each person knowing how to do everything necessary for survival and pleasure, unlike us who are dependent on thousands of people we will never even meet. Tribal people are not dependent on others, yet they have the support and succour of the tribe. We, on the other hand, are not able to survive alone.

At the end of shooting I went with my wife, Christel, and my daughters, Telsche and Katrine – then aged 7 and 8 – to an atoll, Kyangel, and licked my wounds among people whose contact with the outside world was a tramp steamer calling two or three times a year. There we slept in the Abai, viewed the twentieth century from the Stone Age, and became aware of its madness, its grinding pressures, and also its addictive pleasures. Tribal life follows unchanging patterns. I saw that for us, in our world, change is the only imperative: fashion, novelty, progress, news. We crave them. They feed us. Stasis is death and so we hurtle on, faster and faster towards ... what? Bruised and wounded by the rigours of making that film, I contemplated staying on. The healing warmth of the people was like a caress, but I soon longed for movies and marmalade, football results and newspapers, shop windows, and all the other indispensable trivialities of civilization. Film-making is an expression of that neurosis of novelty, that process of inventing impossible problems for oneself and failing to solve them. A film crew of 200 people struggles to overcome these difficulties with desperate seriousness. A colleague of mine, Bill Stair, once said, when we were treating some trivial problem like a major tragedy: 'Wait, it's not a matter of life and death – it's much more serious that.'

Rospo and I have viewed some documentaries on South American Indians: particularly interesting was *The Tribe that Hid from Man*, which was about an expedition trying to connect with an uncontacted tribe in the Amazon. They try to lure them with gift racks of machetes and mirrors, and finally use fireworks to tempt them into the open. That is an alluring notion and will definitely find its way into the script. The astonishing fact is that there are still tribes in the rain forest that no one has made contact with at all.

We debated a thorny problem: language. If we are to enter the Indian world and be close to the characters, we must understand them. Subtitles would distance them. Can we find a solution to this?

JULY 1982 *LONDON*

Dickie Attenborough asked me to meet with him and David Puttnam at Mr Chow's for lunch. They talked about Goldcrest. Would I join them on the board and help to make it a force in the movie world, revitalize British films, etc.? David said nobody had spoken to him since he won an Oscar for *Chariots of Fire*. Lindsay Anderson said, 'I'm very glad for you David. You like that kind of thing.' The English, wallowing in failure, bitterly resent success.

They fired me up with the idea and I gave it my support. I said I had an aversion to formal arrangements, but I would make films with them and urged them to let the thing develop organically. I agreed to meet Jake Eberts, the founder and driving force of Goldcrest, and discuss my projects. We set a further meeting at David's office together with Michael Apted. My lawyer, David Norris, would come to that one. Looking across the rice bowls at these two men, I marvelled at their modesty and geniality. David with his Oscar, Dickie just back from filming his immense *Gandhi*. Do they really care so deeply about the British film industry? David is an enigmatic character (his company is called Enigma Films), of immense charm, adroit and skilful as a producer – a little too good to be true. One cannot escape the suspicion that Dickie is acting out all his roles as mediator, peacemaker, director, chairman, businessman, yet he is redeemed by a true goodness of heart, which drives him to pursue the common good. He has reached

out to me just at the moment I needed it, alone and em-
battled. This is his genius.

I remembered during the looping of *Excalibur* I was lunching with Nicol Williamson at the White Elephant when Dickie
sat down at a nearby table with a group of men who looked
like bankers, businessmen. He was still desperately raising
finance for *Gandhi*. He was playing the role of responsible,
sober producer. Nicol stared across at him with his cold, lac-
erating eyes, then said to me, 'Dickie's disconcerted by me
watching him because *he* knows that *I* know that *he's* just a
fucking actor.' Feeling the real warmth and affection flowing
across to me from Dickie, I felt abashed by these intrusive
thoughts.

What we all yearn for, Dickie, David, I, is a friendly base,
a place of sanity where we can work, knowing that our projects will be backed, knowing that financing will not be
snatched away at any moment, knowing that one can work
steadily among sympathetic people. Most serious film-makers
would forgo their fees for that. That, they assure me, is what
Goldcrest will do.

AUGUST 1982 *ANNAMOE, IRELAND*

Jake stayed the weekend. We played tennis. I took him to
Slane Castle for the Rolling Stones concert. I introduced him
to Mick Jagger, which pleased him no end. I reminded Mick
of a visit he paid to us, in Ireland, some years back. At that
time he was sporting a diamond set into an eye tooth, giving
his smile a sparkle. 'Why do you have a diamond in your
tooth?' asked my daughter Daisy. 'I believe in putting my
money where my mouth is.'

Jake is a fan, a wonderful enthusiast. He is very tall, very
straight, and mouthed the words of most of Mick's old songs.
He takes in everything in an instant – people, situations, relationships. I have given him the script of *Little Nemo*, which
he likes. It is to be directed by a young Frenchman, Arnaud
Selignac. I aim to help Arnaud make it, acting as a teacher
rather than a producer, as I did with Neil Jordan in *Angel*.

Jake shied away from *Broken Dreams*, the script Neil and I
wrote, and which was rejected by every American major. I
told him the story of *The Emerald Forest* and he is intrigued.
We agreed to meet with Rospo in Los Angeles. We will tell
him the story, in detail, and if he likes it Goldcrest will finance
the script.

---

5 NOVEMBER 1982 *LOS ANGELES*

Staying at Malibu with my dear friend, Bob Chartoff. We
met Jake at Edgar's house. Rospo and I make our presenta-
tion. Jake had wanted only to pay for a treatment rather than
a script. We wanted to go straight into a script. A compromise
was reached, whereby we would present a spoken treatment
rather than a written one. Rospo and I were opposed to the
treatment becoming a literary document with shape and style.
I always tell writers that scripts should be badly written in the
sense that the elegant description, the fine turn of phrase,
distance a script from a film.

A script needs to communicate intentions – first to financiers, later to agents, finally to actors and technicians. It is
only when one has backing that it is safe to make a realistic,
practical script. A truly accurate script of a film is unreadable.
In fact, on completion of a picture, we are obliged to produce
a 'release script', for legal purposes, and for foreign versions,
censors etc. It reverses the process. Someone sits down with
the finished film and describes it on paper. These scripts are
totally incomprehensible unless the film is very literary. In
writing a script, most film-makers today go for a simple description of the scenes with dialogue, but without the shots
and technical details, which are fairly spurious at that stage.
Shobal Hashimoto, who worked with me on *Hell in the Pacific*,
told me that Kurosawa was a purist and would not allow a
writer to describe something that could not be shown, such as
imputing thoughts to a character. Hashimoto once wrote,
'The crow flies wearily home to its nest.' Kurosawa said, 'This
is a shot of a crow flying. How do we show it is weary, and
how do we know it is going to its nest?' I develop a secret

script alongside the public one which can be revealed only when production begins.

We spoke the thing through. Rospo, in my absence, had done a lot of research and had encountered problems with the structure we had devised. We spent the last two days going over it, prior to meeting with Jake. The family is established, the child is abducted, then we pick up the story ten years later and discover that the father has spent each vacation searching for the boy. We follow the father's expedition until he encounters his son. This shape provided a solution to the language problem since the audience discovers the tribe through Markham. However, Rospo found that once Markham came upon the tribe, there was no opportunity to sketch in the life, culture and relationships of the tribe. So we have to find a way to introduce the now 17-year-old Tommy in his tribal life, boldly and directly, before Markham meets him. It is not as elegant a solution, and it forces us to confront the language problem right away.

---

6 NOVEMBER 1982

The session of story-telling is scheduled for three hours, and Jake has warned us that there will be a half-hour break in the middle while he gets his photo taken with Dickie Attenborough in front of the billboard that announces to a sleazy section of Sunset Strip that *Gandhi* is a World Event. After the telling, Jake moves quickly against our weaknesses: 'What do you do about the language?' 'How do you make the tribal scenes credible?' 'How do you cast the tribal roles?' I don't have these answers right now. I have to go there and find out. Jake agrees to finance the script. After all the years of vacillation from studio heads, this decisiveness is breathtaking. Of course, this does not mean the film will be made. He declares that he must get backing from a US distributor before agreeing to make the film. This means going back to all the people who have already rejected it. But going back with a script, possible casting, and with Goldcrest underwriting the production, the US studios will reconsider. They will have limited financial risk; the film will be a reality, not merely a fond hope. And Jake has just done it with *Gandhi*. Turned down by everyone, Jake made it happen. Another step along the way.

---

10 NOVEMBER 1982

Edgar has tracked down two professors at UCLA, and arranged to pay each of them $5,000 for advising us. Professor Bennett's speciality is the study of disturbed rain forest – no shortage of that. We spread out the maps and Bennett surveyed the possibilities. We need rain forest, and a dam which our engineer is engaged in building. Furthermore, it must be cut out of the jungle and nearing completion, but not yet functioning. Bennett's cheerful manner was in marked contrast to the chilling story he told of the massive destruction of the rain forests throughout the world.

The movie will be very difficult to achieve, so it is important to find an hospitable country in which to do it. He ranged across Central and Southern America. Colombia and Peru – politically unstable and dangerous. A list of Central American countries was disposed of through lack of rivers, dams, or an excess of armed insurgents. He categorized Brazil and Venezuela as 'stably unstable'. They both had dam schemes. What about Mexico? Chiapas is in the rain-forest belt, Mexico has dams and hydro-electric schemes and has a film-making infrastructure. He feared their rain forest was gone.

Professor Wilbert is an anthropologist and has been visiting a tribe of Venezuelan Indians for thirty years. Their contacts with the outside world have weakened their traditions and they now consult him on the finer points of their rituals and history. He is deeply suspicious of our enterprise and indeed anything that might distort the truth about rain-forest Indians or expose them to temptation or corruption, by which he means us.

He tells shock-horror stories of the diseases – either excruciatingly painful or fatal or both – that hover in wait for us. I suspect he wants to keep us out of his territory. He made a point of saying he had just come from having tests for river blindness. His field of study is Indian remedies. He tests the efficacy of their medicines. 'Do any of them work?' I ask. 'Nearly all do,' he replied. 'What can they cure?' 'A whole range of diseases, including ones for which we have no remedies, for instance, asthma.' The Indians, it appears, distinguish between their own diseases and ours. They use our medicines for the latter category, which includes the common cold and malaria. Strange that they should possess such complex and astonishing knowledge and yet have developed nothing new for hundreds of years. Where and when did they learn what they know, why and when did they stop learning? How, for instance, did they find out that poisonous manioc is edible if boiled three times?

---

18 NOVEMBER 1982 *CHIAPAS, MEXICO*

Bennett is right. There is no rain forest left in Mexico. The climate is already changing. A tourist official told me that when he was boy, it rained every day, now they have a wonderful climate! I am recovering from a horrifying plane journey from Pelanque. The regular thirty-seater was grounded, so they sent two Cessna six-seaters. Three macho young hoods forced their way on to the already full plane, despite being turned back by the attendant. They crowded into the narrow back seat. The pilot took one look at their deadly, dangerous faces, and shrugged fatalistically. I desperately tried to say, 'Let me out of here' in Spanish, but a combination of linguistic incompetence and engine noise defeated me.

As we taxied down the airstrip I reached for the seat belt. Nothing – just frayed ends. The front wheels left the ground, but the heavy tail just dragged along the ground. The airstrip ran out, we bumped over the rough scrub of cleared jungle. The pilot was at full throttle; the machos giggled; I made a rapid reassessment of my theological views. Somehow the plane skeetered into the air. In other circumstances I would have marvelled at the wild mountains and gorges on the route to Tuxtla Gutiérrez, but as we picked a way through storm clouds and the pilot nosed between mountain peaks, unable to get enough altitude to overfly them, I had to concentrate all my attention into a massive act of will, which alone was keeping the plane aloft. My thigh muscles ached from the effort of pressing my feet down on to the floor so as to keep the Cessna airborne.

That over, thoughts of Pelanque came back. The Mayan pyramids, the ruined city lying in the heart of the jungle, is haunting and evocative. Why there? They have stripped away the vines and creepers that concealed it for hundreds of years. The Mayans disappeared without trace. I climbed to the top of the central pyramid and then descended by narrow steps into the chamber at its very heart – its matrix. The weight of stone pressed in like the hand of God. I thought of those stories of razor blades mysteriously sharpening. I crouched there, sensing some kind of force silently at work aligning my cells into some mystic pattern; my mind resharpened, like the razor blades, I would be ready for revelation.

Carvers fret away at soapstone making copies of the Mayan friezes. I bought one representing a scribe, an artist or writer, himself cutting hieroglyphics in stone. I stare at it, asking it to yield up its secrets, but despite the keen harmony induced by the pyramid, I wait in vain. What did the Indians think when they came upon this vibrant Mayan city couched in their jungle? Did they retreat, abashed, afraid? Was it this dream in stone that arrested change in them? Perhaps it was a cultural shock that made them dread change, curse curiosity?

I came across an ITN news cameraman whom I had last met twenty years ago. He had been marauding the nearby Guatemalan border looking for the Indians who were fleeing into Mexico to escape persecution and death. Did the Mayans hunt down Indians too? Probably not. The Mayans seem to be inverted, coldly immersed in their mysterious cosmic dialogue. Surely, they simply ignored the painted faces peering out of the jungle. And did the Indians finally gain heart enough to move in and massacre the dreamers that had come among them? Is there a Mayan icon in the tribal memory?

In Pelanque I noted that there were no mosquitoes, no

netting at windows, no insects around naked lamps hung out at night. Could that be why the Mayans built their city here? Could it be the simple solution to the mystery? There are Indian faces everywhere, here in Chiapas. Strange to see them *en masse* in the streets. Their expressions are clouded, melancholic, disturbing. Imagination casts them as a shadow, as a shade, of all the annihilated Indian nations of the Americas. Their presence is a reproach, and Mexicans eye them with murderous looks. Why does murder always seem to be hanging in the sticky air of Mexico? Although Mexico once had an Indian president, culturally and politically the Mexican Indians seem mute and anonymous, unabsorbed. They saw the Aztecs, the Mayans, come and go. Now they watch the Spanish. The eagle holds the snake in its beak. Who is the eagle, and who the snake?

The Museum of Anthropology in Mexico City has provided me with a mass of information. Detailing the daily life and rituals of many of the tribes of Central and South America in a series of elaborate and imaginative tableaux, it reminds one of the rich diversity of the Indian nations. James Fenimore Cooper and *Triste Tropique* are summoned from memory, and the scale on which this continent and all its nations were ravished. Yet, the question hangs there. Were the Indians a limb of humanity, genetically unable to change, resistant to mutation, or did they reach a state of balance and harmony that made change not just irrelevant, but destructive to that state?

No rain forest, no dam in construction, and something arid, worn out, about Mexico. It is wrong. The story needs a more primal, vibrant landscape. The Amazon beckons.

---

14 MARCH 1983 *PARIS*

In the middle of *Nemo*, and it is taking up most of my time. Arnaud and his crew, indeed the cast, are very young and inexperienced. They are fresh and bright and the project is wildly ambitious. We are shooting it all in a large inflatable plastic dome where the fantasy unfolds in the shape of a miniature Manhattan, a beach, an ocean, a Roman ruin, the *Nautilus* submarine, and an enchanted desert oasis. Jean-Luc Godard visits the set and he remarks slyly that you need to be young and foolish to make movies. As you get older, you can foresee the pitfalls (and pratfalls) that lie in wait. The art of movies, he always says, is the art of raising money. I get him to expand on this. Part of him is Swiss and, therefore, he is partly a banker. The mark of your standing as a film-maker, he claims, is defined by the percentage of the budget you can spend on yourself and your friends.

'It is impossible to make a film today,' Jean-Luc told me, 'but it is possible to go through the motions.'

He is wonderfully subversive, and wickedly funny. Half of what he says, I am sure, is designed to mislead young film-makers.

Rospo arrives today with the first draft of *The Emerald Forest*.

---

20 MARCH 1983

I am spending my mornings at the set of *Nemo* and the afternoons with Rospo. The first draft script has a lot of vigour and the structure is strong, but the characters are still unformed. Rospo has pieced together convincing patterns for the two tribes – the Invisibles (the ones that Tommy has grown up with), and their antagonists, the Fierce People. We started with the notion that these tribes would represent and be the progenitors of the divided nature of man. The Invisibles are gentle, poetic, loving; the Fierce, aggressive, destructive, hungry for territory.

Wisely he has modified these extremities. The Invisibles have preserved their identity by their belief that when they are painted they cannot be seen. Yet they are also warriors. The rain forest is 'the World'. Beyond the jungle is 'the Dead World', a place they despise, full of 'the Living Dead'. All this he has done brilliantly and it suggests to me a solution as to why Wanadi (the Chief of the Invisibles) abducted Tommy.

Our research shows more than 500 cases of White children taken by Indians in North and South America. Sometimes when a child dies, the father, in order to console the mother, will undertake to replace the child. He goes off and usually steals one from another tribe. Occasionally, he takes it from a White settlement. Sometimes, two families are in dispute with the chief, both wanting a son of theirs to succeed him. The chief will then go off and steal a child as a compromise candidate. This has the merit of introducing fresh blood into the tribe. But Rospo's invention, that the Invisibles view us as 'the Living Dead' suggests to me a scene that we badly need. When Markham finally finds his way to his son's tribe, he must ask the question, 'Why did you take my boy?' My solution is very simple. Wanadi says that the boy stepped into the forest and smiled at him, and that he did not have the heart to send him back to 'the Dead World', rather as we might pick up and adopt a stray fledgeling bird. It helps to define them. It is a notion that explains the central situation and yet, if anything, widens the division between the two fathers.

A series of tense and acrimonious sessions with Rospo. He and I have spent weeks and months writing together over the years. He started as my pupil, but now he is ready to direct his own films and he is restless working with me. This kind of collaboration is very intimate. We always start each day by chatting and reminiscing. As we write, so we dredge up characters and incidents from past experience and lay them out for inspection and possible inclusion. We have reached the point where we know too much about each other. We are acutely conscious of each other's weaknesses. One of his is to enslave characters to plot, forcing them to follow a pre-ordained line rather than allowing the clash of characters to define action. I want to be very specific about Jean and Bill Markham, how they have responded to the loss of a child. Rospo believes they should be very ordinary and unexceptional, that it is what happens to them that counts. Also, Rospo is sometimes clumsy, his writing lacking in grace. On the other hand, he is not reluctant to catalogue my faults: I am impatient with exposition; I plunge into the heart of scenes, confusing and alienating an audience that may need a little coaxing to climb on to the rollercoaster; I make characters

too quirky and eccentric. My films are overwrought; I am led
astray by cinematic effects, etc. What makes his criticisms so
infuriating is that they are mostly true.

A truce is called each night as we go out and eat. He likes
La Coupole in Montparnasse, which is the model for Musso
and Frank's, the Hollywood restaurant that he favours – solid
food, no pretensions, noisy, rude waiters. We are kindred spirits. We have a good time together. He has written a script
that he wants to direct. I admire it and am trying to help him
get it made. I have given it to Walter Donohue of Channel
Four, who likes it too. Most people don't.

I decided some time ago that, instead of teaching and lec-
turing to film students, I would help some aspiring directors
get their pictures made. The problem, as with *Angel* and
now *Nemo*, is that the understandably nervous investor ends
up insisting that I supervise the productions. I start out
with a helping hand, and end up as a fulltime producer.
This takes too much time away from my own work.
So I am being careful not to get too involved in Rospo's
piece.

Due to an eccentric childhood in which he was left to roam
the family piazza in Rome instead of going to school, Rospo
avoided the crushing effect that education has on the imagination. He has a powerful organizing intellect that paradoxi-
cally does not inhibit his instinctive side, which can make
wonderful leaps and bounds. He is capable of sustained concentration. He can write for long hours, for weeks at a time.
Yet he is lazy in the sense that he will use any device to make
his working life easier. He first worked for me on *Deliverance* as
a dogsbody, a gofer. I would send him off each day with a list
of chores: looking for props, hotel accommodation, a local
doctor, special extras – it was he who found the boy who
played the banjo. Once, having assigned him a heavy day's
work, I passed by the house he was renting at 11 in the
morning and found him sleeping in a hammock in the garden.
I stormed over to him demanding that he get on with his
work. 'It's all done,' he said with a yawn. 'You should write
a book,' I shouted. '*How To Do Things The Easy Way.*' He
eased his heavy bulk in the hammock, considering it, sleepily.

'That's not a bad idea,' he said. 'The first thing would be to find someone to write it for me.'

After I made *Leo the Last* for United Artists, they asked me what I wanted to do next. I gave them a treatment I had written about Merlin. David Picker, then in charge of production, did not respond to *Merlin*, but asked me instead to make *The Lord of the Rings*, the film rights of which they had bought without having any idea what to do with it. Tolkien's work stirs a great brew of Norse, Celtic and Arthurian myth, the *Unterwelt* of my own mind. It was a heady, impossible proposition. If film-making for me is, as I have often said, exploration, setting oneself impossible problems and failing to solve them, then the *Rings* saga qualifies on all counts.

I had met Rospo in New York, where he was working as an architect. He was trying to write scripts. I recognized a fellow spirit. I brought him to my home in Ireland and we spent six months delving with dwarfs, wallowing with the Golom, tramping Middle Earth with Bilbo, but, most of all, Gandalf filled my life. He was, after all, Merlin in another guise.

Apart from the prodigious and daunting task of making a $2\frac{1}{2}$-hour script from the three enormous volumes, many technical problems had to be solved as we went along, especially ways to render the magical effects. This was long before the *Star Wars* saga, a time when optical special-effects practice had wasted away through lack of usage all over the world. I had always had a fascination for the magic and trickery of the cinema from Georges Méliès onwards. During this period I studied the techniques of the past and then experimented with modern technology to see how it could be applied.

Rospo pasted every page of *The Lord of the Rings* on to four walls in a room in my house in Ireland. We worked in that room, literally inside the book. He made charts of characters, chronologies and elaborate cross-references. We also devised a map of Middle Earth and we had counters to represent the movement of characters across it. After six months of intensive work we had a script that we felt was fresh and cinematic, yet carried the spirit of Tolkien, a spirit we had come to admire and cherish during those months. It was a good and wondrous time. The valley in the Wicklow hills where my house sits is as close to Middle Earth as you can get in this depleted world.

During these six months, United Artists had suffered setbacks, a string of commercial failures including my own *Leo the Last*. It was 1970. The latest crop of British films had failed in the States. Hollywood's love affair with swinging London was over. American producers were packing their bags and looking for stories set in Denver and Philadelphia.

The Lord of the Rings was an expensive project dependent on innovative special effects. By the time we submitted it to United Artists, the executive who had espoused it had left the company. No one else there had actually read the book. They were baffled by a script that, for most of them, was their first contact with Middle Earth. I was shattered when they rejected it. Marty Elfant was my agent at the time. We took it to Disney and other places, but no one would do it. Tolkien had sold the film rights, reluctantly, to set up a trust for his grandchildren. He wrote asking me how I intended to make the film. I explained that it would be live action and he was much relieved. He had a dread that it would be an animation film and was comforted by my reply. His death spared him the eventual outcome: UA gave it to Ralph Baski, the animator. I could never bring myself to watch the result.

All film-makers spend time on aborted projects. Sometimes one fails to solve the story problems of a script, but most often it is because the big studios play the destructive game of developing dozens of projects with the intention of making only one in ten or one in twenty. At any one time in Hollywood 90 per cent of the writers and directors are busy working on scripts that will not get made.

Despite my disappointment at the time, it was a rich and valuable experience. It certainly prepared the ground for the script that Rospo and I eventually wrote and filmed as *Excalibur*. It was also a big influence on *Zardoz*. Many of the special-effects techniques I developed at that time were put to work on *The Heretic*, *Zardoz* and *Excalibur*, and some of the locations I intended for *The Lord of the Rings* found their way into *Excalibur*.

More importantly, I became conscious at that time that movies are the repository of myth. Therein lies their power. An alternative history, that of the human psyche, is contained and unfolded in the old stories and tales. Film carries on this tradition.

The Western is most obviously Arthurian: the mysterious knight who rides in, saves a community from evil, is tempted by love, but moves on. The stories were drawn from folk legends, embedded with myths, passed down the ages. The characters were bold archetypes.

The Western went into decline when writers and directors became self-conscious and introduced psychological elements. John Ford and the others worked from the blood. Sergio Leone's 'spaghetti' Westerns revitalized the form because he consciously reverted to mythic stories, making the texture and detail real, but ruthlessly shearing away the recent accretions of the 'real' West and its psychological motivations. Unfortunately this was not understood in Hollywood.

Shane is the perfect mythic Western. *High Noon* is already a corruption of that; its political overtones make the hero decent and understandable and therefore incapable of carrying mythic overtones.

Sam Peckinpah was the only American director to take the hint from Leone. *The Wild Bunch* is a throwback to a more mythic approach. Heavy reliance on violence as spectacle suggests lack of confidence in the inherent power of the genre.

Butch Cassidy and the Sundance Kid is a sham Western – the heroes are essentially modern characters dressed up as cowboys; its appeal is in its anachronisms in the tradition of *A Connecticut Yankee in King Arthur's Court*.

Hollywood will not make Westerns any more, having decided that audiences are not interested. Of course, they are not interested in the *wrong* Westerns. In *Once Upon a Time in the West* the Western reaches its apotheosis. Leone's title is a declaration of intent and also his gift to America of its lost fairy stories. This is the kind of masterpiece that can occur outside trends and fashion. It is both the greatest and the last Western.

As the Western declined in the sixties, the mythic stories

passed on to the spy film, and when that strain was exhausted the mantle was picked up by science fiction, notably by Stanley Kubrick with *2001*. Myth in all its mysterious, irrational glory was back on the screen.

That movie affected a generation of film-makers. Steven Spielberg is said to have watched *2001* every night while he shot *Close Encounters of the Third Kind*. Such is the speed of things today that within a decade, along came George Lucas with *Star Wars*, demystifying the form and doing for science fiction what *Butch Cassidy and the Sundance Kid* did for the Western. Myth is left hunting for a home.

---

12 APRIL 1983

Finally, Rospo and I have completed our revisions of *The Emerald Forest* and sent it to the typist.

Jake read it and responded with enthusiasm: 'Let's move to the next stage.' A budget. But before we could make even a rough cost assessment we had to decide where the film would be made and investigate the conditions of that country. We were still in the dark. A lot of foreign films are made in Mexico, but we know Mexico does not work for this story. South America is a jump into the unknown.

---

18 APRIL 1983

Since my duties on *Nemo* required my presence in Paris, I suggested to Jake that Michael Dryhurst, my associate producer on *Excalibur* and a long-time trusted colleague, should go out to Brazil (which seemed by now the only country in which all the requirements of the story could be satisfied) and make a survey. Jake authorized the cost of this, which was in the region of £15,000. Michael's task would be to do a general survey to see if the locations, including the dam, could be found; investigate costs, accommodation, transport and other facilities and to discover if competent technicians are available, etc. Michael is an accomplished photographer and I

asked him to make a comprehensive coverage of possible locations. Jake would then have some pictures to help him sell
the film. Without substantial pre-sales to the US and other
territories, Goldcrest will not back the film.

We made contact with Hector Babenco, the director who
made the impressive Brazilian film *Pixote*, and he provided
assistance there, including a production manager to travel
with Michael Dryhurst and interpret for him.

Meanwhile, with the Cannes Festival coming up, I met
with Bill Gavin, Goldcrest's head of sales, and together we
devised a brochure that he could use to start selling. It shows
on the front cover a blond boy looking out from lush jungle;
inside there is a vista of the Amazon, and a brief synopsis
of the story, together with some photos of my past movies
that will subtly suggest the themes of this film: man against
wilderness (*Deliverance*), mythic action (*Excalibur*), etc.

---

25 APRIL 1983 *PARIS*

Meeting with Jake in Paris. Riding his luck, generated by
the success of *Gandhi*, Jake has sold the US rights of *Nemo* to
Columbia for $2,850,000. It means we have to expand the
scope of the film, which was conceived as a Channel Four
picture. I hope it is not oversold. Claude Nedjar, my co-pro-
ducer, is a maverick figure whose quixotic ways extend to his
labyrinthine accounting system. Jake and David Norris are
trying to unravel it. In other ways, Claude is a marvellous
producer. He takes risks, puts his last centime on the line,
reveres talent, infuriates and inspires the crew.

The task is a stiff one for Arnaud, the young director, and
Claude and I consider each day how much we should inter-
vene. We try to provide a framework in which Arnaud's very
special talent can flourish. If he makes a choice, through in-
experience, that would cause a waste of time and money, we
try to turn him away from it. However, to assert his artistic
authority, he often digs in his heels. France has laudable laws
protecting the rights of authors, and Arnaud is not above
drawing our attention to them. Shooting is under way and I

have given most of the help I can until editing begins. Now I am just a reluctant policeman. I stay away from the set, as I did from Neil Jordan's *Angel*, where my presence can only intimidate. Besides, I find it excruciating to watch in silence as the camera is set up in the wrong place; an actor fails to get help with a line, or a move, or a gesture; a scene playing at the wrong pace; a loose composition; time being wasted on an irrelevance; an extra shot being made that will not cut elegantly into the scene; and on and on.

I recall a scene in *Angel* where Danny, the protagonist, pursues his suspect into a wood. Neil wrote and shot an elaborate scene where Danny finds a revolver hidden inside a portable radio in a woodman's hut. He then conceals himself in the back of the suspect's car and, waiting until the car is moving, pops up and puts the revolver to the man's head. There follows a terrifying scene where the man drives faster and faster and challenges Danny to shoot and send them both to hell. I was always opposed to the scene of the finding of the revolver because I found it mechanical and laborious. It offered no insight into Danny's character, nor did it advance the plot. In fact, it slowed the narrative just at a point where it should be gathering pace and tension. Neil felt that since so much is made earlier in the story of Danny finding an automatic rifle, it was vital to show how he comes by a revolver. I pointed out that the film had moved on to another level by this point, that it now had to be driven forward by emotion. The audience is involved and connected by this time, not needing to be convinced by the mechanics of the story. No one will ask where he got the gun as the car careers down an Irish road full of madness and death.

In the cutting room I was able to show Neil that by eliminating the scene, and editing the scenes before and after so that they follow an emotional flow, not a single question would arise about the revolver. And so it was.

Apart from helping to shape the script, putting an experienced and sympathetic crew around the director, watching for abrasive elements that might clash with his vision of the film – there are other ways to help, some of them rather simple and practical.

All directors nurse a dream of an ultimate movie. At each stage, the realities of money, time, the exigencies of casting erode that perfection. But most of us – not just the inexperienced film-maker – hang on to a vague, indeterminate beauty that no amount of time and money could ever realize. We put off as long as possible the brutal necessity of defining its reality. Directors are confronted with an endless succession of decisions and choices, and we all avoid making them until the last possible moment. We hold on to the film in our head because once we cast it, break it down into shots, we are giving bits of it away, and each bit will be altered by its new tenant – sometimes for the better, sometimes not.

It is a jolting experience when we lay out the schedule for the first time on a production strip board. Until now, each sequence has been worked on separately. But now we see the movie at a glance, as a whole, like a musical score.

Each long thin strip of cardboard represents a day's shooting, and is colour coded; blue for exteriors, yellow for interiors, green for night shooting, etc. Down the length of the strip various information is recorded: the scene number and a brief description, i.e. 'Sc. 84a/Piccadilly/Night Exterior/1.3.9.10.12 (each member of cast is assigned a number) 46 Crowd/5 Action Vehicles.'

The strips can be juggled around to make the best use of time and resources, and countless combinations will be tried to squeeze more value out of the schedule. It is for this reason that films are mostly shot out of sequence, since it is always more economic to shoot the scenes that occur in one location in a block. For instance, there may be four scenes in the main character's house, one at the beginning, two in the middle and one at the end. So, we might shoot the opening and concluding scenes of a film on the first day of the shoot. The changes the character will undergo during the body of the film have to be judged as accurately as possible. It is horrendous for actors and directors, but once the deed is done there is a sense of release. Decisions have been made and we are committed. After the agonizing consideration of all the options, for better or worse, it is on film. We have shot the beginning and the end. We have the book-ends – now we can fill in the empty shelf with more ease and less tension, or so one rationalizes. How much better, though, to shoot sequentially, to have the luxury of allowing the story and characters to develop as you go along. But the realities go something like this. The house is 100 miles out in the country. To shoot each of the four scenes separately would involve the following:

Set out at 6.30 am.
Half a day's travel to location.
Set up camera, rig and light.
Get actors into make-up and wardrobe.
Ready to shoot 3.00 pm
Shooting continues to 6.00 pm. (Cannot go longer since crew had early start and would be on overtime. Actors must have 12-hour break before their next call.)
Sequence unfinished.
Continue and complete by noon of next day.
Travel back to base.

The whole operation repeated four times would use up eight days of the schedule. Clearly, this time can be halved by lumping the scenes together.

If the scene is to be shot on a sound stage, one might fare better, but more often than not similar pressures are at work. Stage space is expensive; the scenes must be shot in a group so that the set can be torn down and another built in its place.

Invariably, the first attempt at a schedule comes out with more days than the budget will cover. Days are saved in the manner just described. An extra rest day is required after night shooting, so putting all the night scenes together is clearly a saving. A night shoot is twice as expensive as a day shoot, so is there any way of reducing the number of nights? Could scene X, a night exterior, be shot at twilight without the film suffering? Or could it be done as an interior scene with the windows blacked out so that it could be shot during the day?

Laid out on the board, the strips often give one insights into the script. Should it take three days to shoot sequence Y when it is a relatively minor scene and doesn't warrant so much time? It's much better to find a simpler way of shooting it and allot the time to major scenes that are inadequately scheduled.

If the number of days must be radically cut, then all one can do, after all the juggling, is to go back to the script and make excisions.

Painfully, inch by inch, the gap between the budget and schedule is closed. If, despite all one's efforts, a gap remains, a final sanction is available. One has the option of working six days rather than five days per week. In this way a six-week schedule comes down to five, or twelve weeks to ten.

I have done this from time to time, but never again. A director needs at least ten hours' preparation before each week's shoot. On a six-day schedule, it means the seventh day is wholly taken up with preparation, and there is no space for rest and thought.

Once the schedule is finalized, then comes the detailed work of planning each day's shooting. To Arnaud and Neil (or to myself), clinging to our dream movies, I say, 'Here are the hard facts. In a ten-hour day it is possible to do between four and ten set-ups (separate shots) depending on their complexity.' Of course, it is possible to do more, but only by sacrificing the care and standards of feature film-making.

One hour per set-up is not much. Actors need to be rehearsed, their movements worked out, lighting done, camera movements rehearsed, sets and props arranged and rearranged to suit the action, special effects such as wind machines organized, make-up effects, like wounds, prepared. Finally, several takes are made of each shot. I tend to shoot an average of four set-ups per day, preferring to spend more time on each shot rather than make a lot of 'cover'. If you are sure about how a scene will cut together, you can dispense with a lot of 'cover' shots.

Arnaud had planned thirty set-ups for a sequence and then found he had to do it in one and a half days. After some thought, he said he must have at least twenty-five shots – still too many for the time allocated. Perhaps, I suggest, the scene is longer than you imagine? Why not time out the thirty shots? After a day's work with his cameraman, Philippe Rousselot, he finds it comes to eight minutes instead of the three he had expected. He cuts the scripted scene down to four minutes and reduces his set-ups to sixteen. It still looks difficult to achieve. It is a scene on spiralling stairs in the interior of a rocket ship. Philippe suggests using the Louma crane, a snorkel camera device that allows very fluid movements in confined areas. It is very expensive but they feel that with it they can shoot the scene in two long set-ups and achieve the scene in one day, thus saving half a day. Michel Propper, the production manager, makes his calculations and we find out that it will actually cost more – although time will be saved. Arnaud, however, has fallen in love with the Louma by now. He decides he wants more sinuous camera moves and less cutting throughout the film. Aesthetically, I have to agree with him, but I know that such a style gives less latitude in the editing and he lacks the experience to judge pace on the floor. With misgivings, I concede. It is his film. In these ways the style of a movie begins to emerge.

The commonest fault of film-makers is the failure to cut the script down to length. A first rough-cut is quite often four hours long. This means that half of it must be thrown away in order to get the film down to an acceptable length. In other words, half of the shooting time was wasted. Well, not quite. It is important that the first rough-cut is at least half an hour longer than the eventual length so there is scope in the cutting room to control pace and rhythm. Besides, the film changes at each stage: a scene that feels vital in the script sometimes becomes redundant in the editing stage; a complex tracking shot that looked beautiful in the rushes can seem painfully slow or contrived when cut into the film. Experience teaches you to judge these things better, but there are always surprises. A movie grows and develops organically from stage to stage and you never know exactly how it will turn out.

All over Paris I keep seeing a poster advertising a lecture on the plight of the Brazilian Indians. There is a haunted Indian face staring out at me. It seems to beckon.

Nemo is still shooting in Paris, but Claude brought the cast and Arnaud down for the weekend for the Festival. Goldcrest gave a dinner and Jake spoke with great charm and warmth introducing Arnaud and the actors, little Seth Keybel who plays Nemo, Harvey Keitel, Michel Blanc, the brilliant comic actor, Carole Bouquet in a diaphanous black dress, my daughter Katrine even more outrageously got up, my son Charley who also plays in the film, and my daughter Telsche who wrote the script with Arnaud. Jake described it as the family school of film-making. My children have always helped me on my films, played small roles, worked in the cutting rooms, assisted their mother who often designs the costumes, and so on. A film unit is an extended family and it has always seemed appropriate that the children play their part.

Bill Gavin and Guy East are busy selling Goldcrest product past, present and future. The brochure for *The Emerald Forest* looks impressive and they are negotiating pre-sales with major independent distributors from France, Italy, Germany, Australia.

Jake's policy at Goldcrest is to keep down production costs by giving the film-makers more freedom and an honest accounting (revolutionary concept!) in return for reduced fees; not to spend money on stars; and to try to lay off the cost of the film in pre-sales before shooting commences.

We estimate *The Emerald Forest* will cost between $15 and $17 million. The US market is 60–70 per cent of the world total so he is trying to get $8 or $9 million from an American distributor. Foreign pre-sales will hopefully raise $5–7 million. These are advances against sales. Once the distributor has recovered these amounts, and deducted his fees and advertising expenses, the balance – if any – is split with Goldcrest. European video is worth $1 million, US cable and TV will garner at least $6 million. A tax shelter will be worth $2 million. These pre-sales, of course, are contracts, not money. The distributor agrees to pay that money when he gets delivery of the film. Thus, if Goldcrest covers its bets, it still has to find money to fund the production.

The movie is proving very attractive to the Europeans. If they are drawn by the synopsis, they ask for the script. Neue Konstantin of Germany, AMLF of France and others are doing just that. Bill Gavin is asking top prices.

Meanwhile Jake has been shopping around the US majors in Hollywood and there are three companies interested: MGM, Universal and Embassy (a so-called mini-major recently acquired by Jerry Perenchio and Norman Lear).

The plan is to meet up with them during the Festival. Goldcrest will not give me a go-ahead unless a US deal is made. Nor will they wish to risk more development money. Michael Dryhurst is still out in Brazil and I plan to join him there directly after Cannes. Jake and I are both nervous. The situation at present is that Embassy has put an offer on the table, but Jake is worried that they might well change their minds, and there are onerous conditions attached to it. We have just heard that MGM have cancelled the meeting we were to have with Freddie Fields at the Hôtel du Cap since they consider Jake's terms too tough. Jake cannot give ground on the terms as they are the same ones that Embassy has accepted. The third contender is Universal. Bob Rehme has just joined them and loves the script. Jake and I met him at his suite at the Carlton. He is sharp, witty and a film buff, all rare qualities in a movie mogul. I outline my plans for the film, which he greets with enthusiasm. He quickly sees the kind of movie it could be. 'Let's make it,' he says. Twenty minutes later Jake and I are back on the Croisette. Jake is dubious: 'If he were really buying, he would be much more negative than that.' No one is sure how much power Rehme wields at Universal. Behind him and above him are the heavies, the money men. Universal, traditionally, like to own and control their product worldwide rather than buy in like this. But Jake, encouraged by the enthusiasm of foreign buyers, feels he has enough to go on with and agrees to my trip to Brazil.

---

15 MAY 1983 *CANNES*

Attended a dinner at the Hôtel du Cap in Antibes given by Jerry Perenchio for Lew Grade. Lew, after profligate years, wanton ways and sinking his TV profits into expensive cinema flops, has finally fallen. His empire has crashed about him. Even his sternest critics are sorry.

Jerry Perenchio promoted the Ali–Frazier fights. Later, he and Norman Lear made millions in television with *All in the Family* and other hits. Their joint income is said to run to $1 million per week. There is no way to lose that kind of money except by acquiring a movie company. They purchased Embassy, a sickly mini-major that was once the creature of Joe Levine, who looked and behaved much like Lew Grade, or vice versa.

Perenchio, morose and tense, was always taken with Lew, would like to be like him, I suspect. Lew was 76 years old. The industry wrote him off. But Jerry offered Lew a job and here he was up on the stage dancing the Charleston again while 300 of us guests guzzled caviare and swallowed Dom Perignon at Jerry's expense. Maybe Lew can show Jerry how to be Joe. The evening was topped off with a fireworks display lighting up the Mediterranean outside the window. Lew's wife said, 'Haven't they gone to a lot of trouble?'

There were no other writers, directors or actors present, only studio executives, agents, distributors and producers. They were all very happy in each other's company, a respite from the distasteful necessity to meet and talk with the people who actually make movies.

The Hôtel du Cap is popular on two counts: it is the most expensive hotel in the world and is as far away from the Film Festival as you can get while still claiming to have attended. Most minor studio executives will graft away in their Carlton suites, leaving them only briefly for meetings on the Carlton terrace. But the studio heads stay out at the Cap, occasionally summoning a favoured supplicant to their presence. Neither group would dream of attending a screening unless their studio was presenting a film in competition.

I sat next to Joe Wizan, my first agent, now head of production at Fox. 'Joe,' I demanded, 'how could you turn down *The Emerald Forest*?' He was vague, claimed not to have read it, promised he would. Not long before I had turned down Joe's offer to me of his pet project, *Enemy Mine*, so exonerating him from suffering any moral pressure. He was unmoved by my attempts to stir up feelings of guilt.

I reminded him of an old story. Joe had the task of helping me set up *Leo the Last* in 1969, a difficult script by Hollywood standards. Joe's pal, Jere Henshaw, had just been appointed production executive at a new company, National General (now defunct). Joe had taken *Leo the Last* to all the majors and been turned down. When he heard Jere had this new job, he contacted him immediately.

'Jere,' he said passionately, 'we were at school together, you are my closest friend, you have to do this movie, otherwise I will never speak to you again as long as I live.'

Jere protested, 'Joe, I love you. I love Boorman. But I didn't understand the script. Tell you what. If you can explain it to me, I'll make it.'

Joe understood it no better than Jere. He had a moment's panic before he snapped back, 'Not on the phone.'

Jere fell off his chair because Joe was right there in the room with him.

'So come on, Joe,' I said. 'On our friendship, I'll never talk to you again if you don't make the *The Emerald Forest*.'

'I'll call you,' he said. 'I hate talking about these things face to face.'

---

16 MAY 1983 *EN ROUTE: CANNES-PARIS*

Christel and I are on the overnight train to Paris and tomorrow morning I go straight to the airport to catch a flight to Rio. Now that *Nemo* is finished shooting, except for some miniature shots, I am free to go. We talked to more foreign buyers. Bill Gavin and Jake are delighted with the response. Jake is not so happy about the US deal but will keep negotiating with Embassy while staying open to other offers.

Perenchio is clearly wooing Jake to join Embassy. Jake's track record of hits makes him very desirable. Like many before him, Jake is entranced by Lew Grade who seems to be aiding Jerry in his hunt for Jake. Jake is having problems at Goldcrest, and so may be tempted to leave.

Everyone has Lew Grade stories. I told Jake one or two of mine. When Lew started making movies he approached me with a script about Livingstone in Africa. It was intriguing, but needed a lot of work and research before you could get to the point of knowing if it was makeable.

Lew would have none of my doubts and reservations. We were lunching at his office suite together with the writer and a couple of Lew's executives. 'How much do you want to make it?' he said. 'A quarter of a million?'

'Lew, please,' I protested.

'All right, make it $350,000.'

'I don't know if it *can* be done, even if I did want to do it.'

Lew bellowed out for his cheque book. He made out a cheque for half a million dollars and signed it. He handed it to me. I refused to take it. He got up from his chair and tried to stuff it into my jacket pocket. I fended him off and we sparred for a moment, when with a deft movement he stuffed it between my backside and the chair. I tried to ignore it, but I felt at a distinct disadvantage from then on with half a million dollars of Lew's money sticking up my arse.

He refused to talk about the project itself, the story, the script, the casting – these were details for writers and directors to take care of.

'Let me tell you how I work, John. I don't want to read the script – haven't got time. I don't see rushes. Don't show me a rough-cut.' He waved away such a trifle. 'You make it. You have final cut.'

I felt if I let him go on any longer, my silence would be construed as agreement. I made a feeble attempt to interrupt. I reached out a protesting hand. He thrust into it a cigar that looked capable of sinking the *Belgrano*.

'I know what you're going to say, John. Other studios have given you final cut, right?'

I nodded assent.

'But nobody has gone as far as I'll go. I don't even want to see the picture when it's finished!'

It all came to nothing, but I was won over and became very fond of him.

---

18 MAY 1983 *COPACABANA PALACE HOTEL, RIO*

I am looking out from my room on to that swarming beach. It is dark now, but the pageant continues, and the beat never stops. Rio is exactly as it should be. Sun, sea, surf, sand, sex and samba. Whores of every hue throng the promenade. Laughing and giggling, they grope at you as you come and go. You run a gauntlet of them outside the hotel. Even the muggers are smiling and finger-clicking.

At the airport this morning I went through customs with a group from an American package company called Gay Tours. They all had cropped hair, moustaches, check shirts, tight jeans and shameless eyes blazing with lust. And this at 7 am. Michael met me and by 8.30 am we were entering the hotel through a cluster of boys and girls plying their flesh, the early shift. I took a swim to freshen up. It was already hot, the sand staked out with spreadeagled bodies, many of stunning beauty. With maps and photos spread out, we sat down and Michael made his report.

He has travelled thousands of miles criss-crossing this country, which is as large as the continental USA. There are few roads and railways, especially in the vast northern region that makes up Amazonia. There, it is either river or air. Brazil is a post-industrial country. They could not lay telephone cables to link up these vast distances, so they jumped direct to satellite and the phone service is excellent. The trans-Amazonian highway is a lost cause. In the wet season sections are swallowed up by the jungle. But the air services are comprehensive, modern, punctual and cheap – because so vital. The telephone and aeroplane are giving Brazil a coherence that could release enormous power.

Most of the locations we need seem to be available, but scattered over long distances. Michael found that you must travel hundreds of miles before there is even the slightest change in terrain. There is no one centre in which we can base ourselves and find all we need. There is only one dam that fits our purpose, at Tucuruí, being in the middle of the Amazonian rain forest, whilst the best waterfall is at Itatiaia, 1,000 miles from the dam.

---

19 MAY 1983

Looked at locations in Rio that might serve as the Markham family's apartment and the office headquarters of our imaginary construction company, Amazco, for which Markham works as an engineer on the dam project. Not suitable.

In the afternoon Hector Babenco came in from São Paulo. Hector is an Argentinian who has based himself in Brazil for some years and made his name with *Pixote* and is now preparing to make *The Kiss of the Spider Woman*. He has a booming voice that seems to flood the room. When we got into an argument about the arrangements he has been making for Michael, he raised it still more, sheer volume drowning our complaints. But he seems straight and is certainly well intentioned.

The major subject of the meeting is our deal with his company, HB Films, and the subsequent negotiations with Concine, the government department that controls the film industry. Brazil is strongly protectionist in all fields. A foreign film company must enter into a co-production arrangement with a Brazilian company. Only the Brazilian company can deal with Concine.

Hector wants $150,000 to obtain all the permissions (which are many). This is much too much, he knows it, but he is sticking out because, as he freely admits, he needs that sum to complete the financing of *Spider Woman*. His case is that another Brazilian company was paid a similar sum for the same services on *Blame It on Rio*, which is shooting here now. To our consternation he wants that money free and clear. Everything else he supplies we must pay for. Michael Dryhurst and I retire to confer. Edgar has already looked into the deal done on *Blame It on Rio* and briefed us. We suspect that the high fee was partly for finding cheap cruzeiros to help finance that film.

One of the problems here is that there are three rates of currency exchange: the euphemistically termed 'parallel' rate, which is 30 per cent better than the official rate, and the black-market rate, which might be 10 per cent better still. With inflation at 200 per cent no one will take a cheque. If it takes five days to clear, its value has dropped by 3 per cent. It is a blocked currency. No one can get their money out. But of course there are ways. One way is to take it out on celluloid. If you invest cruzeiros in a movie and it then earns back your money abroad, you have done it. The snag is that most films lose money.

After several calls, including an illuminating one to the producer of *Blame It on Rio* (a catalogue of the disasters, pitfalls, delays and broken promises that lie in wait for us), we conclude there is probably no alternative to Hector. From his confident manner when we go back into the meeting, this is something Hector already knows. Michael tries to contain our losses by telling Hector we will pay his exorbitant fee only when all Concine permissions, and permission to shoot at Tucuruí, are granted. Since we cannot shoot in Brazil without these it puts Hector at risk and minimizes Goldcrest's losses if they should decide not to go forward with the picture.

We agree, shake hands and sit down again to plan our strategy. I like Hector, he is a graceful winner. He hugs me and says as far as he's concerned we can keep the Falklands.

'No, no,' I protest, 'the Malvinas are yours. A couple of years ago you could have bought out those British settlers – $150,000 would have covered it, and Bob's your uncle.'

Hector protests he had no Uncle Bob; but he loved my films, it was a great honour to be assisting me, he just wished he could be doing it for nothing, but – he spread his hands – you know how tough it is to finance a film. I assured him I knew it well.

---

20 MAY 1983 *SAO PAULO*

Possibly the biggest city in the world, 25 million or more.

Where Rio is all fun, São Paulo is all business. Drove through the Japanesé quarter. More than 2 million Japanese here, a community established for fifty years. Hector took us to see the head of Concine. We are given tiny cups of strong, sweet coffee.

Excalibur was very successful in Brazil and I am treated with great deference. He will do everything he can to help, but of course there are many formalities. We must submit our script in Portuguese, as well as a list of all crew and cast members we wish to bring to Brazil together with medical certificates guaranteeing that they are free of a list of diseases that he provided. All known diseases are listed together with some I take to be special to Brazil. For each person we import, 50 per cent of their salaries must be paid to the Brazilian trade unions to compensate those who would otherwise have worked. We must process our film in a Brazilian laboratory – it turns out there is only one, of dubious reputation.

'Who', Michael asks, 'decides to give us the permission?'

He explains that the Concine Committee is made up of representatives of the Department of Internal Affairs, External Affairs, the Employment Department and, of course, the military. They need to be satisfied that the film will not harm Brazilian honour or reputation.

Afterwards, Hector says, 'We have to make a few changes when we translate the script. They won't let you shoot at Tucuruí if you show the dam breaking. It reflects badly on Brazilian engineers.' I protest that it would be difficult to maintain such a subterfuge. Hector drowned out my concern by raising his voice and flash-flooding the room.

'You don't understand. If they found out, they would be flattered that you were gracious enough to want to spare their feelings.'

---

21 MAY 1983

Michael Dryhurst had already made contact with Maureen Bisilliat, whose brilliant photographs of the Xingu Indians we have so admired. I went to see her, while Michael visited a lawyer who had been recommended as a man who would lead us through the bureaucratic minefield of Brazil.

Maureen has a shop selling very expensive Indian artefacts, which she picks up on her photographic forays. She has been visiting the Xingu for ten years and I want her to use her influence to get me permission to visit the Xingu reservation, the size of Denmark, where Indians are able to live out tribal lives in their traditional hunting grounds, protected from outside influences and incursions – which, of course, includes people like me.

Maureen is as shrewd as Hector. She needs to be convinced that my film would advance the cause of the Indians. She has read the script and she is not sure. She complains that Werner Herzog picked her brains and walked off without compensating her. Finally what convinces her of my fidelity is a large fee, which is as it should be. She also has a hectoring voice, but I am beginning to realize that there is such a high level of noise in Brazil that one needs to shout to be heard.

Maureen takes me to see Orlando Villas-Bôas. He is a squat, bearded man, compact and full of power. His eyes glint with humour behind thick lenses. People drift in and out of his house, including a couple of Indians, and an Indian woman who might be a housekeeper or wife. Maureen presents my credentials and translates. He doesn't appear to listen, but watches me, with humorous childlike openness that is, at the same time, shy. He is making his own judgement of my worth. He has been twice nominated for the Nobel Peace Prize, and word has it that the Brazilian Government has discouraged it because what he did was save the Indians from systematic destruction by successive Brazilian Governments.

Orlando and his brother Claudio set out in 1943 as part of an expedition to open up Brazil's western territories to colonization. It took three years to cut a path 300 miles into the Mato Grosso. There they encountered the Indians of the Alto Xingu whose impenetrable terrain had sealed them off from the attentions of the White man. Since then the two brothers have devoted their lives to the Indians and, against tremendous opposition, have managed to force legislation protecting the Xingu territory from the cupidity of ranchers, hunters and prospectors, thus paying restitution for that path they cut into this hidden Eden.

So well have they succeeded that even for Orlando it is very difficult to get me in. To begin with, one must have an invitation from a tribe, then make a submission to the government body responsible for Indian affairs, the Funai, and have medical clearance; above all, one's reason for being there must be of help to the Indians. At the moment the tribes are angry and bitter at recent actions – and inactions – of the Government and are not feeling very hospitable. And, I sense, Orlando has not yet decided whether he should help me or not.

Maureen is voicing her doubts about the enterprise and, as they talk back and forth, I am not sure if they are hers or his. She has summarized the script for him. Can I, an outsider, have any real insight into this culture? Isn't the story just an adventure, exploiting the Indians as entertainment? And the case for the Indians is never properly expressed in the text, she claims.

After being polite and deferential, I suddenly found myself blazing with passion.

'The destruction of the rain forest is expressed by the vast clearing of the area to be flooded by the construction of the dam. The dam itself stops the flow of a river. It is a perfect symbol of man's determination to harness, tame, control, destroy nature. It forces two Indian tribes away from their lands and into conflict with each other. The father who builds the dam is unwittingly the cause of the tragedies that befall his son's tribe.

'The relationship between our modern, acquisitive, greedily all-consuming society and the balanced tribal life proceeding in harmony with nature is perfectly dramatized in the persons of the father and son divided by these extraordinary circumstances.

'It will be seen by millions of people throughout the world, mostly people who would flick channels if it came up as a documentary on TV. And in a sense I understand that boredom because people feel there is nothing they can do. The Indians and the rain forest are doomed. We all know it. It is an inevitable process.

'You know that once your Indians have got steel axes,

they'll never go back to cutting down trees with sharpened stones. You have sealed them off in the Xingu – you have slowed the process. In another generation these last vestiges of tribal life will be gone from the whole world. Maureen set out with her camera to bear witness while there is still time. I need to go there because I want to touch that world, to know something of its truth, because what I am doing is trying to relate the present mess to our tribal past. We were all tribal a couple of thousand years ago. It has been forgotten too fast. We have to acknowledge what is still tribal in us. That was my aim in *Excalibur*, to touch the mythic, archetypal sources that begat us. So my aim here is mythic, not naturalistic. I am not going to film a real tribe. I am going to invent tribes. The surface, the detail must be correct. That is no problem. I can get that from books, anthropologists. But I have to make contact with these people, their spirits.

'I have to go there. I have to touch the past. If you won't help me, I'll walk there.'

I don't think Maureen translated much of that, but Orlando understood, at least my passion. And if he didn't, I'm glad he didn't, because these things are best left unsaid, even Rospo and I in private avoid such overt intentions. It is bad form, bad magic, to say out loud what the whole movie is about. You work towards it, weave the themes into the characters and narrative, until, hopefully, these cannot be picked out of the fabric. Finally, what you have made always surprises you, however close it is to intentions. If we knew exactly what we were trying to make in every detail, we would lack the heart to make it.

Orlando began to talk about the practical difficulties of getting out there as though it were all settled.

He will contrive to send a radio message to the Indian post named for him and try to persuade the great Shaman, Takuma, to invite me. Having listened to my story he believes I must meet Takuma if I am to get it right. He warns that it could be quite dangerous there at the moment.

There are fewer than 200,000 Indians left in Brazil. In 1600 there were 4 million – England's population at that time was only 6 million.

There are still two tribes in the Xingu that have never had contact with other Indians or White men. It is such a tribe that would have taken Tommy. Curiously enough, Orlando has just returned from an expedition lasting six months trying to recover a 7-year-old Brazilian boy who was taken by the Indians. It was documented on film by Adrian Cowell, who also made the marvellous film, *The Tribe that Hid from Man.* I will try to see the kidnap film when I return to London.

Orlando opened a wall cabinet and, with a huge beam, revealed a comprehensive collection of Scotch whisky bottles, malts and blends, every label I'd ever seen – and none of them empty.

Maureen did not translate the toast but I raised my glass, for Orlando and I both knew well enough what we were drinking to – none of the things we had talked of – we were drinking to Adventure!

---

22 MAY 1983 *BRASILIA*

I'm looking down from the plane as we leave the capital, which is laid out below in the shape of an aeroplane – a modern jet with swept-back wings. This is altogether appropriate because the city itself is not much more than an airport. The politicians and bureaucrats constantly fly in and out, and the city lies there, dumped down arbitrarily in the middle of a vast plain of bush and shrub. Comings and goings are its only purpose.

Le Corbusier must take some of the blame, for it is another Radiant City. All functions – commerce, leisure, hotels, shopping – are carefully cordoned off into separate, sterile areas. The long, wide central street that bisects the city looks like a runway and adds to the impression that this is an airport. Even the cathedral (the only interesting building) feels like the chapel at Heathrow.

Because it was all built in the 1950s – what rotten luck to choose that period to build a capital city – it looks embarrassingly dated, like the Festival of Britain caught in a time warp. We thought of basing the Markham family and the Amazco headquarters there, but it is a great disappointment. After just a few days in Brazil I am struck by the gulf between what the country actually is and the official view of how it should be. In Rio and São Paulo life is a continuous celebration that spills out into the tumultuous streets. Its beautiful, vivid people crowd together and make noise and music. They announce the coming of something new; they have stirred the racial pot and here is a new dish, try it, anyone can join, you too can be Brazilian. It is not a nationality, but a new way of thinking and feeling, open, free, spontaneous.

The streets of Brasilia are deserted. There are no trees, the bland buildings offer no shade from a relentless sun. The statement Brasilia makes is, 'We are as dull, as pedantic, as air-conditioned, as orderly, as important, as sterile, as you Americans and Europeans.'

And yet, one senses, in so many ways, for better and worse, Brazil *is* the future. Much more so than the USA, which seems entrenched and conservative by comparison. Perhaps Brasilia is the city of the future, the airport city.

En route for Belém which lies at the mouth of the Amazon.

---

22 MAY 1983 *BELEM NOVOTEL*

The Amazon is seventy miles wide here at the mouth. Forty per cent of the world's rainfall drops on the Amazonian rain forest and the river thrusts fresh water 80 miles out to sea.

This gimcrack hotel sits on the waterfront hemmed in by the *favella* (shanty town) that straggles along the shoreline where hundreds of boats ply up and down the river bringing their jungle fruits and *légumes* to the markets of Belém. Further up are the proper docks where the big paddle steamers and ocean-going tankers call before clawing 1,000 miles up river to Manaus, itself an ocean port. Down town, high-rise apartments and office blocks jut out from the crumbling baroque mansions built by the rubber planters at the turn of the century. The city sits on the river bank, jungle on the other three sides and looks across the delta islands to Macapá, which lies smack on the Equator.

It is hot and humid and every afternoon the rain falls out of the sky to the melodramatic accompaniment of thunder and lightning that would look excessive in a Hammer horror film.

I am quite beguiled by the city: its avenues of mango trees; peeling, flaking, crumbling colonial buildings; cracked, twisted streets; its tumultuous markets; its waterfront – it reeks of the romance of the Amazon.

When Michael made his first visit here, he found a young guy, Caito Martins, and he is our guide. He has been a river trader and knows the jungle, and is now engaged to the daughter of Mr Big of Belém, who owns the newspaper, the TV and radio stations and whose mere nod opens all doors for us. Caito is reckless, unreliable, disorganized and his enchanting manner disarms us. He never takes us where we want to go, always somewhere else and somewhere better.

Michael and I are sure this is the place. We will foray out each day with Caito by boat, air taxi and jeep and try to find all we need. Michael has now been eight weeks on this trip and his wife, Anna, has now joined him.

---

2 JUNE 1983 *EN ROUTE: BELEM-PARIS*

Eleven days have gone by and not a word written in this journal. It has been an extraordinary trip. I am sitting in the plane, going over my notes, sorting out the maps and locations.

What is clear is that the Belém base will work. The dam at Tucuruí will fit the bill if we can get permission to shoot there. It is not quite what one had in mind – the conventional dam in a gorge – but perhaps more interesting. It is a mile-wide barrage across the Araguaia river which runs south-north from the Mato Grosso and joins the Amazon network at Belém. It is only 200 miles from Belém so, by Brazilian standards, close and accessible. It has a tarmac runway and we can bring the crew in by charter jet. 'No problem,' says Michael, giving me his oldest-fashioned look. The dam is surrounded by rain forest and they are clearing some 200 square miles of it for the lake that will back up when the dam is complete. This scalped land very eloquently illustrates the theme of 'the Dead World' – which is encroaching on the Indians' life.

Coming back from Tucuruí in a Cessna we were forced to land on a football pitch in Cametá, a crumbling little river port halfway back to Belém.

Obliged to stay the night, we deplaned with little prospect of comfort or ease ahead of us.

The football match we had interrupted quickly resumed and we looked bleakly about us. The sun was going down. A ramshackle taxi approached and out of it stepped a large round man, balding, with a drooping moustache. He smiled with melting eyes and bowed courteously. We stepped into the taxi and drove carefully away. Very carefully. The car had almost no suspension. One could feel every protuberance in the road under one's feet, thudding and scraping the metal. But Senhor Calixto, as we came to know him, was serenely oblivious to such hazards.

We asked him to take us to an hotel – *the* hotel, it turned out. His sweet smile said, 'Don't ask me to take you there. You will be displeased and will then not think well of me.' He held us with his look, finally yielded, shrugged and drove us there. Each room was a concrete box with a square hole in the wall – no glass, no mosquito screen. The rough, bare, concrete walls had black, greasy dirt ground into the crevices. The only furnishing was a low, wooden platform that served as a bed. On it was an inch-thick mattress, the one I examined unmistakably bloodstained.

We regret having left the resourceful Caito back in Belém. I suggest that we buy hammocks, string them in the trees by the river. Anna, who is Irish, saw a convent on the way in. 'The nuns! The nuns will take us in.' Her face falls when Senhor Calixto gently points out that it is not a convent but a seminary.

Senhor Calixto waves away all other alternatives with great firmness. 'You will sleep in my house.'

It is very simple, but spotlessly clean. He is over 50 but has a young wife and a 6-month-old baby. He treats them both with that special careful gentleness that is so touching in a strong man. He walks on eggshells, afraid to shatter his idyll. He keeps looking at the baby, leaning over the crib, blinking and shaking his head to reassure himself he is not dreaming.

Michael and I sleep in the hammocks on his porch next to a flimsy cage in which he keeps a savage, snarling, hissing jaguar. Senhor Calixto's all-embracing goodness extends to this creature, which he pets and coos at. It responds by tearing at his hands and ripping his shirt sleeve.

He insists Anna has the bed, his wife sleeps with the baby, and we discover in the morning that he sat up all night in a chair because he was afraid his snoring would have kept us awake.

As it turned out, a few snores would have been lost in the cacophony of the jungle night, the growls of the jaguar a few feet away, and visiting mosquitoes that left their marks. But lying in a hammock listening to these sounds, and staring up at the shapeless jumble of stars that crowd the heavens of the Southern hemisphere, I thought, well, here I am. This is it.

Senhor Calixto cooked up a huge breakfast and watched us benignly while we ate it all up. One felt that to leave a single scrap on the plate would deeply offend him. The eggs were fresh from the nest, the bread still hot from the baker, the papaya ripe and the flavour enhanced by the juice of just-picked tiny limes.

He spoke a lot about jaguars and their nature. He hunted them, knew their ways. I took it all in. The jaguar has a place in our story and I am beginning to discover what it should be. He gave me a tooth, a fang, I suppose, of a jaguar, for luck. I shall keep it about me.

He drove us back to our plane, refusing money, even the taxi fare. As we parted, we all found ourselves in tears. I shall never forget Senhor Calixto.

We spent several days exploring the rivers and islands around Belém. Caito has a knack of stepping right into the lives of people we encounter on the way. He is completely open to experience. He is born again each day. He has no malice or aggressiveness, which people sense, so they do not resent the way he leads us on to their land, into their boats and houses. His manner is pushy and aggressive, he shouts, but it is all fake. He cannot conceal his sunny good nature even from total strangers. At the mention of his name people who know him smile and shake their heads.

He is a skilful boatman, but cannot resist taking chances. When we come back at night from the islands he cannot bear to drive the speedboat slowly. The heavy brown water of the Amazon is treacherous with submerged logs, but Caito does not feel we are living unless our lives are at risk, and, of course, he always leaves it too late and we are forced to come back in the dark. We probe into the fascinating channels and rivers, the half-caste Indians watching us from their palm-thatched shacks sitting on stilts in the mud; the endless commerce of traders, their boats piled high with lurid fruits from the forest, pass us with friendly waves.

Then the rains come. We shelter as the river churns and froths from the onslaught and the air is fogged with moisture and the rain is so dense there is no air to breathe. You inhale vapour. You are drowning in your own element.

We run for shelter. Caito marches into a shack, elbows past the family and shows us the pots of sticky white latex they collect from the nearby trees. The man is a fisherman, he trawls in these waters and takes his catch to the market in Belém. He sells that which he does not need to feed his family. With the money he buys manioc, which is a carbohydrate made from a root, a staple of the Indians and adopted throughout Brazil and served in the form of gritty granules with every meal. Fruit they find in abundance in the forest and they offer us samples. Exquisite tastes, flamboyant shapes and colours that I have never seen.

Caito helps himself to whatever he finds in their house. He is always ravenously hungry. He bellows questions at the man and his wife, shouting across the roar of the rain outside. The children stare at us with dark forest eyes.

The latex reminds Caito of a funny story. Manaus and Belém grew rich with the rubber boom, and we all know the stories of Caruso and others coming to entertain them, of how they sent their laundry to Paris and so on. It was fine while they bought the latex from the Indians who they trained to collect it in the forest, but they wanted more. So they sowed rubber plantations. But the balance between growth and destruction in the rain forest is a delicate one. Rubber trees are always spaced out, never found close together. Here Caito begins to giggle. There is a disease that afflicts them, that jumps from tree to tree when they are adjacent, and, of course, it wiped out all the plantations. Caito finds this incredibly funny. Along come some sneaky Englishmen, who steal the rubber seeds, and plant them in Malaya where there is no disease. End of rubber boom in the Amazon. He is roaring with laughter now, wiping his eyes. 'You stole the tea from China and planted it in India. You stole the rubber. You took breadfruit from Tahiti to feed the slaves in the Caribbean.' Our English ways tickle his sense of humour. It makes me uneasy, for here we are again, stealing as usual. Art is our excuse now.

We watch the latex being cured over a fire, a spit turning and the liquid pouring over it, forming a huge golf ball. Smoke and steam cast ghostly wreaths about our conversation.

The rain has stopped. Of course it has got late again, and we are far from home.

Caito starts off at breakneck pace in the speedboat and we fly around the narrow river bends out into the open vastness of the main river where the evening has turned the water muddy orange and a Day-glo sunset is framed by Alpine ranges of black and grey cloud stacked up along the horizon.

We pass an island where all the foliage seems to be crawling like maggots – hundreds of thousands of macaws fight for every twig and leaf screaming at such a pitch that you cover your ears as you come close. They rise up in swarms and subside again like volcanic lava, blackening the sunset, and revealing it again.

We speed on. Miles of water lie between us and Belém, which is a string of lights on the far side of the river. Suddenly, flames light the creosote-black water, resolving into the shapes of tugs pushing a raft of logs, half a mile long. Bonfires light its extremities, serving as navigation lights. There are men. Several shacks have been erected on it. Children play.

Out of these impressions I will fashion a handful of images

to represent Markham's experience of journeying into the heart of the forest in his quest for his son. And I am not unmindful of how tough it will be to get a cast and crew into these places to recapture some of these wondrous moments.

Michael and I have criss-crossed Amazonia in our air taxis, buffeted by storms, always relieved to see the red dust of an airstrip: Santarém, Manaus, up to Boa Vista on the border, searching for the interesting terrain and spectacular forest that we need as a setting for the story. We have found good places, but these are usually hard to get at, requiring boat journeys or long treks over pot-holed dirt roads. The problem is that anywhere accessible by river or road has been logged of its big trees.

We finally found a solution in Carajás, some 350 miles from Belém. A few years ago they discovered the world's largest deposit of iron ore lying under virgin forest in undulating hills to the north-west of Marabá. Just a few years ago, a forest guide, Carlindo Milhomen, was lowered by line from a helicopter into the jungle. With his machete, he cut a landing platform for the helicopter. They made a landing strip and workers poured in. There is enough iron ore to supply the world's needs for a hundred years. But how to get it out? They decided to build a railway through 600 miles of jungle to the port of São Luís.

They scraped off an area some way from the iron ore to build a town, but when they essayed the soil they found copper, then magnesium, then bauxite – a lot of it – then gold and uranium and just about anything else you can think of. It was a massive trove of treasure, but locked in the heart of the jungle. For seven years now they have laboured. They have built a town and an airport, three smelters, hospitals and schools and they are inching the railroad towards the sea. Seven years and hundreds of millions of dollars later they still have not earned a single cruzeiro, still have not got a bucket of ore out of the place. In the meantime, the market in minerals has slumped and it is calculated that the Carajás project can now never make money. But they must feverishly work on for ever, just to pay back the interest, digging away, digging Brazil deeper into debt.

The very same Carlindo who took the first giant step for Brazil as he alighted, machete swinging, from that ill-fated helicopter, is assigned to show us the primary rain forest that hems in the trucks, cranes and bulldozers of the project.

Seeing the forest with his eyes is very illuminating. Here man has hardly set foot. These hills, with no rivers to carry intruders, have been undisturbed for 100 million years. Here is the greatest variety of flora and fauna in the world. Stepping into its jaws in the wake of the silent, watchful Carlindo I witnessed primeval forest, unseen by man. The world in its beginning. We all have a landscape of the spirit, that place in which we feel – not peace but wholeness. Mine is the forest: but northern oak and beech woods. I filmed much of *Excalibur* in one of the few primeval oak forests left in Europe, uncut and unplanted.

This is wilder, more vibrant. Oaks are immensely slow, nursing old grudges and forgotten secrets. The rain forest is rampant, spiteful, tangled in angry knots. Barbed thorns, spiked leaves, resins that burn, poisonous fruits, grasses that clutch you, huge ants that sting like snakes, caterpillars whose hair brings welts up on the skin, tarantulas a foot across wearing mink coats.

Carlindo checks me and stops. A thin shiny black snake slithers lazily across our way.

'The Indians call that a Ten Step.'

I laugh. It sounds like a dance from the 1940s.

'Because', he continues, 'if he bites you, you are dead before you can run ten steps.'

He glances up at the tree under which we are standing. He garners some yellow berries from it and urges me to consume them.

'If you eat these you will be able to make a baby when you are 100.'

I swallowed them down. One moment instant death, the next immortality beckons.

We came to a big tree with buttresses splayed out on all sides supporting 120 feet of trunk and branch in the shallow soil. It is 30 feet across at the base. In its upper branches a whole garden of satellites flourish. Vines hang 60 feet down from its branches, an irresistible invitation to swing on them. I grab one and it immediately snaps high up and drops around me in heavy lethal coils. I weave and dodge and somehow manage to survive.

'How old would it be?' I ask Carlindo.

He explains that there is no way to tell. A tree will grow long and thin, but if there is no gap in the canopy above, its growth will be arrested for years. When a big tree falls a gap of sky appears and all nearby trees start a race to claim it. The Amazon forest has almost no soil. Everything lives on the instant humus that the heat and constant rain produce. A big fallen tree is a bonus of nourishment and the competing trees shoot out roots to it. One will win and very quickly increase its growth and seize the piece of vacant sky.

'How can they know where the fallen tree is?' I ask. 'How can they tell where to send their roots?'

Carlindo shrugs. He spends a lot of his time taking botanists and tree experts around these forests, and no one knows the answer to that, nor to a lot of other mysteries. For instance, trees seem to be able to warn each other of an approaching disease, so that they can develop resistance.

Inside the forest, it is dark and dank. The air is rich, fragrant with the scent of blossom and decay. It recalls death: I visited a coffin in a chapel that was decked with flowers and wreaths. Under the fresh smell of flowers I could detect the sweet corruption of flesh. Here, you walk through the subtle strata of the humid air: a current of hot air gives way to a cooler one, a juicy mango smell becomes the acrid, unmistakable whiff of snake. But under it all is the smell of death, sometimes concealed, sometimes raw and blatant. No wind penetrates. No leaf stirs. You strain to see and hear, every faculty alert, watchful. Never have I felt so intensely alive.

We stop and gaze about us. There is nowhere else I would rather be. It is alien, yet I belong. I am anxious to press on, and Carlindo's machete cuts a way for us. I have an urge to go on and on. Desert freaks describe this impulse, to walk on and on, never to turn back.

Yet, like the desert, it is endlessly monotonous. Only when you come to a river or gorge is there any break or change.

Photographically it poses enormous problems. Light scarcely penetrates. It is grey and gloomy, and so dense that a man 20 feet away is swallowed up by the vegetation. There is no way to tell that this forest stretches for hundreds of miles. Michael shows me his exposure meter. The needle scarcely flickers.

Here in Carajás we have finally found undisturbed rain forest, and in a place into which we can fly the crew and cast.

---

6 JUNE 1983 *PARIS*

Caught up on all the *Nemo* rushes. Spent the day in the cutting room with the editor, Tom Priestley.

Back in time to catch the chestnuts exploding into life in the Jardin des Tuileries. Translucent leaves of such a tender hue of green. The leaves of the rain forest, by contrast, look like olive-drab PVC.

The evening light on the Seine at the Pont Neuf is the brush stroke of a god. The French are busy about their business of refining and perfecting. A few hours on a plane link the beginning of the planet with its highest ends.

---

8 JUNE 1983 *LONDON*

Michael has taken on an accountant, Fred Harding, to make a budget and has been feeding him all the information on costs that he gathered on our trips. We spend two days doing a 'breakdown' of the script. Each scene is analysed on a separate piece of paper, its location or stage set, actors involved, props required, etc., and an estimate of the time needed to shoot it. There are still locations we have yet to find and we lack other information so this will be a rough preliminary budget.

14 JUNE 1983 *PARIS*

Rospo has arrived to work on the next draft of the script. In the interval he has written another script for someone else. He has written and been paid for perhaps a dozen screenplays in the last six years, and the only one that was filmed was *Excalibur*. This is a common experience for Hollywood writers. It is very dispiriting. But he is in good heart. I spent the first session regaling him with my experiences, which of course change many of our preconceptions. I explain the difficulties of shooting inside the rain forest. It will feel claustrophobic, so we must find story devices that allow us to step out and look over the canopy; punctuation points that remind us of the sweep and scale of the forest. We must set more scenes on or near rivers and streams. The scenes at the dam have to be revised to take account of its special characteristics. The observations I made in and around Belém need to be worked into the story.

We had intended to rewrite only certain sequences but we decide to go from page 1 and revise whatever seems necessary. Inevitably, everything starts to change. After three days we are still only on page 32. But it is coming to life.

5 JULY 1983 *LONDON*

Brought the script to the typist in London today and Rospo has gone back to Los Angeles. It is lighter and richer now, with much more texture. I can now concentrate on the budget and schedule with Michael and begin designing the picture.

8 JULY 1983

Laying out the schedule on a strip board with Michael. We have been juggling all day. It comes to seventeen weeks shooting with the main unit, then a further five weeks with a reduced unit that I will take into the remote jungle. On returning to the UK, we have to shoot a model sequence of the dam bursting, as well as other sequences of the dam that may require front-projection shots with actors after the model shots have been made. There are question marks against how we achieve the many animal scenes in the film. Tommy's spiritual animal is an eagle and there are scenes where he goes into trance and sees with the eye of an eagle. The camera must fly and swoop over the roof of the forest, soar and hover. (This is part of my plan to find ways of experiencing the rain forest and escaping from its clammy confines.) I have a mixture of devices to achieve this, including the most obvious – helicopter shots. We are making enquiries about falconers, some of whom do occasionally manage to train eagles.

Oxford Scientific Films make astonishing natural-history films. They have developed new techniques for micro-photography. They came to my attention when I was making *Zardoz*. I was looking for images that could represent brain impulses, DNA codes and molecular biology, which I wanted to project on huge screens as Charlotte Rampling and Sara Kestelman investigate Sean Connery's mind. Shots of plankton did the trick. Since I introduced Oxford Scientific Films into the world of feature films, they have never stopped working on them. When I made *The Heretic*, which was full of optical effects, I sent the great Al Whitlock from Los Angeles to instruct them in the use of blue-screen techniques. The film required a locust swarm in an Ethiopian desert. There were several elements to this shot: a desert set on the stage at Burbank; Al Whitlock's matt painting to enhance the horizon; the distant locust swarm, which was achieved by putting iron filings on a sheet of glass and by moving a magnet behind them, so they appeared to 'swarm'. Oxford Scientific were to photograph flying locusts in close-up against a blue screen and these would be superimposed on top of the other elements.

We have been up to Oxford to talk to Peter Parks. He says he can build a model eagle that would be mechanically articulated. He would shoot it against a blue screen, matching its movements to the helicopter flying shots that we would make over the jungle. The two would then be married together. Although I hope to find a trained eagle to do most of the shots, this technique would allow us the illusion of the camera moving in intimate proximity to the bird. It is the same technique used to make Superman fly. Effective special effects nearly always involve a mixture of techniques. The trigonometry of the brain is ruthlessly clever. If there is something wrong, it will detect it. The beholder will not know what is wrong, just that something *is* wrong. So we must trick the eye and brain by shifting from one device to another and creating a perfect illusion. The spoilt audience, sated on sensation, sits back and says, 'OK, amaze me. Take me on a trip, but don't you dare take me for a ride.'

The blue screen must be an exact hue of blue and illuminated and exposed very precisely. It must, in fact, perfectly match the blue emulsion layer of the film that will neutralize it and allow the background shot to print through. There are all kinds of technicalities involved, but it is most vital to match the lighting of the foreground and background. The light source must come from the same angle and it must be the same kind of light, that is to say hard or diffused, and have the same colour temperature. If not, it will look fake.

Finally, Michael and I sat with a great list of unresolved issues and the rambling, endless strip board. The daunting scale of the enterprise is evident. The budget will certainly come out at the top end of our $15–17 million prediction – perhaps more.

The bureaucracy involved in shooting in Brazil looks more tangled at every turn. We have been meeting with David Norris, who looks after business affairs at Goldcrest, trying to unravel the legal and financial problems. David was my lawyer for years. He is brilliant and inventive and can usually find a way through problems. His solutions are often complex and he draws beautiful charts with arrows pointing at coloured boxes, which I pretend to understand. He has instructed an American bank that operates in Brazil to find a company that wishes to unload cruzeiros at a discount. Until we get some idea of what the cruzeiros will cost us it will be impossible to finalize the budget.

We have to put a crew together resilient enough to withstand six months in the equatorial jungle. Not easy. There are so many movies being made in London that every inch of stage space is booked out for months ahead. Many prefer now to work on commercials since they shoot for only two or three days, are highly paid, and can then take a week's rest. It spoils them. On the other hand, I want only people who *want* to go, who relish the adventure, who know that a tincture of danger sharpens the senses.

Casting lies ahead, much of it in unknown territory – Brazil – and beyond that we must recruit and train the tribes.

We looked at each other and the thought passed between us: did we really want to punish ourselves like this?

The thought could not be spoken. Fred Harding was still buried in figures. He wears a bemused smile that never leaves his face and his handwritten figures become more and more illegible. That smile makes me nervous.

Still, a long way to go before the final decision to Stop or Go.

---

12 JULY 1983 *PARIS*

We screened the first rough-cut of *Nemo* today at the LTD Laboratories. Claude, Tom Priestley, Arnaud, Telsche, Michel Propper were there. Of course, all the optical effects are missing. The music has yet to be recorded. All the dialogue has to be 'looped' since it was not possible to record usable dialogue in the *boule*, our plastic dome. The dome was supported by air pressure and the noise of the machine is on the soundtrack. So it is a *very* rough cut. It is comprehensible only to those of us who know it well and can fill in the gaps with imagination.

Yet, the first time you see a film put together, however loose and rambling it is, however lacking in refinement, you know if it plays or, at least, if it *will* play. Up to this point, you have been editing it sequence by sequence, giving each the timing and pace it appears to need. Now you judge the relationship between sequences, the relative weight and strength of performances, the movement of the narrative and so on.

Nemo is difficult to judge, more so than most, because it has

the free-associating form of a dream, and depends on enchanting us moment by moment. I found that it does cast a spell,
yet one feels detached from the characters, remote, as in a
dream. Since there is not a strong narrative to hold one to it,
we are dependent on the wit, the invention, the beauty of
each scene. Some scenes sustain this better than others. Yet I
was moved at the end. As a dream world with its own rules,
it parallels the strangeness of our planet, and expresses what
every child feels at some time: 'Why have I been put down on
this ridiculous planet? It doesn't seem to make sense or have
any meaning. I feel very sad and lost, and so does everyone
around me.' Yet, on the way, there are pleasures and wonders
and distractions and, most of all, laughter.

It will not be easy to find an audience. By today's standards
it lacks the high energy action that young people expect, and
it may seem too childish for adults.

I am impressed with the work of Philippe Rousselot, the
cameraman. He has been a good support to Arnaud, offering
ideas when needed, but never intrusive. He is an artist and
has the pragmatic good sense that most good artists have. I
am considering him for Brazil. He lacks the experience of big
international pictures, and there would be the problem of
integrating him into an English unit. On the other hand, I
like to break up these cosy patterns. We shall need fresh thinking out there. British crews are as good as any, better than
most, but they are full of little ruses to make their lives easier,
to extract more money. However much they may love or
respect the director, there is always, at least, a skirmish in the
class war: the director and producer are the bosses who are
trying to screw them.

We will have a mixed crew anyway – British and Brazilian
– and, if I ask Philippe, he would want to bring his gaffer,
Jean-Pierre Baronsky, who in turn would want his electricians.
There are wretched problems in mixed crews. Paul Henreid
told me a story about Michael Curtiz during the making of
Casablanca. Curtiz suddenly decided he needed a poodle for a
scene. The prop man and assistant directors ran in all directions, searching and making calls. Meanwhile, Curtiz and
Bogart played chess, which they always did during delays.

Eventually, an animal wrangler arrived with a selection of poodles for the director to choose from 'Not a poodle!' he screamed. 'A poodel! With water!'

I fell into these problems with a mixed crew myself on *Hell in the Pacific* where I had an English art director, Tony Pratt, an American cameraman, the great Conrad Hall, and a lot of Japanese. Film techniques are the same throughout the world and the language of film is international, yet in the detail there is boundless scope for misunderstanding.

Hell in the Pacific was about an American airman and a Japanese naval officer, Lee Marvin and Toshiro Mifune, who find themselves washed up on the same atoll in the South Pacific after a naval battle. There are no other characters and, of course, no spoken communication is possible between them. It was certainly an example of my adage about film-making being the process of inventing impossible challenges for oneself and failing to solve them.

Writing the script required a special approach. I recruited Shobal Hashimoto who was a principal writer of several Kuro-sawa pictures, among them *Rashomon* and *The Seven Samurai*. He sat in one office at Goldwyn studios in Hollywood; I sat in the adjoining one, and the third was occupied by Alex Jacobs whom I had brought from England to work on *Point Blank*. Alex was a brilliant structuralist, but a very urban man and a bit lost when asked to pitch his imagination into a jungle island. But, then, so was our American airman, so that was all right.

I would sketch out a scene and give it to each writer. They would work on it from the aspect of their character and then pass it back. Translators rendered it back and forth in the two languages, and gradually a script grew where each character behaved according to his background. My idea was that it should be two films. As they muttered to themselves, or shouted at each other, a Japanese audience would understand one half of the movie and an English-speaking audience the other half.

Making the script was tremendously difficult and we were often stumped by its inherent problems. When we were in Japan between drafts, doing research, I said to Hashimoto,

'Ask Kurosawa what he would do if he was making this film, with these severe limitations.'

Hashimoto put the problem to the master who pondered it for some time. Hashimoto waited patiently and finally the solemn answer came, but with tongue in cheek.

'They are not alone on the island. They meet a girl.'

I often regretted not taking his advice.

One day Hashimoto said, 'Look, I have an idea for a fresh approach to the story. Give me a week on my own and let me see what I can make of it.' I agreed reluctantly, and I must confess slightly suspiciously, since he was an obsessive gambler and I knew the proximity of Las Vegas was a terrible temptation to him.

My suspicions were ill founded because he returned after a week having done an extensive rewrite. When it was translated, I discovered that without changing the structure at all he had rewritten the existing scenes turning the film into a rather broad comedy.

When I told him he was on the wrong tack, he shrugged philosophically and dutifully returned to the old system. In due course we completed the screenplay and the Japanese version went off to Mifune.

We all assembled in Palau and started shooting. On the very first day Mifune started to cavort in a very strange manner. When I corrected him, he became very stubborn. For me to tell him he was wrong in front of the Japanese crew put his honour at stake. However much I explained, when it came to a take, he just reverted to his own interpretation. I had to suspend shooting. We all went back to the ship on which we lived, and spent hours going through the scene step by step. He and Lee got drunk and there was a lot of shouting. At last we got it right and for three days while we shot the scene, all was fine.

When we started a new scene on the fourth day, the trouble started over again. Mifune was simply not playing the same scene as we were. He was behaving like a buffoon. I thought he was drunk. We clashed again. Shooting ground to a halt. Lee was distraught. Alarm spread to the financiers as we got hopelessly behind schedule.

Eventually I realized that Hashimoto had given Mifune what I called the 'Las Vegas' script.

By the time we were able to get the proper script translated, the damage had been done. Mifune felt his honour obliged him to continue to oppose me. We fought every inch of the way. Lee became dispirited – or full of spirits. The crew's morale plummeted. And racial frictions flared up, particularly between the Japanese and the crew of the ship, which happened to be Chinese.

My relationship with the producer, Reuben Berkovitch, collapsed under the strain and I banned him from the set (the island); since he was very nervous about catching tropical diseases, he spent his days on the ship arguing with Captain Wong about how things should be run on board. One night it all came to a head and Captain Wong, in his cups, challenged Reuben to a duel with billiard cues snatched up from the table that provided the only entertainment on the ship. He actually called Reuben an Imperialist Jewish Running Dog and it turned out that although he came from Taiwan, when the chips were down, the Communists were to be preferred to the Americans. Blood will out, I thought, as Wong flailed his cue. Christel and I, with Telsche and Katrine, were living in a hut on the island and when I arrived the next morning to rendezvous with the crew, I found the ship had weighed anchor and set sail, my crew and cast aboard. Lloyd Anderson, the production manager, went back and forth between the bridge and Reuben's cabin and eventually a compromise was reached and they turned back.

Shortly afterwards, a camera platform we had built on the barrier reef was smashed down by a rogue wave and Conrad Hall and I were cut up on the needle-sharp coral. I got coral poisoning in a knee, which caused an infection that nearly lost me a leg. The island medical officer (they get one year's training in Fiji) cut out the infected part and drained it off. I was out of action for several days.

The producers seized the chance to fire me and went to Mifune in great jubilation to convey the good news to him. He told them he would work with no other director.

'But you hate Boorman,' they said. 'Yes. That is true,'

Mifune replied. 'But at the tea house in Tokyo, Boorman and I agreed to make this film together and we sealed that pact with many toasts in sake.' (I remember being carried back to the hotel.)

When I started work again, carried in a litter by four Palauans, I felt a new warmth and closeness to Mifune. But everything was exactly as before. We fought like cat and dog. It was a matter of honour and had nothing to do with personal feeling.

By chance, *Hell in the Pacific* has been revived and re-released in Paris this summer. Christel and I went to see it on the Champs-Elysées. We took Daisy who had never seen it. She was 1 year old when it was made. She is 16 now.

Normally when I have finished a movie, and it has opened, I never see it again, but I wanted to remind myself of how Connie Hall and I had dealt with the problems of shooting in the jungle.

By a further happenchance, Lee Marvin and his wife Pam are here in Paris making a movie. We have talked a lot about those times over the last few days, and the faces of Lee and Toshiro stare out from bus shelters all across Paris.

---

15 JULY 1983

The preliminary budget comes out at £8,450,000, which includes Goldcrest's overhead and the completion bond fee of $4\frac{1}{2}$ per cent, which Goldcrest will receive, having agreed to take the risk themselves. Most US majors do the same. Going to an outside company to guarantee completion is expensive and creates a lot of difficulties; in particular, the financier and the producer lose a degree of control. The guarantor will want a representative looking over the shoulder of the accountant and breathing down the neck of the producer. If the director wants to shoot something unplanned or make changes, the guarantor will disclaim responsibility for any overage. If the film gets behind schedule he will suggest cuts in the script and schedule. He has the right to take control of the picture if it goes substantially over budget and can fire the director and producer. A film can go over budget for all kinds of reasons, sometimes good ones. The director and the studio occasionally decide the film needs more money when they see the rushes. They may decide a piece of casting is wrong, find another actor and reshoot three weeks of work. There have been a lot of over-budget pictures that were great successes. Billy Wilder once commented, 'Nobody ever said – "I must see that movie, I hear it came in under budget." '

One of Goldcrest's conditions for making the film is that we qualify for the Eady benefit. This is a levy on cinema seats taken on all foreign films (effectively American ones) and divided up among British films released in the same year. The more successful your film, the more of the levy you get. Eady is not worth much today, partly because cinema attendance is so poor in the UK. But if a film qualifies for Eady it also qualifies for a form of tax-shelter investment that the government has sanctioned, but which is to be gradually phased out. In effect, it can mean 10–15 per cent of the budget. A film qualifies for Eady if 80 per cent of its labour costs are British (or EEC, since no discrimination is allowed under Common Market law). There are some other variations to the 80 per cent formula, but they are minor and technical.

Our dilemma is this: if we take a minimum British crew and employ Brazilians for the balance, we save money, but do not qualify for Eady. If, on the other hand, we increase the British contingent, the cost of the picture goes up and the advantage of the tax shelter is eroded.

For the most part, film companies make a tax deal and, although it effectively reduces the price of the movie, they do not pass it on to the producers. Goldcrest have agreed to do so in my case.

This is Jake's way: a partnership. It is wholly in the spirit of our early agreement. I have spent well over a year now working on *Nemo* and *The Emerald Forest*. I have received no remuneration. I invest my time and skill, as Goldcrest invests its money. We are partners and we share all the advantages. The US majors notoriously 'load' your picture with costs in such a way that they never have to pay out net profits unless the film goes through the roof. Because everyone knows that profits will not be paid out, directors and stars insist on high fees up front as a way of punishing the studio in advance for not paying fair profits. This pushes up the cost of movies, and in turn reduces the possibility of profit.

I have often given up a fee in order to get a picture made: *Excalibur* and *Zardoz*, for instance. You work two or three years without pay, gambling on the film being a big enough success to shame the studio into paying you out. Mostly the studio balks at the final fence and says it will make the picture only if you can cut the budget. With perhaps only a month to go, your emotional commitment is such that you do it. There are few cuts that can be made at this stage, the director's fee is one that can.

The economics of a typically successful film would be as below:

	$
Negative cost of film	10,000,000
(How much it costs to make exclusive of interest, marketing)	
Prints for US release	2,000,000
Advertising (including TV)	7,000,000
	19,000,000
Interest, charged 2% above prime (Prints and advertising costs are quickly recovered, but production costs are out for two years or more) Therefore, 14% on $10,000,000 for 2 years	2,800,000
Total Cost	21,800,000
Let us say the picture is a big hit and earns $40,000,000 at the US box office. Half is retained by the exhibitors.	
Received by distributor:	20,000,000
Distributor deducts 30% fee	6,000,000
leaving	14,000,000
Cost of prints and advertising deducted	9,000,000
	5,000,000

This sum ($5,000,000) goes to pay
off production costs. So after a
successful US run the film still
recovers only one half of its
production costs.

It now plays in foreign (anywhere else other than the USA and Canada) territories and takes a further	20,000,000
Here the exhibitors keep 60% leaving	8,000,000
The distributors take a 40% fee	3,200,000
Leaving	4,800,000
Prints, advertising and costs of dubbing into foreign languages, shipping costs, subtitles	6,000,000

So the foreign release puts the
picture $1,200,000 further in debit.
Now there is still $6,200,000
unrecovered.

Because the film was such a success, the distributor is able to make very good sales to cable TV, for video cassettes and TV amounting to	9,000,000
Distribution fees here are only 25%	2,230,000
Leaving	6,770,000

This appears to be enough to pay
off the production costs but these
ancillary incomes will be paid a year
or two down the line so you have to
add another year's interest at 14%

on the unrecovered	6,200,000
which is	888,000
	7,088,000
less	6,770,000
	18,000

So it seems the film is still not in
profit. $18,000 is still to be
recovered.

How has the studio done to date? It
split the net profits 50–50 with the
producers, that is 50% is divided
among the stars, director and
producer, and writers. The studio
will often lay off half of the negative
cost to an outside investor and give
up half its profits. The poor studio
has ended up with only 25% of the
net. However, it has been able to
get a tax shelter of $1,500,000,
which, since the film has broken
even, becomes profit.

It has made a small profit on its mark up on the interest	40,000
It has received discounts from press and TV groups it advertises with of 10%	1,000,000
Its distribution fees are	11,400,000
Tax shelter of	1,500,000
Total income from the film	13,940,000
Its risk going in was	10,000,000
Less outside investor	5,000,000
Total risk	5,000,000

For this investment, which is now paid back, it has received
profits of $13,940,000 within two to three years. Out of this it
has to pay its overheads and distribution costs.

But part of the $10,000,000 budget, in fact the biggest item,
was a 15 per cent overhead charge – $1,500,000. So its in-
vestment was really only $3,500,000. If the studio makes ten
to twenty pictures a year the overhead charges will cover its
production and distribution costs, so that the $13,940,000 rep-
resents clear profits – but not quite. Not all films do as well as

this, and some of them are total failures. The losers must be set against the winners.

If this film had looked like failing, the studio would have set about minimizing its losses. It would quickly slash the spending on advertising, sell it fast to cable and TV, and concentrate on trying to get back as much as possible of its $3,500,000 cash cost. Most studios today have covered their downside before shooting starts. Pre-selling cable or TV can cover their cash outlay. The secret of the game is having free counters with which to bet.

All our friends are congratulating us on having one of the hit pictures of the year, and we are desperately wishing we had taken a big fee rather than a share of the profits.

Goldcrest's slogan is 'Fulfilling the promise'. Ruefully, I am hoping that this is not a hollow boast, that this one is different.

---

19 JULY 1983

I have been trying to find a production designer to start working with me. There are eight or nine sets to make, the miniatures to be supervised, as well as the Indian villages to be constructed. It requires flair, but above all organizational ability. British and Brazilian craftsmen will have to be integrated, a warehouse or hangar found where we can build sets, and most of the things we need must be shipped out months in advance.

Tony Pratt, who did *Excalibur* for me, but perhaps more pertinently *Hell in the Pacific*, is not available. I tried to lure him away from his current project, but to no avail. He is designing a film called *Santa Claus*.

Richard MacDonald, a wayward genius, did *The Heretic*, but is busy too, and complex logistical work is not something he savours. Tony Woollard did two films for me, including *Leo the Last*, in which he did superb work, but he is off shooting in Australia.

I talked to Stuart Craig who just came back from designing *Greystoke* in the jungles of the Cameroons. He loved our script and agreed to do it, but he is involved in *Cal* for Goldcrest and David Puttnam which he is designing and producing. Its start has been delayed and he has had to cry off.

Today I saw Michael Seymour whose credits include Ridley Scott's *Alien* and a picture for Nick Roeg, *Eureka*, in which I found the design quite brilliant. In fact, for the first hour, I thought it one of the best pictures ever. The movie faltered when it suddenly switched from telling its story in a series of searing vivid images to a courtroom drama.

When you are considering a technician you do not know, the accepted procedure is to call up people with whom he has worked. Nick Roeg gave a strong recommendation.

Jake said, 'If Ridley likes him so much, why isn't he doing *Legend*?', which is Ridley's new film. I asked Seymour. He told me that at one stage Ridley was going to make it in the States, and so got an American designer.

Seymour starts right away. He will break down the script and then rendezvous with me in Brazil.

---

22 JULY 1983 *PARIS*

Dinner last night with Sam Fuller at the large apartment he and his wife Christa are renting while he completes the thriller he has been making in Paris. Sam was King of the Hollywood 'B' movie. A one-time *Front Page*-style newspaperman, his most famous adage is, 'Film is war.' Certainly, being harangued by Sam is like enduring constant machine-gun fire.

I once met Sam in a hotel in Rome where he was scouting locations for *The Big Red One*, the story of his combat in World War II. One of the great experiences in the movie business is listening to Sam telling the story of a film he plans to make. I was spellbound while he described every shot, played all the characters. Waiters recoiled as he lobbed grenades at the bar, took cover behind a sofa, slit throats, raped and pillaged. It was 2.30 in the morning before we reached the fade out and as we went up in the elevator he described the background to the end credit crawl.

It was a master class: how to build tension, the use of tracking shots, pacing, interplay of characters. It was spellbinding and exhilarating. Lying in bed afterwards, I wondered how he could bear to go through the drudgery of shooting when it already existed as a perfect *performance*.

Later, when he was shooting part of it in Ireland, I watched him work. He was still dominating the actors and crew with a non-stop barrage of anecdotes and admonitions. Instead of calling action, he fired a shot in the air from one of two .45s he kept in his belt.

After each take he would turn to the camera operator, cigar clenched in his teeth, and snap out, 'Did you get it? Forget it!'

The only person I ever met who could out-talk Sam was his wife, Christa. A double bombardment could leave you shell-shocked for a week. But such is Sam's fund of wit and wisdom, I never once heard him repeat himself.

So it was that my wife and I presented ourselves for dinner to discover two other directors already in attendance – Claude Chabrol (with his wife and ex-wife Stephane Audran) and Andrzej Wajda. The dinner was excellent, although Bertrand Tavernier is easily the best cook of any director I know.

It was a fine thing to be among directors one admires. When directors gather, they usually fall to talking about money, how to get enough of it to make a movie, and of how movie-making is a kind of exile – as we invent and people our own places, so we vacate the real world.

From *Ashes and Diamonds* to *Man of Iron*, Wajda snatches moments from the Polish body politic. His films are like wounds, smeared with fresh blood. They are made fast and furious. Now he seems baffled and cautious. What can he do, cut off from Poland? I searched his face for humour, irony, bitterness, running his movies in my mind at high speed to catch a likeness, but I could not connect them with the man who sat before me. Sam and his films are indivisible; Wajda appeared as a shadow of his. Sam was abandoned by Hollywood and languished for years in the wilderness. It was the French new wave – Chabrol and others – who wrote about his films and because of their recognition he has enjoyed a revival of fortunes.

Chabrol is wholly delightful, constantly clowning, generous, sensitive to those about him, very comfortable in the company of women. He is one of the few who loved *The Heretic*, and wrote and spoke of it extensively. Although he does not resemble his films, he has qualities in common with them: his love of the macabre, the ironic, the sensual textures, the humanity. I suspect Claude's sense of the ridiculous is too highly developed to be able to conduct the struggle to get pictures made with any earnestness.

Of course, one must be totally serious about film-making, and at the same time not take it seriously at all. It is hard to know how to get that balance right.

---

2 AUGUST 1983

Dinner last night in Les Halles with Philippe Rousselot. We sat outside in the warm night air, and ate oysters, something I would never do in England in August. At the end of it I offered him the job. He is slight, but all muscle, sinewy, wiry, alert. His eyes are keen, take in everything, but are kind too. He is unFrench in his attitude to food. He orders whatever I do. I tell him how impossible it is to shoot in the jungle, of the heat and humidity, the five-month schedule. But I cannot dampen his enthusiasm. He announced his intention of learning Portuguese. Since his English is excellent, perhaps he will help to bind together the different national groups.

---

3 AUGUST 1983

Michael Dryhurst in Paris yesterday. We spent the day going over the budget and finalizing plans for our trip to Brazil, which begins in three days. David Norris will go with us and we will try to set up a Brazilian company and buy cruzeiros. The cost of the film depends on the terms we can get, and if we cannot keep the budget down, the picture will not be made. It is all still in the balance.

6–7 AUGUST 1983 *EN ROUTE: GATWICK–SAO PAULO*

While David and Michael deal with the lawyers and bankers in São Paulo I will go to Rio to begin casting. The plane journey is a chance to spend time going over all the contractual issues with David and reviewing the various outstanding problems. The flight is eleven hours. I planned to use a good part of the time to work on my script, but our discussions soon decline into gossip. The lofty overview one feels at the beginning of a long flight is so quickly trivialized by the distractions provided. We succumb, weakened by alcohol. The night has passed. A couple of hours' sleep. It is light now. We will land soon. I can see the coastline of Brazil.

10 AUGUST 1983 *RIO*

Back in the Copacabana Hotel where, outside my window, the spectacle continues unabated, as joyful and depraved as ever.

Flavio Tambellini is an elegant young man, son of a Brazilian film producer, who himself is a screenwriter, assistant director and casting director. For three days he has been bringing actors in to see me. I have a video camera set up in the living room of the suite, the windows closed against the barrage of sound from the beach. We have seen, auditioned, over a hundred actors.

Flavio has first of all brought me all the actors of Indian descent. We also have other roles, non-Indian, to fill. These are much easier. Apart from the American family, which I will cast in the US, all the other parts must be filled in Brazil.

Without knowing their work and without, in many cases, sharing a language, casting poses problems.

My solution is to improvise scenes with each actor, which I record on the video camera, and then review at night. It is exhausting but very revealing. Brazilian actors are open and expressive. They present themselves, expose themselves, right away. In the savage economic climate of Brazil, theatre struggles to survive, few films are made, most of these are pornos, and the remainder done on pitiful budgets. Over these actors hangs the oppressive shadow of Globo, the Brazilian TV net-work that is the fourth largest in the world. Most actors are indentured to one or other of the plethora of soap operas that dominate the channel. Whereas in the States the soaps are relegated to the afternoons with just the occasional one – *Dallas* or *Dynasty* – breaking into peak viewing hours, in Brazil the soaps rule. The evenings are lathers of soap, punctuated only by sport, usually the quasi-religious ceremony of a soccer match.

As in all other spheres, Brazil leaps into the future without shame or embarrassment or a backward glance. Looking out for actors, I have watched a number of these soaps. Occasion-ally, writers and directors are using the form to do interesting work, without feeling the need to apologize, or have tongue in cheek. Good or bad, TV dominates here as elsewhere in the world. In the *favellas*, families sit on wooden crates, nursing malnourished children – watching television. Most of it is trash and most actors spill fake emotion into the shanty towns like cheap booze.

Casting is always interesting. Actors soak up whatever is in the air. They are a barometer of the emotional and psychic life of a nation, reflecting, as they do, those about them. And these Brazilians are tender and loving, poor but dignified. They have zest and fire. Not wit, perhaps, but verve. Not great intelligence, but quickness of mind. Uninhibited by tra-dition, they are ready for change, adept as all Brazilians are. This gives a great lightness to life, but there is always the sense that at any moment it could all spin out of control. It is a pleasant contrast to English actors. I struggled to find actors of heroic mould to play in *Excalibur*, for most of them are cautious, inhibited, entrenched and cannot give themselves. There is a technical excellence, but they are mostly mean-minded and dreary. I do not share the widely held reverence for English theatre. In most London theatres there is a mutual hostility between actors and audience. Neither wishes to be there; they are simply going through a ritual in a futile attempt to recapture an ecstatic past. Theatre actors seem much more insubstantial than those in movies. I feel like a shadow myself as I sit there in the theatre.

I have found only one man who could play Wanadi, the Indian chief and father to Tommy. His name is Rui Polonah and he played Indians for Herzog – small roles in *Aguirre, Wrath of God*, and *Fitzcarraldo*. Flavio tells me he had a bad drinking problem. He did an impressive improvisation. He has a wonderfully expressive face, and a gentle, quavering, fluting voice; a quirky manner with just a hint of danger lurking under it. His body is soft and flabby. We would have to put him on a strict training programme. It is worrying that he seems to be the only option for the part. These sessions help me to penetrate Brazil: through these actors I get intimations of the *Zeitgeist*. My foremost intuition is that this country *is* what the United States *thinks* it is.

The immigrants to the USA were supposed to turn their backs on Europe, but they hang on to their past. It is always disconcerting to a European when Americans say, 'I am Italian' or 'I am Swedish' with such pride. They cling to what distinguishes them from other Americans. They foster and indulge the most crass national foibles of their forebears: the sexual jealousy of Italians, wild Irish tempers, etc. They did not melt in the pot.

In Brazil they really melted; in fact, melting seems to be what they like doing best: Indian, Carib, European, Japanese – the genes swirl together, dancing to the samba beat, with never more than a pitying glance backwards to those sad, suffering souls who begat them to a life of sun and fun.

---

11 AUGUST 1983

Further meeting with Maureen. Our trip to Xingu is still not certain. We have asked the British Embassy to intercede. Orlando is pressing the Funai also. Takuma, the great Shaman, has agreed for me to visit his village. Orlando has advised us to take a fishing net as a gift. It must be of a very specific nature, size and mesh so that it corresponds to the one that (traditionally) they made with vines. We are turning São Paulo upside down to find it. Meanwhile, my application is processed slowly by a suspicious Funai.

I had a long meeting today with José Possi. He is a chore-
ographer and has been recommended as someone who might
contribute to recruiting and training the tribes. He was once
married, but is now gay. People chop and change here. He
shows me the tapes of his work – dance shows, modern ballet.
They are strong and real, refreshingly free of theatrical exag-
geration.

I told him how I want to work. He will have to organize
workshops in Rio and Belém. We will advertise for Indian
types. Possi must devise a series of exercises so that we can
judge their physical grace and prowess, their expressiveness,
their concentration. I do not wish to use tribal Indians. Training them to work on a movie would corrupt their way of life
and be quite immoral.

The selected ones will go into training. We will take more
than we need in order to allow for those who, inevitably, will
not stay the course.

We estimate the whole training process must last three
months, the last part including daily application of body
make-up and feathers and living naked in jungle conditions.
Possi is tough, and practical. He is a pro. But he has a dreadful
voice. If Hector's voice fills the room, Possi's cuts like a chainsaw. It is on one note, only the volume alters. When he raises
his voice, I imagine acres of rain forest crashing to the ground.
He is asking a lot of money and he wants it paid in dollars. It is
impossible to underrate someone who values himself so highly.

---

14 AUGUST 1983 *EN ROUTE: SAO PAULO-BELEM*

David Norris has gone back. On his first night we ate raw fish
at a Japanese restaurant and he was violently sick. He dragged
himself to his meetings and then fell back into his bed at the
Maksoud Plaza Hotel. He has now gone back to England
with surely the slightest exposure to Brazil it is possible to
have. He is forming a company called Goldcrest Filmes Limitada which has purchased a Brazilian company by exchanging stock which ... At this point I lost track and my mind
drifted to other thoughts. As David explained the arrange-

ment his spirits visibly lifted, since its complexity apparently has a pleasing geometry. He recaptured my attention when he concluded by saying that on his return he would deposit £2 million in Brazil for the purchase of cruzeiros. Citibank would then invest this money hoping to keep ahead of inflation. Surely, I thought, such a commitment would mean no turning back for Goldcrest.

In my entire career I never once had the good fortune of a studio saying 'Yes, we'll make the picture. Here's the money. Off you go.' The closest was Lew Grade's cheque under my backside. No. You must inch the financiers towards the brink. You continue to spend more and more of their money, edge them into commitments until they find they have spent so much it is cheaper to make the film than abandon it.

Before inflation, they used to say of Hollywood, 'There's nothing as scared as a million dollars.' After all, movie-making is the process of turning money into light. All they have at the end of the day is images flickering on a wall.

When I was making *Point Blank* in Hollywood, I insisted on using the tiny Arriflex camera rather than the huge cumbersome studio Mitchell that was standard then. One day the studio heads were to visit the set. My wise and talented cameraman, Philip Lathrop, advised me to use the big camera while they were around. 'If they see all that money disappearing into that itsy-bitsy camera, they're going to get very nervous.'

By the time David had explained his brilliant plan he was quite cured and went back to London brimming with health. I love his spirit. We have been confidants for years, but now, alas, we must be circumspect because we are on different sides.

He totted up the score – the pre-sales to Embassy and foreign distributors, the tax shelter, the TV and video sales, the savings on cruzeiros – set against our current budget – we come out $4 million in profit before the film is distributed. Nevertheless, I remind him, there is the small matter of actually making the movie. This is the one messy indeterminate in an otherwise perfect equation. I told him I would try not to spoil it all.

Michael and I plan to take a lease on offices in Belém and

a warehouse that will serve as workshops for set building. Another commitment. David agrees. It is beginning to look solid. I feel a tremor of dread.

---

20 AUGUST 1983 *EN ROUTE: BELEM–BRASILIA*

I seem to write most of this journal on aeroplanes. As the crew begins to grow, so the demands on one's time increase. Michael Seymour arrived in Belém to join us. He wore a jungle-green safari suit with matching luggage. Marcos Flaksman, a Brazilian art director whom I met in Rio, came up to join us. Flaksman art-directed *Blame It on Rio*. He speaks excellent English, and I am hoping that he and Seymour will work together since Marcos's local knowledge will be invaluable.

Since my first visit to Belém Caito has been at work solving problems and creating havoc in equal measure. He has obtained permission to use a government building as the Amazco offices and even to fix our emblems to the top of the highrise. This was especially tricky as part of it is used by the secret police who are very touchy. Also, he got the whole top floor of an apartment block that is still raw concrete. We can take over the entire thing, decorate it as we wish, have 'wild' (moveable) walls to accommodate camera and lights, with extra rooms for catering, make-up, etc.

Went back to Tucuruí so that Seymour and Flaksman could take detailed pictures of the dam from which the model can be constructed. Now that I have adjusted the script to suit the location, I was able to tell them exactly where I would place the camera. Then a trip to Carajás for further explorations. We need a river with some rapids that is about 50 metres across with jungled banks. The Carajás project is enclosed in barbed wire with armed guards. Just outside the gates we discovered that a *favella* had grown up, as they always do on the fringes of these places. Inside, a stern military morality is imposed – the Brasilia mentality, you might call it – with separate clubs for married and single people, curfew, rigorous medical checks, any street life ruthlessly repressed.

Once outside the gates, you are back in Brazil. A wild chaos of wooden shacks houses forty-seven whorehouses at the last count, bars, blaring music and continuous street football.

Inside the fence nothing grows. Nothing must mar the total sterility. All the food is canned or frozen and brought in from outside, while out here is the familiar riot of fruit and vegetables. Chickens and pigs run in the muddy streets, and everywhere are children. The national costume of Brazil is nylon soccer shorts for boys, usually red or blue with two white stripes down the side – and nothing else. Girls favour a one-piece stretch nylon swimsuit with a cotton skirt over it. Girls love to put colours together like orange and pink, yellow and blue. And, of course, T-shirts. The slogan T-shirt has swept the world, and such is the speed with which commerce converts originality into banality that what a few years ago was special, élite and distinguishing, is now available to everyone. Thus, here in the Carajás *favella* one saw an illiterate boy wearing a Harvard T-shirt. One of the more popular T-shirts is emblazoned with AGENT ORANGE, which is widely used as a defoliant. It was employed to inhibit the jungle from clawing up the pylons and power cables they laid from Tucuruí down to Belém. They left empty drums of it lying about which the poor settlers along the way picked up and used to store water. Over a hundred people died. God knows what the long-term effects will be on others, indeed, on this community in Carajás where it has been used in clearing the place.

The Indian tribes of this area have been driven off; the women often taken and pressed into prostitution. Everywhere one finds elements of our story being played out in life.

There were remains of an Indian village at the river by the *favella*. An old man was farming the land and had two dug-out canoes. He in one, his son in the other, we paddled upstream for a couple of hours. At one point on a rising bank, a man appeared with a rifle. Our old guide (old? – none of us could keep up with his paddling) advised us to hug the near shore so that he would not see us. He was wanted for murder and took pot shots at anyone coming up river.

These river excursions are absorbing. Each bend reveals something new: a sudden profusion of blossoms cascading into the water, a pair of parrots explode screaming from a tree, a snake glides across the front of the canoe and up an over-hanging tree with a single movement, at ease in both elements.

The banks have been slashed, trees cut; it is sullied, broken – finally disappointing. Hot from the effort, we plunged into some gentle rapids, at least Marcos and I did – Michael doesn't like to swim and Seymour is still a little tentative. They always tell you not to bathe in Amazonian waters.

When we got back a bunch of girls from the whorehouses were bathing naked. They flashed their bodies at us, striking overt sexual poses and screaming with laughter. How do they manage to make it seem so innocent?

On the way back to Belém we made a slight detour to land on the football field in the little town of Cametá where Senhor Calixto lives, circling his house and waving our wings to attract his attention.

He came out to the field and Michael Dryhurst and I gave him a pair of binoculars we had bought him in London. He was overcome. We all embraced, and more than one tear was shed.

Now I am on my way to Brasilia. I will rendezvous with Maureen and tomorrow morning at dawn we will set off in a small plane for the Xingu. It is as though everything so far has been leading up to this moment. I am excited and a bit apprehensive as well.

---

21 AUGUST 1983 *XINGU*

I am writing this by torchlight lying in a hammock in the house of Takuma, Shaman of the Kamaiura tribe. It has been an extraordinary day. Maureen and I left the hotel at dawn for the airport. We reported to the office of the air-taxi company from which we were renting a plane. The arrangement was for them to fly us to the grass airstrip at the Posta Villas Boas, where the Funai maintains an officer charged with taking care of one section of the Xingu Indians. The pilot would come back a week later to fetch us.

A situation developed that has characteristics I am starting to recognize in Brazil. First of all, no one seemed to know anything about our flight. After Maureen had bent a few ears, someone of authority emerged and demanded to see written evidence that we had permission to visit the Xingu. We produced our letters and papers which they studied closely and laboriously. Gradually it emerged that they did not want to send a plane there at all. The Xingu tribes are very angry, almost in a state of war, with the Funai. The last plane that went in was captured and the pilot held hostage against various demands the tribes are making of the Government, including the dismissal of the President of the Funai, no less.

The plane was finally released after fourteen days and had arrived back in Brasilia daubed all over with war-paint. It is a dramatic emblem of Xingu hostility, sitting as it does in the heart of the capital.

Our pilot is a slight, thin man in his fifties who seems remote and nervous. He does not inspire confidence. Maureen harangues him mercilessly: if she, a mere woman, is ready to go, why not he?

Finally we set out, flying over the tundra almost due north for three hours. Down below fires raged across the dry bush. It was the burning season. Even at 3,000 feet we could smell the smoke. As we got nearer the pall of smoke began to obscure the topography. Our pilot, who was beginning to reveal a wry sense of humour, had not been there before and began to zig-zag, peering down none too hopefully. I took the map and he descended to 2,000 feet. There was a river below us that we hoped was the Xingu, and I tried to reconcile the twists and bends with the meandering blue line on the map. At this height and with such limited visibility, we could not see enough of it to be sure. He followed the flow of the river and we simply curved back and forth with it. The problem was at a certain point we would have to leave the river, which flowed south to north, and turn westwards towards the Posta. But, of course, if we did not turn at the right point we would miss it altogether. Just to make things more interesting, the fuel gauge was sinking at an alarming rate. The pilot said, with a smile, that we had sprung a leak and would have to land shortly with or without an airstrip.

I held my finger to the point on the map where I thought we were, so as not lose my place as I leaned over the side. When I looked back I saw that sweat was running down my finger on to the paper. The river bends seemed to coincide with the map and I said I thought we had reached the turning point. He said if we don't turn now it will be too late, the fuel was sinking fast. So he turned. The ground looked very rugged and broken, certainly nowhere to land. When the pilot, Joao, calculated that the airstrip should be below us, there was no sign of it. He started to fly in a big circle. Suddenly, among the trees an Indian village appeared, like an apparition from an earlier age. A circle of nine domed, thatched houses, each 60 to 90 feet long and perhaps half as wide. I saw figures moving about, but none seemed to be interested in us. It was a thrilling sight and I quite forgot the map as I craned back to keep the village in my sightline as long as possible. Joao nudged me and dipped the plane. Ahead was the airstrip. It was overgrown and clearly not much in use. Near it were some shacks and a single brick building with an antenna; they were clustered under some shady trees along the bank of a small river, a tributary of the Xingu. We landed on our last gallon of fuel.

A young couple with a baby, the Funai officer, came to greet us. In their wake, a straggle of Indians. Some with T-shirts and jeans, others naked except for necklaces. They were a sorry bunch, deformed, unprepossessing – I felt a stab of disappointment, but we were still dazed from the flight and quite glad to be on solid ground at all.

It turned out that these were the sick and crazy who drifted to the post and hung about there. One man had been driven from his tribe because he was too ugly. The young couple were hungry for news of the outside world. Their generator was broken and they could not operate the short-wave radio. A year ago on leave in São Paulo they had seen *Excalibur*, so I had a calling card.

They gave us some fish and manioc, and we swam in the river. We had brought soap and matches for the Kamaira and we gave some to them, which caused great delight. They ran to the river, soaped themselves and took all their clothes with them and washed them too.

There was a barrel of aviation fuel at the post. The pilot said he would first have to discover the fuel leak. If he could not repair it he would try to get the radio going and ask for a rescue plane.

It was a three-hour journey to the village where we were to stay and it was too hot to walk there in the middle of the day. We chatted and dozed in the shade of the trees. Taking Orlando's advice, I had brought nothing with me except a hammock, which I would leave as a present, plus the boxes of soap and matches together with the fishing net, which altogether made a heavy burden.

The post owned an old tractor and trailer which had gone off to fetch a group of warriors from the Kamaira which had been on a fishing trip. We could hitch a ride with them part of the way and then they would help us carry the presents.

They duly arrived. Thirty men, naked but heavily painted with their hair matted down with *urucu*, a red paste made from the dye of a vivid scarlet berry. They were pressed together and Maureen and I climbed up among them. Their catch of fish was wrapped in parcels of palm leaves bound with vines. They carried bows with long barbed arrows and harpoon spears. They smiled and fixed us with the strangest, seeking, probing eyes, open and innocent, yet infinitely mysterious. The *urucu* had a musky, fermented smell, but pressed together as we were, there was no discernible body odour from the men and their breath was sweet and fresh. A few spoke some Portuguese, learned at the Posta, and Maureen understood quite a bit of Tupi. They knew her, of course, and soon began plying her with questions about me. How many children did I have? Don't tell them you have twins, she said, it is considered unlucky. They usually kill one at birth.

They became more excited and I found it difficult to gauge their mood, which was certainly teasing and provocative, and perhaps hostile.

Maureen translated bits and pieces. One needed a wife and said he would take Maureen. They found this very funny. Another said, no, that was not possible because they were going to cook her and eat her since they had not caught enough fish for the tribe's needs.

When we arrived in the village – which was similar to the one I had seen from the air – there was great excitement. Takuma was quite brusque. He knew from the various messages that had passed back and forth with Orlando that we had brought a net. He demanded to see it. It was unpacked and laid out near the men's house in the centre of the ring of domed houses. There were angry shouts and cries of dismay. Despite all our efforts, the net had the wrong gauge. We made strenuous promises to rectify it, which were greeted with great scepticism. The mention of promises sent Takuma off on an angry tirade. The warriors began making a chilling clicking sound by rattling their bows against the arrows.

We judged it politic to display the cartons of soap and matches. These were greeted with considerable enthusiasm, and diverted the general attention from Takuma's vehement speech. Seeing he was losing his audience, he abruptly turned on his heel and entered his house.

Even with the tribe in this volatile condition, their delicacy of behaviour was impressive. Nobody grabbed at the gifts. Instead they were laid out in neat rows in the centre. The women and children, who had been very much shyly in the background, now edged forward. They paraded up and down looking at the presents, then they picked them up to examine them. Little by little they took up their portions and drifted back to their houses.

Maureen led me into Takuma's house. It is 90 feet long and perhaps 40 feet wide and 30 feet high. There is an interior structure of crossed beams on which a woven lattice of vines and branches rests. Over it all is a thatch of leaves that curves down to the ground. There are no walls or windows and only a tiny entrance, so the structure has a pleasing purity, being an unbroken elliptical dome.

It is dark inside, the only light coming from a number of fires and the daylight entering the two openings, which are opposite each other at the centre of the building. Between them is a large fire with a great flat griddle on which manioc pancakes are being made. There are perhaps ten families living within, each having a cluster of hammocks and its own cooking fire. They are all kin to Takuma. The smoke drifts up into the high ceiling where there is a vent that allows most of it to escape.

Takuma indicates a place near the entrance where we may hang our hammocks. We have brought cotton ones with us. The Indian hammock is made from fine woven vines and is stained a dark red colour by the *urucu* and black dye which rubs off from their bodies.

The sun is going down. Maureen says we should go to the lagoon to wash while there is still light. We take our soap and toothbrushes and head for the lagoon which is 200 yards away. The elders are smoking in the men's house and do not acknowledge us as we pass. The lagoon is limpid, the sun settling into a hazy mist at one end and a sharp crescent moon rising in the east at the other.

I step into the water feeling reverence for the lagoon, which is sacred, trying not to ripple the glassy surface. A memory is triggered. I was 16, making a journey alone up the Thames in a kayak. Camping on Runnymede Island. Awaking to a dawn of such stillness as this. Stepping into the water, sensitivity acutely sharpened by days without language, I felt a oneness with that place, realizing that it was a place of power, not chosen by chance for the Magna Carta ceremony. It made me aware of the spirits of places. I entered the water with great care so as not to ripple its perfect smoothness. If I succeeded, I felt I would live forever and discover hidden truths. And I did succeed, a head moving across a mirror where the liberties of man had been won. That experience, so profound, sent me searching for images, through cinema, to try to recapture what I knew that day.

Soon the water is fractured by villagers. They are washing with our soap. I swim far out into the lagoon. Thirsty from the hot journey, I open my mouth and drink each stroke, fish-like. The warning voices, 'Never touch the water', seem distant, irrelevant. I feel quite safe. I know now, as I knew then at Runnymede, that if I am in such harmony, no harm can befall me. I am drinking the Amazon, but it is drinking me too. We are the same.

Back in Takuma's house, we are given some fish and manioc. It is fresh river fish cooked in leaves over an open wood fire. The manioc is crisp, and quite tasteless. It serves as a plate for the fish. We eat it with our fingers. Dietitians are baffled as to why these people are robust and healthy when their diet is so restricted. No vegetables – no meat – just an endless repetition of fish and manioc; a few berries if they find them by chance in the jungle – nothing else. Other tribes in the Xingu eat monkey and other meat, but not this one.

It is all Maureen and I have eaten today, first at the Posta, now here. It will be interesting to see how one's system responds to it: no sugar, no coffee or tea, no alcohol, no fruit or vegetables.

So far I find the food is quite satisfying. I feel no hunger nor craving. What I do feel is awkward and uneasy. My clothes, albeit only shorts and T-shirt, seem an affront to their nudity. Both men and women are quite naked. All body hair, what little they have, is plucked or scraped, so as not to impede the application of body paint. The absence of pubic hair gives them an innocent, child-like vulnerability.

The Indians of the Americas, at least the ones from the tropical and sub-tropical regions, have been libelled. Their shameless nakedness posed a theological threat to the Church and her missionaries. When we were all cast out of the Garden of Eden, we were supposed to feel shame and cover ourselves. What could be concluded from the shamelessness of these Indians? Either they were not human, or they were still living before the Fall. With the handy excuse of not wishing to offend the public sensibility, the nudity was hushed up and – as soon as possible – covered up.

Until that fateful expedition of 1943, the tribes of the Xingu were cut off from the world, so were spared the ministrations of the missionaries. The discreet artists of the past painted over the exposed genitals and the world never knew. By the time the Xingu Indians were found, the camera had taken the place of the brush, and the truth was out. Emerging from the Second World War, people were scarcely shocked by a few naked Indians, so the Xingu have kept their ways and go still without clothes.

I am embarrassed to know so much about these people. They have been studied in every aspect by anthropologists.

Daily Life as Drama in a Brazilian Indian Village gives a detailed account of these very people with whom I am living, including a set of tables showing extra-marital sexual activities and the paths they use when they defecate. Many I know by sight from Maureen's photographs. Yet the essential mystery is overwhelmingly more powerful than the specific knowledge. It is a time machine. I have stepped back into the Stone Age.

When the sun is down, the air cools quickly. The men come in from their smoking and talking. The little fires cast moving shadows on the lofty roof. People lie in their hammocks or wander about talking softly. I noticed that there is almost no talk during the day. This is clearly the time.

Takuma came over and had a long talk with Maureen. The Indians have a catalogue of grievances. Only a portion of the public money allocated to the Funai reaches the Indians. The rest goes on administration or is directed into the pockets of certain officials.

When the World Bank helped to finance the dam at Tucuruí, they gave money to resettle Indians displaced by the project. The help was bungled and inadequate and most of the money was embezzled.

Roads have been cut through the Xingu, contrary to the law protecting it. A well-placed bribe allows rangers to nibble at the perimeters of the reservation.

The most recent row concerned Jacques Cousteau who has been shooting a big documentary series on the Amazon. He wanted to dredge and excavate the sacred lake in the hope of finding early Indian relics. This was vigorously opposed by the Indians. Since Cousteau was friendly with the President, a lot of pressure was exerted. The head of the Funai arrived in the Xingu and made a threatening speech that inflamed tempers still more. The Indians decided to cut off all contacts with Brasilia and all visits were banned and Cousteau never got to see the sacred lake. Killing interlopers and taking hostages is becoming widespread.

The Cousteau contretemps touches Takuma in a special way.

Orlando tells of learning from a chief, Tamapa, that their oral traditions spoke of a secret sacred pool that would be discovered only by a *pajé* (shaman) of great spiritual strength who had the courage to dive into its waters. Many years later, Tamapa's own son found the lagoon and dived deep into the waters and brought up remnants of an ancient Indian culture. The son's name was Takuma, now the greatest *paje* of all the Xingu, the very one who stands before us.

When you see the dignity and respect with which even the simplest tasks are accomplished, one can imagine their horror at having divers and dredgers in the sacred pool. Besides which, Maureen says that Takuma is very jealous of his reputation and prefers to be the only person courageous enough to dive into the pool.

---

28 AUGUST 1983 *EN ROUTE: BRASILIA–RIO*

The pilot, Joao, could not contact Brasilia for help so he set about trying to repair the plane himself. Fortunately, he is a trained engineer as well as a pilot. It took him some time, but he fixed it. He is a keen fisherman and brought his rod with him. He caught many fish and the degenerates at the Posta came to rely on him for food so he decided to stay on and wait for us. All three of us are quite relieved to be leaving safely, what with the faulty plane, the incipient violence, and the inherent dangers of such a journey. We are very light-hearted. It has been one of the great experiences of my life. Whatever else happens, the movie will have been worthwhile for this alone.

Just when we are feeling we have made it, Joao says he is beginning to feel feverish. Last night, he says, a bat bit him in the neck. He shows me two puncture marks. It is a scene from a Dracula movie. We all know how it goes on from there. He slumps over the controls and I have to land the plane. Then we find there is a killer bat inside the cockpit. Maureen tries to fight it off as the plane lurches towards the airfield. We are going to crash. I woke up with a start as we landed in Brasilia. It was hard to remember where the dream had begun. I looked across at Joao and the puncture marks were indeed on his neck and he was still very feverish. The air-taxi company were glad to see their plane.

I made no further entries in this diary after the first night in the Xingu. Writing just seemed antithetical to life there. I tried to be inconspicuous, practising a self-effacing technique I learned in my documentary days. I took no photographs until they invited me to do so, and then only very few. I find taking pictures distances me from experience.

The last few days have been so extraordinary I hardly know how to express my feelings. I can't imagine ever seeing things quite the same again.

After Takuma's talk that first evening the house settled down for the night. A collective tiredness took over and the soft droning conversations petered out and we all fell asleep together. This experience was repeated each night, this drifting off together, and I slept deeply and dreamt old, mythic dreams. Unfamiliar – their dreams, perhaps.

The burning hot days give way to cool evenings and, finally, cold nights. The chill seeps through the thatch about four or five o'clock in the morning. It was still dark when I awoke. People were stirring out of their hammocks. Maureen and I followed them down to the lagoon. The morning sun made a thin red slash on the skyline. Shivering, they plunged into the water, which, having retained its heat, was like a hot bath. We splashed around waiting for the sun to come up. Big wood fires were lit on the beach and we gathered round them drying ourselves. And how else? No towels, of course. The absence of things is what strikes an outsider most and the happy corollary of that, a total lack of litter.

We went back to the house and as the orange light of the sun slanted through the entrance, a lovely girl came in wet from bathing. She stood by the fire and swung her mane of black hair in an arc, slapping it on to her back and then forward. Caught in the sunlight, the water drops took fire, hung in the air and then fell hissing into the flames. An image for the movie.

I was always asking what would happen next. What was planned for tomorrow? Would there be dancing tonight? They were perplexed by this thinking. At one level, life would go on as it always had in unchanging patterns. It was simply obvious. The women would go off to the manioc patches and bring back the heavy roots that looked like turnips. They would boil them and then start the hypnotic scraping and grinding that painstakingly turns the manioc into flour and the juice into a delicious, slightly sweet soup. The men would go off to the river and fish, smoke and talk at night. All other time is spent in preparing feather ornaments, making necklaces from seeds and painting their bodies in elaborate patterns.

For no apparent reason, the mood would suddenly shift. Someone would start to chant. Dancing would begin. An elaborate ritual would ensue.

One morning, two warriors blowing on 7-foot-long flutes and with rhythmic steps began to circumscribe the village. Behind each man was a girl, one hand on the man's shoulder, keeping in step with him. They entered each house in turn playing continuously. The flutes make a deep, dark sound – no more than three notes. It is tedious to the Western ear, but its power lies in repetition. This ritual went on continuously for five hours, an astonishing physical feat. Little by little the flutes become hypnotic, possess the tribe, and yet everyone goes about his business. No one acknowledges the four figures, two men and two girls, going in and out of their houses. It has the discordance of dream.

My test came one day when Takuma came to me very early, it was still dark, and told me I could join him and the warriors on a journey to find logs for the *quarup* or ceremony of the dead. It would be very hard. It would be better for me to stay in the village with the women. I went with them. For three hours we tracked into the jungle at a fast lope. Takuma led the way, intense and very conscious of his importance. Maureen kept up most of the way. She is very resilient.

Takuma's seething anger over the Funai's treacherous behaviour soon surfaced. The Indians have become politically conscious. Some of the younger anthropologists have recruited civil-rights lawyers and the Indian cause is widely reported. Takuma reminded Maureen of two men who had come to the village and had not fulfilled promises. He told each of them when and how they would die and they had duly obliged. It was a dark hint, I felt, about the fish net . . .

Eventually, we came to a part of the forest that was where Takuma deemed the special trees could be found for the *quarup*. The men split up and searched. A wickedly funny old man who communicated with me in mime carried a length of twine and measured the girth of the trunks which had to be exactly right. The first four we cut proved to be flawed. One had rot inside. Two more split as they fell and another was not perfectly smooth. We needed six of these, one for each of the people who had died during the year, and whose bodies were temporarily buried in the centre of the village. Each trunk would be decorated and the ceremony would release the souls to the stars, after which the bodies would be burnt.

The trek back with the logs in the blinding heat was almost unendurable. Nothing was eaten all day. We got back after nightfall. There was no food on offer, only manioc, since there had been no one to fish that day. I began to realize how hand to mouth their existence was.

The next day the hostility towards me had melted away and I felt a great warmth. The couple from the Posta came up to visit and told the Indians what I did. Takuma was fascinated and insisted that I explain my work. It is not easy to describe a movie to a man who has never seen one or watched television. I struggled and he listened intently. I told him how one scene would stop and another begin, in a different place and time as it does in a dream. He lit up, grasping that. I told him of some of the tricks and wonders we got up to. Finally he was satisfied. 'You make visions, magic. You are a *paje* like me.' After that there was a sense of complicity. He would bring me a root or berry and show it to me, telling me of its properties. He had many ways to get into trance, some deeper and longer than others. The commonest way for the Kamaiura is tobacco, which of course came from the South American Indians in the first place. They cure wild tobacco and roll it into long cheroots. They inhale the smoke violently, hyperventilating on it. It causes them to vomit. After two or three bouts of retching, trance is achieved.

Although their daily life is monotonous and unchanging, their spiritual life is an endless, unpredictable and sometimes dangerous adventure. There is no division between the

material, the ritual and spiritual worlds. It is all one, a con-
tinuum. Living with them was like a dream, shifting and
changing. They are connected to all the animals and plants
that share their environment.

Increasingly, I felt Takuma was in possession of a knowledge, a consciousness, that far surpassed my own. A closeness
grew between us and we felt a great affinity. I began to sense
his thoughts and feelings. I had the distinct conviction that he
could project them into my mind. When we left he pronounced us brothers in a simple and moving moment. I could
return whenever I wished and when I did he would give me
a bench carved in the shape of my animal. Everyone is connected with the spirit of a particular creature.

'What is my animal?' I asked.

'Your animal,' he replied as though it was perfectly obvious
and he did not deign to name it. The only intimation I have
is that when they painted me it was with the markings of an
eagle. This was a strange moment. Just as they prepared to
cut the *quarup* trees they told me that I should not witness this
naked. Since I was the only person with clothes, it was puz-
zling. To them, someone without ritual paint is considered
naked.

---

30 AUGUST 1983 *EN ROUTE: RIO–LOS ANGELES*

After the Xingu, Belém and Rio seemed a nightmare. I had
severe withdrawal symptoms. The harmony, grace and tranquillity gave way to chaos and mass neurosis. We have paid
a high price for progress.

Michael Dryhurst has gone back to London together with
Seymour. We have received provisional consents from Concine, the film board, and Electronorte, owners of the dam at
Tucuruí. Both are subject to approval of the script, which is
still being translated into Portuguese.

THE XINGU

△ *The injured plane.*

The lagoon. ▽

The rituals.

△
▽   *Cutting the trees for the Quarup.*

△▽ *Cutting the trees for the Quarup.*

△ *John Boorman's spirit animal.*

2 SEPTEMBER 1983 *LOS ANGELES*

The search for a boy to play the all-important role of Tommy was proving more time-consuming and less fruitful than Markham's efforts to find the same person, with casting directors looking in both the USA and Europe.

Two days of intensive casting sessions with Melissa Skoff who has been rounding up boys. Not only disappointing, but depressing. These boys are phantoms, as though a cunning computer had succeeded in reproducing human beings so cleverly it was impossible to detect the fraud, yet it had left out just about everything that is important about a human being.

We also saw children to play the young, 7-year-old Tommy, who will be abducted, and his sister. I cannot cast the young boy until I have the older Tommy, since they must resemble each other, so we are getting a short list together. Lots of delightful kids. Whatever it is that happens to them happens later.

It is a big operation to bring two children all that way. US law is stringent. They must have a parent, a teacher, a social worker. They must work only four hours a day; all laudable, but difficult for us, and expensive. Perhaps I can find some American kids in São Paulo or Rio.

I have deluged Rospo with my impressions of the Xingu and back we went to the script again.

10 SEPTEMBER 1983

Jake was in LA and we went to Columbia together to show them stills from *Nemo* – or *Dream One* as we now call it – and discuss plans for its release. We gather in the office of Marvin Antonowski, Head of Marketing. He handled *Gandhi* and other successes and is luxuriating in an air of languid arrogance that is the unmistakable mark of a hot executive in Hollywood.

On Thursday night, dinner with Jerry Perenchio at Michael's Restaurant in Santa Monica. Edgar and Jake come along and Perenchio turned up with a girl and his boy assistant whose extreme youth and self-importance suggested that he had just come from being bar-mitzvahed. Jake was hoping that this meeting would finally cement the deal for the US market.

I regaled them with my experiences in the Xingu and tried to bring the story alive for them. A lot of Dom Pérignon was sluiced away. The boy was getting drunk and making abusive remarks. Meanwhile the girl turned out to be some kind of story editor. She made a series of detailed and inane criticisms of the script, most of which were inspired by an outraged feminism. Why didn't the wife go along on these trips to find the boy? After a few sharp exchanges, I turned to Jerry and said, 'Who is this girl?'

He said she was a script editor. I said I thought I'd been invited out to dinner. If he wanted a script conference, let's clear away the food and do that.

An example of the boy's contribution to the conversation was, 'Who gives a shit about Indians?'

Jerry tried to make signals to the boy to shut up. He kept running his finger over his lips in a button-up gesture. The boy thought there was food on his chin and wiped it with his napkin. I learnt next day from Jake that Jerry, on the pretext of going to the toilet, told a waiter to pretend there was a telephone call for the boy. When he got him outside he told him if he breathed another word he was fired. I was so angry by now, I was sinking pretty low myself. I demanded to know if the two kids had ever written a script or directed a film. Jake was white-faced and Edgar's mouth dropped open.

Jerry said, 'OK. Take on someone your own size. I've got some points.' He took out a sheet of notes from his pocket.

'Put them in the post,' I said. We left.

Edgar said gloomily, 'I guess we have to find another distributor.'

Jake is very close to Perenchio and when in LA stays at his home on the beach where nine servants are on hand to tend to Jerry's every whim. He has two tennis pros on stand-by at his tennis court over the weekend in case he decides to play. He has bought Embassy and wants to make it into a major movie studio. He is trying to lure Jake into joining him.

Apparently he was quite unruffled by the dinner and the deal is still on.

---

12 SEPTEMBER 1983

We had a further meeting with the professors of UCLA. Wilbert feels he must withdraw since he cannot approve of our putting together characteristics of various tribes to make up our own invented one. Bennett has prepared a memorandum of medical advice for us. Most of his warnings came too late for me. I also have an irrational aversion to taking preventative drugs. I am ready enough to gulp them down when sick, but the notion of pumping oneself full of chemicals in case the system is attacked later is anathema to me. I used to take gamma globulin in the tropics. Antibodies from a spectrum of a thousand people reinforcing one's own immune system is attractive, like turning up with a battalion rather than alone, but AIDS makes me nervous of anything derived from plasma.

Both professors have been helpful, recommending studies and books, correcting errors and omissions in the script. They are a bit patronizing about my profound experience with the Xingu. They too have witnessed many extraordinary mystic events, but academe would be sceptical of such reports, and they have their reputations as men of science to protect, so these things go unreported for the most part.

---

16 SEPTEMBER 1983 *PARIS*

Spent the first two days of the week in London, then here to complete work on the fine cut of *Dream One*.

On Monday worked on the budget with Michael Dryhurst and Fred Harding. We met with Terry Clegg who is production controller at Goldcrest and in the past has worked in the same capacity as Michael Dryhurst, a job that used to be called associate producer in England but is now coming to be known by the American title, line producer. The responsibilities of a producer and a line producer will vary from film to film. The important distinction is that the line producer is hired, usually at a weekly salary, to supervise the running of the production, whereas the producer is usually involved in developing the project at an early stage, puts up his own risk capital and raises the finance. He is paid a fixed fee, but only if the project gets off the ground.

There are all kinds of producers. In Hollywood there is a category known as 'packagers'. They buy best-selling books and plays, put them together with an attractive combination of director and writer and take the whole thing along to a studio and sell it at a profit. Although their names appear as producers, they have nothing further to do with the film. A line producer is brought in and he and the director take over. The packager then busies himself putting the next one together.

Then there are the very substantial producers like Richard Zanuck and David Brown (*The Sting*, *Jaws*, etc.) and Chartoff–Winkler (*Rocky I, II, III, Raging Bull, The Right Stuff*, my own *Point Blank*). Bob Chartoff and I have remained close friends though our last film together was *Leo the Last* in 1969. He offers me a lot of his projects and asked me to direct *Rocky*. He has framed my letter telling him that the *Rocky* script is old-fashioned, grossly sentimental and that audiences would never swallow it.

Bob has a deal at MGM that means they pay his overheads – offices, secretary – put up the money to purchase film rights, and, because of his important status, pay him an annual fee. In return, they get first refusal on all his projects. He buys books, but most often finds writers and commissions original scripts. Bob is a producer who follows his pictures through. With a less experienced director, the brilliant Phil Kaufman on *The Right Stuff*, he is there every day on the set. On his Scorsese pictures he mostly stays away from the shooting, viewing the rushes and passing on his comments.

Like many other established directors, I prefer to produce my own films since I try to develop the film from its beginnings and see it through to the very end, which includes checking prints, foreign-language versions, marketing. On *The Emerald Forest*, I am lucky to have Michael Dryhurst who has

long experience as an assistant director and production manager. He has worked all over the world and we have been
together on four projects, most recently *Excalibur*. He shields
me from a lot of detail, but makes sure all the important issues
are put before me. I seek his opinion on many things. He
knows where I am weak and watches those areas carefully. At
the moment, he is pressing me on the issue of the casting of
Tommy, rightly identifying it as the crucial problem at the
moment and knowing that I will put off a decision as long as
I can. He has an acid wit, is very tight on spending (the crew
call him 'Drypurse'), and is always trying to lose weight. He
will cut lunch and then eat chocolate biscuits all afternoon.
When the pace gets hot he sometimes tends to hide and write
people memos when a personal word might be better, but he
gets through a prodigious amount of work quietly and without
fuss.

At the other end I have Edgar Gross, a Harvard-trained
lawyer, who has looked after my business affairs for seventeen
years since I started working in Hollywood. I gave up having
an agent some ten years ago. Edgar has been my sole representative in the business since then. He negotiates all the contracts (mine, the leading actors'), and co-ordinates the financial aspects, liaising with the movie company. He also checks
all the legal elements, of which there are many. For instance,
we have suddenly been challenged on the title of the film. The
American studios have an agreement to register titles, and if
someone has a title too similar to your own, and registered it
after you, then you can seek to prevent them from using it.
This agreement has obvious advantages in preventing confusion. MGM has a title with the word 'emerald' in it. They
have to convince the arbitration committee that their film will
be made within a year and that the titles are similar enough
to create confusion. Eventually, a compromise was reached
when Embassy reregistered the title as *John Boorman's The
Emerald Forest*.

Edgar is a tough negotiator and very persistent. He grinds
down the opposition by endless attrition. If a studio executive
fails to return his calls, he phones him at 7.30 in the morning
at the man's home with the moral advantage of already being

in his office. David Norris says Edgar always has fifteen pages of comment on any contract, never less and never more. David, himself a formidable negotiator, waspishly accuses Edgar of running out of stamina after fifteen pages. Edgar has sued most of the major studios on behalf of his clients, usually for disputed profits, sometimes for control. None of the cases ever reaches the courts. The fights in the town are ruthless and rabid, but they don't like the outside world intervening. I have given Edgar the title of executive producer on *The Emerald Forest*.

Hollywood today functions and is run by a small group of people who are in adversary stances yet mostly interchangeable: eight or nine studio heads, another forty-odd executives, perhaps sixty top agents, a dozen influential lawyers, as many business managers, a hundred active producers. There are directors and stars with great power over their own pictures, but they do not influence the way the town is run.

Most agents eventually tire of massaging their clients' egos. They have two escape routes, either become a studio executive, or an independent producer. The latter is much riskier. When a studio head is looking for an executive, he inclines towards hiring an agent because (a) he was probably an agent himself, and (b) agents are the people he talks to every day. Effectively, agents weave a cocoon around the studios so that they can reach directors, writers, actors, only by way of the agencies. They all talk to each other all day on the telephone. So agents are the only people they know and with whom they feel comfortable. People who actually make films are in another business. While they are off on location in Alaska and Texas and Africa and Europe, the producers and agents and studio executives gossip away, wheeling and dealing, nervously watching the grosses of each new movie and constantly revising the unwritten lists of directors and stars who are 'in' and 'out'.

A studio head or executive who does not come up with hits is fired or, euphemistically, becomes an 'independent producer' at the studio he used to run. In effect, this means he is given an office and a secretary, but all his projects are rejected. He languishes there for a year or two, by which time his sins are overshadowed by the greater ones of his successors. Sooner or later there is new turmoil and he lands a job at another studio. Occasionally, tiring of the game, he goes back to the agency business, thus completing the circle.

Writers and directors often become producers so as to retain control over their material, but for the most part producers and executives are those whose only experience of making pictures is making deals.

John Ford used to say you should point a finger only at French pastries, lavatories and producers. There are many stories denigrating the producer: to the writer who is late delivering a script, 'I don't want it good, I want it Thursday'; to the assistant director who tells the producer that the director has asked for fifty horses for a scene, 'Tell him he can have forty and order thirty.'

Antonioni, when he was visiting Ireland, came to dinner at my house and we were exchanging horror stories about producers. He was trying to make *L'Avventura* and Dino De Laurentiis heard about it. He called Antonioni and arranged an airline ticket for him to fly to Rome. He said, 'You tell me the story. If I like it, we'll make the picture.' Antonioni is a very shy, laconic man. He duly told Dino of how the girl, Anna, disappears on an island, and the rest of the film is a search to find her. At the end of the telling, Dino said, 'Well, what happened to Anna?'

Antonioni replied that he did not know.

'Who wrote the story?'

'I did,' said Antonioni.

'You wrote it and you don't know what happened to her?'

Antonioni admitted that that indeed was the case.   Dino held out his hand. 'Give me back the price of the air ticket.'

I was fortunate enough to have David Deutsch as my first producer. He liked my TV work enough to offer me what became *Catch Us If You Can*. He is an urbane, intelligent and sensitive man, enthusiastic and supportive. I did not realize at the time what a rare specimen he was. He has not made many films in recent years. He is probably too decent to be a really successful operator.

Here in Paris, the *entente* is not too *cordiale*, at least between

Goldcrest and Claude Nedjar. All the deep-rooted prejudices between Brit and Franc flare up when there is trouble. Goldcrest's accountant, Andy Parsons, can never agree figures with Claude and Michel Propper.

I buried myself with Arnaud and the editor, Tom Priestley, at the studios at Boulogne, working on the fine cut of *Dream One*. There is something slack at the centre of the film. The extravagant characters and situations on the edges are wonderful and inventive, but the middle is soft. And because it is all shot inside the *boule*, is it not finally claustrophobic in the wrong way?

Gabriel Yared will do the score. He plays us the themes on the piano. They are captivating. We decide on a big orchestra, which will help to expand the film and give it more breadth, and alleviate the confined feeling.

---

30 SEPTEMBER 1983

Drove from Paris to Ireland loaded down with our belongings. This is the last time we will be home for many months. There is a lot to do. I have spent most of the week rewriting the script, particularly the Indian scenes.

In Paris, I had a long session with Philippe Rousselot, going through the script, giving him a general idea of how I intend to shoot each scene and describing each set or location. From these discussions a tone or style will gradually emerge, which will be a response to the story and the Amazon. Philippe will come with me on the next trip to Brazil, see the locations, and get a clearer idea of my intentions. He will then have to decide very soon what lighting equipment he needs since it will have to be shipped out, an operation taking at least six weeks. Brazilian customs are notoriously difficult to negotiate. They have been known to hang on to shipments for six months, a prospect that makes my hand tremble as I write.

During the next few weeks before we return to Brazil, Michael and I have to recruit a crew, order equipment, revise the budget and schedule and, above all, complete casting.

I am working with Mary Selway, the casting director who

did *Excalibur* for me. I have enlisted her help in trying to find an actor to play Tommy. She has been looking in schools and drama clubs and we have seen many boys together. They are quite different from the American contenders. They are mostly scrawny, very few having the developed bodies one saw in California. They are eccentric, introverted, caught up in private mythologies, many exhibit a fierce, hostile intelligence. They seem to have great assurance about their absence of conviction. Their lack of expectation about working, about the world, lends them a curious strength. They are not eager to please, and they lack charm. They are disturbing, making one ill at ease. They do not connect with anything in my experience. Not one of them has the innocence, the openness and physical prowess I am looking for. It is chilling to see iron in such young souls.

I am often asked how a casting director functions. Typically, we start by discussing each character and the style of the film. She then makes a list of possible actors for each role, starting with the obvious ones, then others less well known who have recently impressed her, and finally some wild thoughts – a singer, comedian – that give one a jolt. Further discussion produces a short list that we interview, do readings with, sometimes shooting screen tests. A lot of actors these days have a video tape with excerpts from their work. The casting is so crucial, if you make a mistake the film can be doomed from the start.

Talking about the characters with actors is a process of discovery. Even if you have invented the characters yourself, how well can you know them? Indeed, on the page there can be little more than indications. Until an actor occupies the role, it really has no existence.

We intend to shoot screen tests with a short list of half-a-dozen boys. It will also serve to test the body make-up and decoration that we will use for the Invisible and Fierce tribes.

Timna Woollard, a friend of my daughter Katrine, is the daughter of Tony Woollard, the film designer. The two girls have always, since the age of 7, made fantasy clothes, painted pictures and painted each other. Timna studied Fine Art at St Martin's and has developed a style in which she paints huge, stylized landscapes, puts Katrine or her beautiful sister, Emma, in front of the picture, then paints their bodies in a way that links them to the background. She photographs or films the results.

I have commissioned her to try to design a style of body paint for the Invisible tribe. I have given her many books of reference pictures. In the story, our tribe believes in its powers of invisibility. Their green paint, derived from a rare mineral, must give the impression of camouflage. There is a contradiction here because, photographically, they must be visible, yet suggest invisibility.

With Katrine's help, Timna is experimenting with different paints and colours and patterns. Using my son Charley as a model, she photographs the results, we discuss them, and she tries again.

---

4 OCTOBER 1983

We are installed in offices at Twickenham Film Studios. We will direct our preparations from here and return to do the editing and post-production after shooting in Brazil.

Michael Dryhurst has taken on Judith Bunn as production secretary. She worked in India on *Gandhi*, so is battle-hardened. Together they are hand-picking the crew. They recommend Paul Engelen and Peter Frampton for make-up. They did *Greystoke* in the Cameroons, which is also in the rain-forest belt that girdles the Equator – the real Green Belt.

A construction manager and key craftsmen – carpenter, rigger, plasterer, etc. – are critical posts. Names come up; characters are assassinated. Between them Michael and Bunny have horror stories to tell about most of the candidates – greed, laziness, unreliability, lack of stamina, ill-health. There are those who don't want to leave their wives, and those who are desperate to get away from them. Some will work only if their girlfriends are given a job.

A production secretary is a mother to the crew; they go to her with all their problems, so she comes to know their foibles and weaknesses. 'Bunny' has a scathing wit, and no one is spared. She treats Michael and me like erring schoolboys, but is endlessly forgiving. We look up to her. She is over 6 feet tall and quite beautiful.

Reluctantly we decide to bring location caterers from England. This is very expensive, particularly as they will need to bring a water-purifying unit. But stomach upsets, diarrhoea and hepatitis can decimate a crew and bring production to a halt. Bunny tells of one technician during the shooting of *Gandhi* who came in one morning with the solution to the diarrhoea problem. He said he simply flushed his dinner down the toilet, thus cutting out the middle man.

5 OCTOBER 1983

A banquet tonight to celebrate the fiftieth anniversary of the British Film Institute. As a governor, I had a hand in choosing the first Fellows. We hope to make the award each year. Dickie Attenborough, John Brabourne, Verity Lambert and I were the group charged with deciding who they should be. No one wanted to make the first move. Tony Smith, the BFI's director, said, 'Who would you most like to have dinner with?'

I started off the bidding with Andrei Tarkovsky. Much too highbrow. Dickie countered wickedly with Michael Winner. It was like the judging in ice dancing – the top and bottom marks are discounted. We got to work on the middle ground. We played ping-pong with a lot of names, but finally agreed that the first group should be obvious and august. Dickie, with his marvellous sense of occasion, said we must have Orson Welles because he would lend such presence and give a rousing speech, which he did. I wore red shoes to the meeting to espouse the cause of Michael Powell. There was a slight hiccup there because it meant we would also have to honour Emeric Pressburger, Powell's indivisible partner, which added to a swelling list.

David Lean was unopposed. Ingmar Bergman and Federico Fellini would have made too perfect a nap hand, so Marcel Carné squeezed in for European cinema and Satyajit Ray, as he so often does, stands in for the Third World.

As Claude Rains said in *Casablanca*, 'Round up the usual suspects.'

The Guildhall gathering was extraordinary. Every director, film star, producer of note was there, as well as top cameramen, editors, art directors, critics and screenwriters. Jake and I sat together and gaped at the heroes of our youth, pointing them out to each other, two awestruck fans wondering how we ever got in among the stars.

---

6 OCTOBER 1983

Jerry Perenchio sent over one of his production executives, Jeff Young, and I spent the day with him. He arrived with some trepidation since news of the savaging of his colleagues in Michael's restaurant in Santa Monica has become legend in the company. He brought with him Embassy's collective thoughts and objections.

I have endured many script conferences with studios over the years. Mostly, they are awful. The criticisms are usually of a general nature and seek to subvert the screenplay to the conventional wisdom of the day. 'Why couldn't he be Black?' – when they were looking for Black audiences. 'Why couldn't he be a woman?' – when they suddenly discovered that half the audience was female. Now it is, 'Why can't he be a 17-year-old kid?'

'Well, he does have grown-up children.'

'Yeah, I guess that is a problem.'

More sex (the liberated 1960s), less sex (the fearful 1970s), more violence (then), less violence (now).

'What about a car chase?' (then).

'Not another car chase!' (now).

Given these past experiences, Jeff takes me by surprise. He has studied the script, he is well prepared, he is relentless. We go through it page by page. He questions every line of dialogue, criticizes the characterizations and challenges the structure. He is wildly enthusiastic about the story and as we read the scenes of Markham taking leave of Tommy, or Wanadi's death, he is overcome, and his eyes fill with tears.

He touches on a number of important points: the first being the language. He is in favour of the Indians speaking their own tongue (Tupi) and using subtitles. This is such a major issue that I know it must come from his bosses. Since 25 per cent of the audience is scarcely literate, it is either brave or foolhardy. I told him of my plan to devise a new way of doing it, having each actor shadow his own Tupi words with an English translation. I told him I would make tests and show them when I go back to LA.

He asked what others have asked: wouldn't Tommy remember some English? After all, he was 7 years old when he was taken. The fact is, our researches show that in the many cases of abduction at that age, the original language is completely forgotten, as indeed are the early experiences. At that age memory depends on repetition within a familiar culture. Taken into an alien environment, memory quickly fades. Jeff argues that if Tommy has a smattering of English, he and Bill can communicate and the audience understand them. This solution has attractions and of course it is an option to which Rospo and I had given careful consideration while we were writing. Even more attractive is the idea that a child can be changed and totally absorbed into this tribal life. The heart of the film is when Tommy returns and meets his mother. She can no longer communicate with her son. The scene dramatizes the problem most modern mothers have in connecting with their sons who often seem as remote from them as Tommy actually is.

Tommy's training in shamanism equips him to solve the problem in a spiritual, but non-verbal, manner. He gives Jean the experience that enables her to release him. Letting a son go – as opposed to abandoning him – is painfully difficult in the modern world where there are no rituals to help and guide us. In Tommy's tribal life we witness his progress from boy to man and his tribal mother's traditional understanding of her role in that.

Rospo and I have chosen the more difficult way, but one that can give the film much more resonance.

Jeff's most helpful criticism was to do with the character of Jean. Rospo's concept was that Jean's obsession with her lost son had turned her into a sick woman. Her husband continued the search as much in response to her distress as to his own desire to find the boy. Although this heightens Tommy's eventual success in curing her as a *paje* it makes her a bit of a drag early on.

Here we have surfacing again the criticisms made by the lady story editor at Michael's. I am forced to concede they are right, but it poses a problem. Then Jeff made a remark that resolved the difficulty: there is no dramatic need for conflict between husband and wife in the early part of the film. They can have similar feelings about the quest for Tommy. But if they agree, how does the audience know their state of mind? Thinking about it, I believe there is a way. I will use an outsider, Werner, to challenge their motives in continuing their search.

At present, Markham meets Werner, an anthropologist, by accident during the fateful trip. If I introduce him earlier, he can provide the function that presently is served by the conflict between Bill and Jean. I undertake to make Jean less of an invalid, more robust and normal, and Jeff is satisfied. He will go back and recommend that Embassy proceed.

'Why doesn't Jean go with Bill into the jungle?' Jeff then asks, pushing his luck, and I hear again the strident voice of the feminist lobby at Embassy.

'She does have another child to take care of, and she is in a foreign country. Don't you think it would be irresponsible of her to leave Heather behind?'

It is enough to satisfy him. But the real reason is that an engineer from Texas would not share the views of a Hollywood story editor on the role of women. He would not dream of dragging his wife along on trips like these. Fashionable attitudes force their way into films, often against the characterizations.

An obvious example is smoking. A few years ago, actors were constantly lighting each other's cigarettes, blowing smoke into carefully placed back light, and stubbing them out to demonstrate resolve or frustration. Now, nobody smokes on screen, which is wholly good for obvious reasons, but it has deprived screen actors of an entire repertoire of expression.

Today, the command 'Stand by to shoot' sees them extin-
guishing their cigarettes for another smokeless, blameless
scene.

---

13 OCTOBER 1983

Took time off from these interminable casting sessions and the
briefing of each new crew member to have lunch with Adrian
Cowell who made the documentary *The Tribe that Hid from
Man* and his latest *The Decade of Destruction*, which he is completing at present. He showed Michael Dryhurst and me the
rough-cut. It was astonishing. There, on the screen, is our
story! I had heard about it from Orlando Villas-Bôas and here
he is on film, leading the expedition to find the kidnapped
boy.

The action takes place in one of the new settlements where
the Government has given tracts of forest to landless peasants.
They clear it and try to grow crops. One of these settlers,
while hunting in the jungle, shot an Indian or two. The
Indians mounted a revenge raid and killed two youths and
abducted their 7-year-old brother. The boys' father succeeded
in tracking the Indians for some way, but eventually lost
them. Adrian Cowell heard that the Funai was mounting an
expedition. He joined it with a camera crew and the film is
the result of that trip.

Cowell is an attractive, bearded man, watchful, involuted.
His voice is quiet and his manner tentative, yet there is unmistakable authority, a magisterial calm.

He has known Takuma for eighteen years. We exchange
notes. He warns me that Takuma is dangerous. He learned to
hunt with him when he first went to the Xingu and has since
seen many manifestations of his power. He gives us advice
about Brazil. The customs will seize your equipment, he
warns. What about disease? He takes a kit of assorted drugs
and a book of medical symptoms. When he succumbs to fever,
he leafs through the book and swallows whatever seems appropriate. He stopped taking malaria tablets long ago. He goes
there for six months at a time. On one occasion he and his

crew were cut off from contact with the outside world for ten weeks. He is married with a family. What do they think of these trips of his? They don't like them but they have come to accept his way of life. He casts a look around the noisy Italian restaurant. The London traffic frets away outside the window. This is not his element. He looks haunted. He is a man apart. Not the flamboyant explorer of story books, but one who must search and probe, wedded to the wilderness.

In his kidnapping story it eventually transpired that the Indians had killed the boy shortly after taking him. He kept them awake with his crying and finally one of them stuck an arrow in him to shut him up.

---

21 OCTOBER 1983

We now have a short list of five boys and we will shoot tests next week. Seymour is building a jungle set on a stage at Shepperton Film Studios. Timna has refined the body make-up.

Neil Jordan and his young producer, Steve Woolley, came to see me this evening to ask my advice about the film they are trying to make, *The Company of Wolves*. It comprises a number of stories on the Red Riding Hood/Werewolf theme linked to the fantasies of a pubescent girl. It is clever and inventive and, I said, one story too long. Yes, they were thinking of dropping one. Good. Steve, who founded Palace Video, has a shrewd touch for public taste. He saw *Angel* at the first screening in Cannes and immediately approached Neil and me to distribute the picture. I was in favour but Channel Four put it through the BFI which marked it as a minority film.

They were planning to shoot *Wolves* on location, but I urged them to do it in the studio where a consistent style of fantasy could be better achieved.

Because the script moves from story to story I told them it must have a very strong connecting theme or *leitmotiv*. What did I think that should be? It should be sensual, erotic, I said. It is an ambitious, bold enterprise. I wish them well.

I have been helping Arnaud with the looping sessions of *Dream One*. This is the process of rerecording dialogue that for one reason or another is of unacceptable quality. On location shooting, heavy traffic, for instance, can make the original recording inaudible. In the studio, squeaking camera equipment or a whining lamp can be distracting irritations that would puncture the ever fragile illusion.

It is called 'looping' because the old method was to break up a scene into strips of film 30 seconds long. Each one was joined into a loop that runs continuously on the projector, repeating itself, so that the actor could practise synchronizing his lip movements and performance to match the original. When he and the director are satisfied, the next loop comes up and so on until the scene or scenes are completed. These are then fitted together by a sound editor who can also make minute adjustments for any discrepancies of synchronization.

Many actors have a fear and loathing of the process. Months after they acted the scene, they are thrown into a dubbing studio and, often without guidance, try to recapture their emotional interpretation while in the grip of panic about achieving synchronization. The loop goes round and round and after several attempts it ceases to have any meaning, rather as a word does when repeated over and over.

Peter O'Toole once said that his idea of hell was to have his entire life broken down into 30-second sections and be forced to loop himself for eternity.

A lot of actors hate to see themselves on the screen and won't watch rushes or even the finished film. Richard Burton claimed to have seen only two of the sixty-odd films he had made.

Looping means confronting oneself and one's performance and it can induce disgust of the hellish proportions imagined by O'Toole. On *The Heretic*, it proved very difficult to get Burton to do his looping at all, given his horror of facing himself. Finally, he announced he would do it in Rome. To soothe his reluctance, we had to provide him with tickets for himself and his then wife, Suzy, from New York, and a suite at the Excelsior for three nights. I estimated his loops would take a day. I waited at the dubbing studio for him to arrive. Finally, an hour late, he appeared. He looped with a furious speed and accuracy, faster than any actor I have ever seen. It was done in an hour and a half. As with the performance itself, he followed whatever directions I gave, never arguing or discussing and never making a suggestion.

In 1970 Reeves Sound Studios in New York installed the first computerized looping system known as ADR, or Automated Dialogue Replacement. It is now standard equipment in all movie-making centres. The computer rocks the film back and forward without having to make it into loops. The chosen takes can be selected and remembered by the computer and the whole scene played back instantly so that it can be judged and, if necessary, adjusted and amended.

When I came to this stage in making *Deliverance*, Jon Voight was strongly opposed to looping on the grounds that the actor gives something at the time, an immediacy, a spontaneity, a truth, that cannot be recaptured.

'But surely,' I argued, 'on stage you are obliged to reproduce it every night.'

'No,' he contended. 'On stage you are giving an original performance each time out.'

My argument went like this: it is not the actor's voice that you are hearing when it is reproduced on film. It is electrical impulses recorded on iron-oxide (rust) coated on plastic, which are reconverted into a simulation of the voice. If there is any flaw in the several stages of the system, and there always is, distortion occurs. It is imperfect. Film is a mechanical process, and it follows that we should use all its mechanical possibilities to perfect the final result. The position of the microphone is never ideal since it has to be kept out of shot. The best take visually may not be the best for the voices. In the dubbing studio, the actor and director can devote themselves to the performance without the distractions of camera, props, and intense pressure of time. Just as the film process involves constant rewriting, reshooting, re-editing, I like to spend time revising the performances in this way.

My method is this: after the film is cut, I review the

performance with the actor. The film was shot over many weeks, and usually out of sequence. There are inevitable discrepancies of emphasis. These can be corrected. When Voight saw the potential of the system, he embraced it. We remade the entire voice track of *Deliverance*. I have done so ever since on all my movies. The knowledge that this is possible gives one tremendous freedom while shooting: speed, mobility, and the actor is less inhibited, knowing he can correct and improve his performance in the heel of the hunt, as it were. In difficult physical scenes, I can talk the actors through: 'Edge to your left ... don't stop ... keep going ... marvellous ...' I am there, urging them on, cueing actors into shot, encouraging, alleviating the actor's agony of standing alone in front of the lens.

European cinema, the Italian cinema particularly, has always added the dialogue afterwards – often ineptly – but it made the films more fluid and visual. Fellini once said to me conspiratorially, 'If the Americans ever find out about looping, we are finished.'

I have never failed to convince an actor of the value of looping. With ADR it has become part of the creative process, and no longer an evil necessity.

All major films are dubbed into foreign languages and to protect my movies, I control these, casting the voices and supervising the sessions. Many directors turn their backs on foreign dubbing, preferring not to witness their films being vandalized. I take a different view. D. W. Griffith believed that film was the universal language promised in the Bible that would bring about the millennium. Such hopes lie dashed. Films were silent then and it was an easy matter to translate the written titles. But one of the attractive things about movies is that they cross frontiers of nationality and language with such ease. The fact that films are subtitled and dubbed is something to be embraced. It should modify our way of making them. If the grammar and language of cinema is well used, the movie will work in any version. In a cinema in Brazil I saw a cluster of illiterates listening to a friend who could read, speaking the subtitles. In Moscow I met an interpreter who knew every frame of *Deliverance* because she had

spent a year travelling Russia with it, speaking a translation
live to each audience.

Peter Marinker is an actor who specializes in revoicing foreign films into English. He is an accomplished actor, and also
a dubbing director. He has been working on *Dream One* and
I am discussing with him the special problems of *The Emerald
Forest*. I want to make an experiment to see if we can devise
a new convention: the actor would speak in Tupi (the Indian
language), then loop himself, 'shadowing' each line in English.
Instead of reading subtitles, the audience would experience
the original language, yet hear the line in English in the
actor's own voice and with the appropriate emotion and
meaning.

---

10 NOVEMBER 1983

For the last two days we have been shooting the screen tests
of the five boys for the role of Tommy. The jungle set was
quite convincing and we tried a variety of body paint and
decoration. I got each contender to move through the foliage
so as to judge physical grace, poise, as well as the degree of
'invisibility' that the make-up imparted.

Then they each performed a scene between Markham and
Tommy. I wrote the scene especially for the test but I am
thinking of adding it to the script. The scene has Markham
recovering from fever in the Indian village. He tells Tommy
of the many years he has spent searching for him. Tommy is
conscious of Markham's sadness. He relates it to the experience of hunting: 'Yes. It is good to hunt, to track an animal.
And when you catch it you should feel happy, but no, you
feel sad.'

There is a lot of subtext in the scene. Although they are
close, in an intimate moment, they reach out across a divide
of experience which makes the contact poignant and bitter-
sweet.

11 NOVEMBER 1983

The rushes of the tests were depressing. The boys were awkward, arch, artificial. It embarrassed me to watch the screen.
Except for Charley, none of them was actually 17. Their ages
ranged from 19 to 23, and it showed. Only Charley had the
simplicity and directness that made the character and the
situation credible. On the other hand, his lack of technique
limited his effectiveness. The whole exercise seemed so contrived.

Philippe Rousselot came from Paris to light it and his work
was the only encouraging feature. His lighting was subtle and
atmospheric. He was sensitive, quick and good-humoured
throughout. Philippe said, 'Tests always make you doubt the
script.'

14 NOVEMBER 1983

Today, Marinker and I went into the dubbing theatre with
Charley and looped the English into Tupi. It immediately
gained a credibility. I used Charley's test because it seemed
the best. He managed the technicalities of looping quite well.
Then we experimented with the 'shadow' idea, and it appears
to work, although it requires careful and precise 'fitting'. At
least we have done enough to know that dubbing into Tupi
from English is wholly successful, so I can shoot the film in
English and still have all my options open. I will take the tests
to LA and show them to Jeff Young and the other Embassy
people. I hope it will reassure them on the language issue.

15 NOVEMBER 1983

A meeting with Gilles Lacombe, art director of *Dream One*. I
had approached him to make an estimate for building a working model of the dam in the *boule*, the inflatable plastic dome
in which we made *Dream One*. Gilles succeeded in providing
an artificial sea with a wave-making machine and perhaps he

can use that accumulated experience to solve the immense problems of a dam-burst.

Gilles is a bizarre character, lives in a commune with his collaborators, the 'Productions de l'Ordinaire'. He dresses in an extravagant manner. At a very tense production meeting on *Dream One* he arrived with a hat that sported two human hands. When he approved of something that was said, he pulled a wire concealed in his pocket and the hands clapped. His solutions are always original.

His plan for the dam is quite elaborate. The big problem is to build up a large head of water behind the dam and to find a way to release it instantly so that it will hit the dam all at once. His clever plan is to construct the dam so that it will succumb to the weight of water. He aims to protect it by a huge sheet of plate glass. At the given moment a small explosive charge would shatter the glass and the water would burst through the dam. He insists that because the plate glass is flush against the side of the dam, it will withstand the pressure.

His estimate for three takes is £600,000, three times the figure we have in the budget. Quite a bit of this money goes on the engineering, but much more on constructing the models of lights, ladders, vehicles, cranes and engineering detail. I told him his figure was more than we could afford, and that I would have to seek another tender. It is expensive to rent the *boule* for the three months of construction involved, but at least it means that the shooting can be done during the day. The scene itself takes place at night, so that if we built it out of doors we would have the expense of a night shoot.

---

16 NOVEMBER 1983

Maureen Bisilliat is visiting. She is on her way to the Frankfurt Book Fair to sell her latest photographic opus. I have given her introductions to some publishers. She is still mulling over the possibility of doing a picture essay on the making of the film, and perhaps a film documentary. She is interested in the film unit as a tribe and in our plans to create our own tribes. She is very demanding, but I never quite know what exactly she is demanding.

---

17 NOVEMBER 1983

It is proving difficult to find a good camera operator. In America, the director works out the shots with the camerman and the operator merely takes over the mechanical function. It is difficult to judge the subtleties of the light through the viewfinder, so most cameramen prefer to use an operator so they can watch the scenes with the naked eye, and now the unions insist on it. In England, there is a somewhat different system. The director works closely with the operator and plans the shots with him. There are many highly talented operators, but one, Peter MacDonald, towers above the rest. For many years he was teamed with the great and much-lamented Geoffrey Unsworth. Most directors select the lens for each set-up and line up the shots with the actors. I always design the composition and exactly define the camera movement, so why is the operator important? A good one like Peter will always enhance and improve the shot, adjusting the position of extras and props and being acutely aware of anything that goes wrong. He also organizes the equipment required for each shot, and plans ahead with his chief 'grip' so that he can begin laying tracks for a subsequent set-up or prepare the crane. He will constantly strive to enrich the frame and be concerned, together with the continuity girl, in matching one shot to the next. While I rehearse the actors, he will direct the prop men and special-effects people to make sure everything is working. Finally he has the dextrous physical task of operating the camera movements. Unfortunately, Peter is not free, nor is Bob Smith who worked on *Excalibur*.

Michael Dryhurst has recommended Gale Tattersall, a young operator, and Peter MacDonald endorses him. He has done a lot of low-budget pictures and many commercials, but never a production on the scale of *The Emerald Forest*. I liked him right away. He is a movie buff, which is surprisingly rare for a film technician. He is intense, clearly a worrier. He has a nasal Liverpudlian voice and although he is 30, his career suffers from his extremely boyish appearance. Does he have the authority to command a crew? He strikes me as the sort of person whose anxieties make him vulnerable to catching any viruses in the air. Will he have the resilience to last the course? Despite these doubts, I find myself offering him the job.

We then fell into a long technical discussion about the camera equipment we should take to Brazil. Because of the remoteness, the heat and humidity, we agreed it was essential to have a camera maintenance mechanic with us. On *Hell in the Pacific*, in Palau, our mechanic worked all night, every night, stripping down, cleaning and repairing. Today's equipment has many more electronic elements and they are particularly vulnerable to damp heat.

I was hoping to find an operator adept at using the Steadicam, which is a special camera and involves a special skill. Gale does not have this skill, so I have decided to send him to the States to be trained by the inventor of the device, Gareth Brown.

There are three ways in which we can move the camera to follow action:

(i) Running the camera along rails. This is effective for fast tracking, but its limitations are that the camera can go only in a straight line and the angles are restricted because if you shoot straight ahead or straight behind the rails will be seen.

(ii) Crab dolly on boards. As the name implies it can be steered sideways, in arcs, go up and down and generally affords very fluid movements on a smooth, specially prepared surface. It is also a very heavy piece of equipment.

(iii) A crane. Mounting the camera on the arm of a crane allows a great deal of flexibility, particularly for achieving elevation. It is even heavier and bulkier than the crab dolly

All these devices involve cumbersome equipment and require reasonably good surfaces. We shall need them all in Brazil, but in the jungle there will be many situations where none of these solutions will be practical. I must have constant camera movement in the rain forest. Because the jungle is so uniform, the only way to give a sense of depth and life is to constantly change the spatial relationships.

The Steadicam is mounted on a harness strapped to the operator. A clever series of balances and counterweights gives the camera a stability. The operator can walk or run with it, crouch in the back of a jeep, and achieve steady pictures. However, it requires special training and dexterity – and strength. It is widely used now and there are some skilful exponents. Bertrand Tavernier shot an entire film on it. But no one has ever been able to use it with the brilliance of its inventor, Gareth Brown. He is a tall, rangy man, full of ideas, with a passionate curiosity about life.

He made some astonishing shots for me on *The Heretic* in 1976. At the time the camera was still in the prototype stage. It had cost him a lot of time and money to develop it. At one point he approached Panavision, one of the foremost camera equipment manufacturers, and tried to sell it to them. They examined it carefully, rejected his offer, and set about making their own version. It proved more difficult than they thought.

As Gareth was getting strapped into the camera at Burbank to do a shot for *The Heretic*, a figure leapt out of the shadows and began taking pictures of the Steadicam. It was Gottschalk, the President of Panavision, no less. He was a flamboyant character who wore gold bangles and necklace chains with pendants before such ornaments became standard Hollywood dress.

So, skilfully camouflaged in red shirt, flowered silk scarf, tight jeans constraining more than ample flesh, and crocodile boots, Gottschalk flashed his camera and then fled. Gareth ran after him, trying to get the Steadicam going to record evidence of this flagrant industrial espionage. It was a great triumph for the Steadicam. Gareth, wearing the camera, was actually gaining on a man running flat out and carrying only about 40 pounds of excess fat. Gottschalk just made it to his car and got away, but not before Gareth was able to record his shame on film. Poor Gottschalk was later murdered (not by Gareth), and Panavision eventually made their own device called the Panaglide.

I have become increasingly uneasy about Michael Seymour. Since returning from our trip to Brazil he has been working on designs and storyboards, interrupted by the need to build the jungle set for the tests, which he did extremely well. However, there is a lack of rapport between us. He does not see the story or Brazil as I do. Despite detailed discussions, his drawings come out differently from my intentions. It has been worrying me for some time, and today I decided to talk to him about it, to express my doubts. In other circumstances, I could let things go on and see how they work out, but with our departure for Brazil imminent, I must act promptly and, in the absence of fact, on intuition. I explained all this to Seymour. It was a measure of our lack of close understanding that, despite various hints, he was quite unaware that any problem might exist. It was this lack of sensitivity that decided me to terminate the relationship. I like him, respect and admire his ability, and there was no acrimony in our discussions.

Getting fired is something to which technicians are ruefully resigned, and it happens to most of them at one time or another. It usually concerns some careless error that costs an expensive delay, but it is often to do with personality clashes. Making a movie is so highly charged that these problems are inevitable. Tony Richardson was making a film with Richard Burton, who was persistently late for his calls. Tony plucked up his courage and went to see him and told him that he was fired. They shouted abuse at each other and Tony left the room slamming the door. Only then did he remember he was on Burton's yacht. He was obliged to go back to the stateroom and ask for a boat to take him ashore. With the passage of time, they both came to relish the story.

On a big picture like this it is usual for the designer to work with an art director who will implement his designs. I had hoped that Michael Seymour would work with the Brazilian, Marcos Flaksman in this way, but he insisted on an English art director, Simon Holland. Simon worked on *Greystoke* in the Cameroons and loves the rain forest as I do. He is tall and pale with narrow, Viking features. We are of the same blood, northern forest people.

Since it is too late to find another designer, I decided to ask

Simon to take charge, working in concert with Marcos Flaksman. He has agreed. I feel very relieved, and much more
comfortable.

---

19 NOVEMBER 1983 *EN ROUTE: LOS ANGELES*

Michael Dryhurst has gone ahead to Brazil trying to spur
things along. We still await permission from Concine,
although they have now had the script and schedule for some
time. David Norris has bought £2,500,000 worth of cruzeiros
and the Citibank in São Paulo has put them to work. At present
they are earning something over 200 per cent interest, hopefully keeping up with inflation. We now have a company
called Goldcrest Filmes Limitada.

Terry Clegg, Goldcrest's production supervisor, will meet
us in Brazil to satisfy himself that our arrangements are in
order.

We have shipped a lot of heavy equipment and it should
be on the high seas by now. Melissa has lined up a new batch
of boys for me to see in Los Angeles. I will also try to cast Bill
and Jean Markham. Rospo is waiting to work on the script.
I have written the new scenes involving Jean and revised the
character of Werner. I will then go on to Brazil where Possi
will have candidates for the tribes to show me. I have sent
Simon Holland on ahead to visit the Xingu with Possi. (Not
so difficult now I have an open invitation from the tribe.) I
want them to have that experience before they start work. I
will tour the locations with Simon and Marcos, and then sit
down with them to design the sets. Philippe Rousselot will be
with us and Michael Dryhurst. A lot of decisions will have to
be made. We plan to start shooting early March.

In the hold of the plane I have a print of *Dream One*.
Columbia has bought the US distribution rights. Tomorrow
they are staging some previews, which I will attend. Arnaud
is with me, and Jake meets us there.

Four screenings of *Dream One*. The first one, for very young children, went well. The second, for 12–14-year-olds, and the third, for the 15–34 age group, were terribly disappointing. People were just not ready to enter the film or accept it on its own terms. They were irritated and hostile. Columbia has a roster of guinea-pigs, their demographics carefully analysed, and they are invited by telephone. Afterwards they are asked to fill out cards testing their responses to the movie.

Now that Columbia is owned by Coca-Cola, they have gone mad on market research. I suspect that this pseudo-science is a convenient shelter behind which insecure executives can hide. Apart from this in-house preview system, they market-test poster ideas, displaying several alternatives and asking people which one attracts them. They regularly telephone people and ask them which current movies they are aware of. After this they run a TV ad for a movie and then telephone another sample to see if the 'awareness factor' of the movie they are promoting has improved.

Many studios are going even further; before making a final decision to finance a picture, they send out researchers to supermarkets and ask people if, for instance, they would go to see a film about an extraterrestrial stranded on earth who is adopted by some suburban kids. Perhaps this was why Columbia decided not to make *E.T.* after they had spent $1 million developing it. Even for Steven Spielberg, it is not all plain sailing. Even he, of the Midas touch, has to overcome the market researchers.

Why people decide to go to a movie remains a total mystery. There have been movies that have had brilliant previews, everyone loves the film – but when it opens nobody will pay to see it. There are a lot of movies that people do not actually enjoy and yet feel a compulsion to see. One astonishing scene can be enough – some cathartic mayhem, a spectacular special effect, a performer who touches a nerve.

Very occasionally there are 'sleepers', films that start poorly then gradually build up to success over a long period, but most hit pictures are hits from the first matinee on the opening day. The word gets out somehow or other. The majority of movie-goers do not read reviews, so is it the advertising, the title? Some stars still have pulling power, but none of them can get an audience into a film they do not want to see.

I recall watching *Star Wars* on Hollywood Boulevard on its opening day. There were lines around the block, yet no one knew anything about it. Even people in the industry thought it was about conflicts between movie stars.

Richard Zanuck told me a story. He was head of Twentieth Century-Fox when *M*A*S*H* opened. He was in New York with his partner, David Brown. He decided to walk down to the theatre for the first matinee. David Brown said, 'It will only depress you. There has been no publicity. There are no stars, an unknown director. It is teeming with rain. It's a good picture, but it will need time to build.'

Nevertheless, Zanuck put on his raincoat and walked down. When he was 200 yards away he saw people standing in line. He broke into a run. They were lined up around the block, enduring the rain.

'How do they know?' he cried. 'How the hell do they know?'

He still has no answer.

Research shows that after the first week, it is word of mouth that sends people into the cinemas, but what of those very first audiences? Why do they decide to swamp one movie and avoid another like the plague? They have already decided they like the hit movie before they see it. They are rooting for it to succeed. They wait in line sometimes for several hours. They have an investment in it being a success before they see the first frame of the film.

My theory is this. The opening-day crowds are always the same people, the movie buffs. These people have an underground network of gossip and information. Producers and studio heads guard a film from public gaze while it is being made. When they screen the finished product, doors are locked, only a privileged few executives view it. They always forget that the projectionists are watching in the booth, many of whom are movie buffs. They call each other. Buffs know them and call up to get information. They report on the daily rushes, on the rough-cut, and on the finished film.

So it is the buffs who are there on opening day, and they rush out to tell their friends. After the first showing of *The Birth of a Nation* people ran into the street and seized passers-by to tell them the news. Weeping, they pleaded with total strangers to go in and witness it. Ah, if only . . .

A picture can open big, but does it have 'legs', they ask? It can falter, tail off. Each week the drop in takings is measured. If it drops by more than 10 per cent per week, it will not stay the course.

My source of information is Tommy Culla, a Hollywood legend. He sees everything, reads everything. He keeps elaborate files and cross-references. When a studio announces a project, Tommy puts a tentative gross rental against it. As it is developed, cast, shot, he adjusts the figure. His accuracy is astonishing. He is in touch with the projectionists – daily. His predictions are unnerving. His life is films. No one knows more about the game than he. He is contemptuous of the poseurs and monstrous egos that cripple and strangle the business, and he reveres talent. He rages against mediocrity: 'The picture was so bad,' he once said, 'when they showed it on Pan American, people were walking out at 35,000 feet.'

The Deer Hunter has a very substantial wedding sequence. Tommy said, 'It went on so long I was embarrassed not to bring a gift.'

I test scripts on Tommy, show him rushes and rough-cuts. He judges everything by his own high standards. He never spares my feelings. He has worked for several studios but cannot restrain his brutal honesty. In a community that is in the business of telling lies to each other, and kidding themselves, they would rather not know what Tommy thinks.

So it was with some trepidation that I asked Tommy along to the fourth screening of *Dream One*, together with a few other friends.

He pronounced, 'It's tasty. It will do business.'

'But, Tommy, the preview cards were not good.'

'What do they know? Those jerks are not the audience for this picture. What else can you take a kid to see, and have fun yourself?'

That seemed to sew it up.

Christopher Isherwood and Don Bachardy were entranced by it. Of all the people I met when I first came out to Hollywood, theirs is just about the only marriage that has survived.

Bob Chartoff liked it without being overwhelmed. Rospo loved it. So it is capable of making friends. I go to bed less depressed than I might have been. Poor Arnaud was shattered. After the early blows, he looked completely punch-drunk, but somehow staggered through the day. He had to lose his virginity sometime. What a pity it had to be rape.

---

21 NOVEMBER 1983

Gave Rospo my revisions and the notes of my meeting with Jeff Young. We talked them over, and then went together to Embassy to meet with Jeff. I showed the language tests and both Rospo and Jeff were intrigued with the experiment. They agreed that it allowed us to keep our options open.

Spent the rest of the day with Melissa. Still no Tommy.

---

22 NOVEMBER 1983

Melissa has put together a pile of videos showing the work of actors and actresses for the parts of Jean and Bill. It is taking hours to view them, even just sampling. This is a facility that was just not available a few years ago. It is a valuable aid. Each new piece of technology starts out as an expensive novelty, and within months it becomes an absolute necessity.

In the past, we would borrow films from other studios, ship them over and view them in one of the studio's preview theatres. Then I would run around town watching current movies, sometimes sampling four in an evening.

Why then, with this video facility, does it take so much time? Why does it take longer to make a movie every time a new, time-saving device is introduced? There is an immutable law at work. The computer was going to bring about the paperless office. Since Edgar went over to computers, his place is drowning in paper. The computers spew the stuff out everywhere.

We have cameras that are lighter, easier to load; film stock is faster, needing much less light; the huge lamps have been superseded by miniaturized versions – yet schedules get longer and crews larger. Of course, the answer is that instead of trying to save time, these devices allow us to attempt more difficult shots and effects. Film has been described as the 'art of the possible', and every year more things become more possible.

---

23 NOVEMBER 1983

Meeting with Jake and Edgar. There are many points to discuss. Our deal was that I would take no fee from *Dream One*, and Goldcrest charge no overhead. The sale to Columbia, the Channel Four commitment, the French investment and the tax shelter would put us into profit before the film opened. Now there seems some doubt about the tax shelter. Apparently, Goldcrest's auditors have told them that they cannot enjoy the benefits of tax shelter and I suppose they are not going to do it just for my sake.

Because of Jake's successes, he has received many offers from the major studios who are ready to pay him a huge salary. There are now quite a few studio executives who earn more than a million dollars a year. They have overtaken the directors and producers and are closing fast on the stars. There is a reason for this: while most films lose money, the film studios make bigger and bigger profits. If that sounds contradictory, it also says something about creative accounting.

Jake is under pressure inside Goldcrest because the parent company, the Pearson Longman Group, is horrified at these large salaries. They refuse to pay Jake even a third of the money being offered him by the Americans. Because of the success of Goldcrest, the Pearson's appointed chairman, James Lee, is muscling in on Jake, who founded the company and has run it since it started. Jake is too engaged in the front line to watch his back in the corporate game. He is frustrated by

Pearson's attitude. He borrowed money to get the company going and is still in debt. If he left the company they would have to acquire his shares, making him a rich man. He has a powerful emotional attachment to Goldcrest and to people like me with whom he has forged relationships, but it looks to me that he will go. His departure could pose a lot of problems.

---

24 NOVEMBER 1983

My options in casting the role of Markham have been severely curtailed by Goldcrest policy. Jake is totally opposed to paying stars a lot of money. He just won't do it. He says the picture is the only star, spend the money on that. Cannes showed that we could get top advances from territories without a star. It is a refreshing attitude.

Most of my life I have been in the position of *having* to cast a star to get the picture going. However, in this case, it is hard to find a brilliant 40-year-old screen actor who is *not* a star. Now that the budget is set I have to find someone I can afford, because a star would increase the cost to a point where Goldcrest might decide the film is too expensive to make.

So stars who could play it – Robert Redford, Robert de Niro, Clint Eastwood – command between two and six million dollars, and are clearly out of the running. Jon Voight and Donald Sutherland are brilliant actors and I would love to have either of them in the part, but their price is well over a million dollars.

Jake took the same line over *The Killing Fields*. Sam Waterston was cast for very low money. Why not use Sam, Jake suggests? He is wrong for this. I need less of a racehorse, someone with more juice, a solid Texas engineer.

Melissa and I scanned the videos; we looked at all the actors playing TV leads. There is a terrible sameness about most of them. They have rugged good looks and they set out to charm and seduce rather than enter a role and act it out. They are in the business of surviving. They develop tricks for getting through the scenes. What else can they do, the way American TV is made? Many of them are capable of much more, I am

sure, unless the bad habits have spoiled them for ever. Burt
Reynolds had come off three TV series when I cast him in
Deliverance. He was full of tricks. At the end of the shooting,
he said, 'John, I did this picture under false pretences. I can't
act. I was just faking it.'

It is the kind of humour that makes him so special. I
said, 'Burt, if you can fake it that well, don't bother to start
acting.'

In fact, Burt's approach to scenes was facile, but Voight
had the opposite tendency. He would worry every scene to
death. So Jon forced Burt to dig deeper, and Burt pushed Jon
into being less ponderous. What is treacherous about an actor
who is clever but shallow is that he will impress you moment
to moment. Only when you put the film together do you see
the lack of substance.

Peter Rawley, an English agent working in LA, persuaded
me to meet a client of his, Powers Boothe. I had seen him in
Southern Comfort and in a television film as Jim Jones, the
murderous evangelist. He seemed brilliant, but rather unsym-
pathetic and humourless. Peter said, 'You must meet him. He
is sensitive and subtle. He has qualities he has not been able
to show on screen.'

When he walked into Melissa's office I felt a shock of recognition. He simply *was* the part. We didn't read. We just
talked about the story. I told him my idea of what Bill Markham should be like. And behold, he became the character in
front of my eyes. Some actors can do that, but it is rare. I am
obsessively cautious about casting, I like to spend hours with
an actor, meet him several times, look at him in different
lights, consider him over a period.

When Ned Beatty walked in, I offered him the part of
Bobby in *Deliverance* after two minutes. He had never been in
a movie, or on television. I had never seen him act. I just
knew. Lee Marvin as Walker in *Point Blank*, Nicol Williamson
as Merlin in *Excalibur*, were the other rare occasions when
lightning struck.

Powers comes from small-town Texas. As he stands before
me, he assumes the square set of an engineer. In his eyes is
the hint of pain and melancholy of a man who has lost his

son, and the obsessiveness of a father who, after ten years, will not give up the hunt.

As soon as he leaves, I call Edgar and tell him to make a deal with Boothe's agent. I said, don't play games. Just offer him the full figure we have in the budget.

---

25 NOVEMBER 1983

Things are moving fast. Jake has taken the big step. He has left Goldcrest and joined Embassy. I told him about Powers Boothe. His attitude was typical of his style, 'If you love him, I love him.' The attractive part of the deal with Goldcrest, which compensates for the low fee, is that I have total control of casting and indeed all creative controls, including the final cut.

Goldcrest have a problem, though. Their deal with Embassy gives the American company the right of approval of the role of Markham. It turns out Embassy does not like the idea of Powers Boothe. Guess what, they want a star. Strictly speaking, it is Goldcrest's problem, not mine. But if Embassy withdraw it would leave us searching for a US distributor and Goldcrest would lose the $9 million Embassy are putting up for the right to distribute in America. That would probably mean cancellation. So I have to concern myself with this matter. Jake said, 'Leave it to me.' It is his first task as an Embassy executive. He called me back some hours later, a very shaken man. Perenchio, and his chief executive, Alan Horn, finally succumbed to pressure, but it was a close run thing. It comes hard to Jake, no longer being his own man.

---

28 NOVEMBER 1983 *SAO PAULO*

We have advertised widely and masses of people have turned up for auditions to be part of the tribes. Possi and three assistants have been screening them and I am being presented with a comparatively short list – some hundreds – seen at a series of workouts. Possi tongue-lashes them into shape with his chainsaw voice. If you did not see it with your own eyes, you would swear he was using a loudhailer. These sessions start with an hour or so of calisthenics and then theatre games that bring out character. The physical effort certainly breaks down defences and exposes character. Movement and body language tell a lot. I pass among them with Possi and we cull and select. There are some good prospects. We will have further auditions in Belém where there is a much greater Indian population.

Since everything in Brazil is done to music, Possi has hired a percussionist to keep the beat going for these sessions. His name is Junior Homrich. He sits cross-legged on a mat surrounded by a variety of congas, drums and tablas, flutes and shakers, a one-stringed instrument with a gourd as a resonator called a birenbaum, and other arcane instruments. Many are of Indian origin, some Carib. Like most things in Brazil, the percussionists are the unique result of a blend of cultures. Junior is one-quarter Indian and has studied indigenous music in tribal conditions, as well as percussion at Woodstock. He provides sound effects – insects, rain, bird calls, as well as rhythm and melody. I find what he does very exciting and it suggests an approach to the musical score, although that is a decision for much later. Meanwhile, Possi and I decide to keep Junior with us right through the tribe training.

---

10 DECEMBER 1983 *BELEM*

Completed yet another tour of locations with Philippe Rousselot, Simon Holland, Marcos Flaksman and my location manager, Gerry Levy. Terry Clegg, the Goldcrest man, came with us. It was very much nuts and bolts: where to put the vehicles, what lights and equipment we need at each site, transportation problems, permissions.

Michael and Fred Harding have revised the budget. We have secured offices and telephones in Belém, and rented a warehouse where we can build the sets.

Terry Clegg pronounces himself very impressed with our preparations. After a long session on the budget and schedule he had only minor criticisms. He feels we should import a British transportation manager, shrewdly seeing this area as crucial in our complex logistics of swinging 150 people, and tons of equipment, across the vast distances of Brazil.

Simon, Marcos and I got down to the set designs. The most important is the *shabona*, the living quarters of the Invisible People. The enclosed dome favoured by the Xingu is attractive, but claustrophobic and difficult to light. There is another style, used by some tribes, which has an open centre. This links it better to the outdoors. We are searching for a site with enfolding, overhanging trees so that it will have a hidden look, yet the light will filter through, dappled by the leaves, into the central area where we can stage some of the rituals and dances. The play of shadows, the darkened living areas, will enhance the hidden, half-seen nature of the Invisible People.

We spent a lot of time plotting the ideal dimensions. Before I build such a vital set, I have a model made up. Using a periscope device, I can examine it through a lens, at eye level, that is, an inch or so from the ground. This gives me a good indication of what the shots will look like and how the camera can move. Then I will have Marcos set up temporary stakes and poles defining the area before finally deciding on shape and size.

Although Caito secured us permission to shoot at the building on the Belém waterfront that would serve as our Amazco offices, it is impractical to shoot interior scenes there, so that we must build the interior offices set somewhere else in a way that matches the exterior of the waterfront building. I want it to have a view across the river to the jungle, just as the apartment does, so that when we are inside, the rain forest is always present, always powerfully asserting itself. To achieve this we will photograph, on a plate camera, the view from the waterfront building, and then have the negative sent to London for enlarging into a giant transparency 40 feet long, 20 feet high, which is known as a Translite backing. This will be shipped back to Brazil and mounted on the set outside the office windows. A battery of lights will be rigged behind it. Dimmers will allow Philippe to alter the density of the light to suggest burning noon or stormy twilight.

Certain night scenes in the forest will also be made in the warehouse. Simon and Marcos will take impressions of trees and reproduce them in plaster on the stage, so they will match the ones the audience has seen during the day in the real forest. It is the kind thing that seems crazy to an outsider. We come 5,000 miles to find rain forest and end up shooting in a tin shed with plastic trees. But these scenes require rain-making and lightning effects and to rig up this kind of equipment in the heart of the forest at night would be very difficult and dangerous, and so little detail is seen that the effort would be quite disproportionate to the result.

When journalists come on a set, they love to scribble about this kind of apparent craziness. It confirms their prejudice that movie-making is prodigal, that directors prefer the fake to the real thing.

Judging a film director by watching him work on the set is like writing about an architect by observing a building site.

---

14 DECEMBER 1983 *EN ROUTE: BELEM-LONDON*

Possi came up to Belém for more auditions and we found a few more good tribespeople. My respect for Possi increases by the minute. The people he is dealing with are spontaneously unpredictable. It's not just being late; it is getting the day wrong, or becoming involved in some other activity that drives the training session quite out of mind. I find it difficult to be hard on them. They disarm me with their gentle and affectionate manners. Not so Possi. He is brutally tough. He has a rehearsal room next to our offices, and we shudder as we hear his voice reaching maximum volume, a point at which people fall to their knees, weeping.

Rousselot, Dryhurst, Holland, Flaksman, Caito, Fred Harding, Gerry Levy and I have been conducting a marathon two-day production meeting, with Terry Clegg observing. Preceding this, Michael Dryhurst, Fred Harding and I had made some savage cuts to the schedule to get the budget back under the $17 million mark. What I dreaded has come to pass. I have been forced to shoot a six-day week rather than five. I swore I never would, but it seems the only way to lop weeks off the schedule. When you are away on location you have to pay technicians for the Saturday whether they work or not, therefore *not* to work becomes expensive. A six-day schedule saves us two and a half weeks. The equipment rental charges, the salaries and hotel expenses save around $400,000. Poor Fred Harding is obliged to leave the room every half an hour to vomit. He has been throwing up for two weeks. He still smiles and carries on with the budget, but his handwriting becomes more and more illegible. He has become so nervous of local food that he eats only eggs.

A production meeting is always a jolting and gruelling experience. We go through the script page by page and everyone fires questions at the director. How many extras here? What proportion of men to women? How many children? What ages? What vehicles do you require? What time of day should the scene be shot? Does Markham wear the same costume here as in the previous scene or has he had time to change? How many camera set-ups for this scene? Will you need tracks? Where can we put the catering truck? Where will the crew eat? The dinghy, should it be aluminium or wood? How many wet suits will we need in the cold-water rain scene? How many members of the crew will need to get wet? We still don't have a location for this scene.

There are many questions that I cannot answer. It makes me conscious of how much there is left to do. So many locations still to find, casting to complete, rehearsals and tribe training, the costuming, the make-up.

Stanley Kubrick has a reputation as an obsessive perfectionist. When he gets into a subject he soon knows more than the experts. His conversational style is interrogation. Apart from making several truly great films, he has also pushed back the technical frontiers. He uses every new device and some that he invents himself and, of course, with everything quicker and lighter, each movie he does takes longer and longer to make.

On *Barry Lyndon* the unit was preparing to ship out to Ireland where shooting would soon commence. The production manager kept pressing him to have a production meeting: 'We must know what you need shipped.'

Stanley demurred. There were so many things he had yet
to resolve. As the PM kept pressing, he eventually agreed, but
he said if there was a question he could not answer he would
ring a bell and they would pass on to the next issue. The PM
readily agreed. What kind of bell should it be, Stanley pondered? The PM winced. He knew the signs. At this stage,
Kubrick had teams of photographers out taking pictures of
every field in Ireland with a tree in the middle! The PM said,
'Stanley, I'll get you one of those little bells you have on the
table to call the servants.'

Stanley said no, such a bell would offend the class sensibilities of the participants.

'A buzzer, like on a quiz show?' offered the PM.

Stanley thought it would be irritating. He preferred a more
melodious sound. 'I tell you what,' said Stanley, 'have the art
department to go out and get an example of every available
bell and I'll choose one.'

In this way, Kubrick gained several days' grace and was
able to delay the misery of a production meeting.

We have left Caito in charge of the office in Belém with a list
of a million chores. Possi goes on with recruiting and culling.
As the tribespeople develop, we hope to cast the smaller roles
from among their number. Marcos Flaksman is recruiting a
team of assistants and draughtsmen and will start work on the
designs that Simon and I have left him with.

This flight leaves Belém at 2 am, so before leaving we all sat
down, some ten of us, and had a late dinner with lots of wine.
The river fish from the Amazon are delicious. We had a fine
night. It was very warm. We felt much affection and respect
for one another. The work is in hand. We have done what we
ought to have done.

David Begelman, in his days as an agent, had a genius for
making soothing remarks to his clients that they could interpret in the best possible way yet did not commit David to a
position. After a screening, David would say to the director,
'It's all up there on the screen' or 'It's exactly what you
wanted it to be.'

To the frustrated actor or director waiting nervously for a deal to be concluded, he would say, 'We are exactly where we ought to be at this point in time.'

I got up to make a little speech, Brazil and its wine encouraging me to be more emotional than I would be elsewhere. I spoke of my love of the country, the Amazon, my affection for the people, and particularly for those ten that sat at the table; of the brave enterprise we were engaged on, of the good work we had done in the last weeks, and I concluded by saying, quoting David Begelman with due attribution, 'We are exactly where we ought to be at this point in time.'

'At this point in time,' Michael pointed out, 'we should be getting on the plane.' The hours had fled, and there followed a mad dash to the airport.

---

19 DECEMBER 1983 *LONDON*

A few busy days in London, before returning, via Los Angeles, to Brazil, this time for eight months, by which time the film will be in the can, or Goldcrest broke and my reputation in ruins.

Made revisions, cuts, revoicing on *Dream One* to satisfy Columbia. Signed up the last members of the crew. We are all required to have an extensive medical examination to obtain a Brazilian work permit, this includes blood, urine and faeces tests. Our crew members are required to deliver their samples to our doctor. When I arrived at his surgery this morning, his receptionist was quite hysterical: 'Would you tell your crew that we only require small samples.' Apparently huge turds keep turning up.

The doctor is giving them a range of shots and vaccines, gamma globulin, and putting them all on malaria tablets. For better or worse I have declined all except yellow fever and cholera since you need certification of these to enter Brazil.

Before each film the principal actors and the director are required to have an exhaustive medical examination for insurance purposes. If any one of us died during the shooting, the film would be either abandoned or severely delayed and the insurance company wants to be sure that we are not about to die or be debilitated by illness.

When I went to MGM in 1966 to make *Point Blank*, they had their own doctor, permanently employed. He had been the 'royal' physician to Louis B. Mayer and he was famous for a medical speciality that must be quite rare. He could keep an actor alive and on his feet for the duration of a shooting schedule, however sick or whatever the disease.

Of course, we shall employ a doctor to be with us all the time on the set. The insurer would insist, and I would want to anyway. I am in favour of using a Brazilian who will know more about local conditions and tropical diseases. Michael is not so sure. We took an American doctor, Hampton Fancher with us to Palau on *Hell in the Pacific*. He was a marvellous, hard-drinking character, with a glass eye, one lung and a missing testicle, but it was the island medical officer, with just a year's training who saved our lives, mine included. He even removed a spleen from one of the ship's crew. After he operated on me, I came round in the ward, which was a thatched hut with open sides. The patients lay on mats in their customary manner. Next to me, I noticed our film doctor flaked out. He had been delayed in the local bar and hadn't made it for the operation. At dinnertime, the wives arrived, lit fires in the middle of the hut and cooked up fish for their men, a novel form of hospital catering.

One day Lee Marvin and I went out to find Hampton, who had gone missing on the island. He wasn't in the local bar, the Boom Boom Room, where we expected to find him. Lee, who is an expert on these matters, looked round the back of the corrugated iron shed that served as a urinal. There, lying on the slimy, cracked concrete, was the good doctor, the glass eye staring up at us, otherwise insensate. Trying to shame him into consciousness, Lee bellowed out: 'Where's the dignity of the medical profession?'

Regaling Michael with this story convinced him that we should employ a local man in Brazil.

I had a meeting with Gale Tattersall, the operator. He is

back from his course on the Steadicam and Gareth Brown pronounces him proficient. Apart from a fairly standard set of equipment – the main Panavision camera with a set of lenses, including zooms, a lightweight crab dolly, tracks, two Arriflex cameras and the ancillary devices that go with them – we will bring some specialist items. A camera mount that smooths out the vibrations is required for the helicopter. It is expensive, especially as we will be obliged to keep it for the duration. Gale has the clever idea of adapting the Steadicam so it can be used inside a helicopter, thus saving a lot of money. He is working on this with our camera mechanic.

We decide to take a 'hot head'. This is a device that allows us to put the camera on the crane arm and pan, tilt and focus it remotely. Normally the operator and focus-puller must ride the crane with the camera. The hot head allows us to use a much lighter, more transportable crane. The snag is that it involves complex electronics and takes several hours to prepare for a shot. But we need a number of crane shots, particularly to simulate a swooping eagle for Tommy's trance visions. It seems the best available solution.

Gale's nervousness is now bordering on the frantic as he tries to get everything together and properly test it all. So much equipment is arriving at his flat that his wife is threatening him with divorce.

20 DECEMBER 1983

I had a long meeting with David Norris at Goldcrest going over the outstanding contractual matters. My deal is that once they have approved the script, schedule and budget they are obliged to finance the film. The budget is just about finalized – it can change only marginally now. Terry Clegg has made his report and certainly indicated to us that it would be favourable.

After our meeting I went to see James Lee who is now running the company in place of Jake. He was charming but a little cool. He is concerned that we still do not have the final approval of Concine. I pointed out that they would not give it until they had a final list of all crew and cast members with satisfactory medical reports. We have received repeated assurances that this will be forthcoming. We have paid $42,000 to the Brazilian trade unions to get their agreement for us to bring technicians into Brazil, and have guaranteed to employ a large number of their members.

He was also concerned that Electronorte might withdraw permission to shoot on the dam if they discovered we were going to blow it up. (Only the model, of course.) I had to admit this was a risk and quoted Babenco's explanation, which he did not find as amusing as I did.

Columbia's disappointment with *Dream One* and Jake's departure have certainly chilled the warm welcome I used to get in the corridors of Goldcrest. Mr Lee did not express any great enthusiasm for *The Emerald Forest*. Fortunately, things have gone much too far for him to pull out at this stage. I estimate he would have to write off £2 million for the privilege of cancelling the project. Since the pre-sales cover the budget, Goldcrest really have no financial exposure. David remains an enthusiastic ally.

---

21 DECEMBER 1983

Saw *The Genius of Venice* at the Royal Academy. It is awesome and inspiring. The movement of light, the balance of colour, texture and emotion are caught in sweet harmonious compositions. There is story content as well – in fact, all the elements of cinema except movement in time. It made me yearn to be shooting, making. The feeling of surfeit at seeing too many masterpieces usually leaves one debilitated, too crushed to do one's own work, or hungry for 'junk' – not so today. The exhibition was like Venice itself, of a piece, balanced, whole. Each picture illuminated the others, revealed them, just as images in a movie should serve the film. It led me to define what annoys me about beautiful shots in movies – it is their ego, their narcissism. We want no narcissistic shots in *The Emerald Forest*. Philippe is wonderfully free of that disease which we see so often in modern cinema. A cameraman once said to me, 'I have to be very careful, one good shot can ruin a bad movie.' Today's films and commercials are full of spurious beauty. They intimidate and depress the audience as expensively dressed models do.

---

21 DECEMBER 1983 *pm*

Dinner with Daisy, Katrine and Christel. Daisy in one of her black moods. She and Christel need a huge emotional eruption in order to make parting possible. We will be gone eight months. Daisy goes to Paris after Christmas to resume her studies. I shall miss her savage eye and kind heart. Christel is apprehensive, but excited too. This is the stage where she keeps telling the girls where deeds and keys and jewellery are hidden, in case she never comes back. Charley will come out with us, initially just as a member of the family, with the possibility of playing Tommy.

---

2 JANUARY 1984

A day spent at Twickenham Film Studios. Michael Dryhurst was stuck in fog on his way back from spending Christmas in Portugal, so our planned overlap day did not work out. He will stay on in London to supervise the despatch of crew and equipment. I spent the morning dictating memos to Norma Paulsen who will hold the fort in London when we are all gone and be responsible for shipping items, despatching bodies and maintaining communications. I am awash in insurance, shipping, permissions, budget problems, medical exams, visas, permits, etc. The work involved in making a movie is out of all scale with the final result. The effort is so disproportionate. Especially with a film like this, which is also an expedition. Yet an air of excitement prevails. A group of people break out of their lives and venture into the unknown. The best part of making a movie is this exploration. The fellow feeling, the closeness and warmth that common cause gives rise to are very rewarding. I like to put myself and others under intense pressure, and in making a film everything is concentrated, just as film itself is. Each film is like living a whole new life and we are all ready to be reborn. Freddie Raphael once said that people love making movies because it is an activity that suspends all thoughts of death.

---

3 JANUARY 1984 *EN ROUTE: LONDON-LOS ANGELES (BRITISH AIRWAYS)*

Goodbye to London and Europe for eight months. Finally, after eighteen months of writing and research, three trips to Brazil, one to Mexico, four to Los Angeles, I'm leaving to make the film. The struggle to get it off the ground is over. Now it is finally a reality, and a year of work stretches ahead from which there is no escape. Now the desired moment has arrived I find myself depressed, like a prisoner being led away for a sentence. From now on, there will not be a day free. Never a chance to sleep late, decisions always to be made, not even the luxury of getting drunk can be risked. I try to take exercise each day, running three miles and getting in some tennis, so that I can sustain the health and stamina to last the course. Next, is ten weeks of intensive preparation, rehearsals, casting, planning. Then seventeen weeks of shooting, six days per week – with the seventh spent preparing the following week's work. After that, several weeks of second unit shooting. The months of editing I look forward to. At that stage all the heavy work will be done. There will be time for reflection, to try ways of putting the picture together. At that point the film belongs to me again. I will have retrieved it from the cast and crew, and I won't yet need to give it to the world.

---

4 JANUARY 1984 *BEL AIR SANDS*

All day working on the script with Rospo. He was surprisingly relaxed about all my rewrites, accepted the quite sweeping changes with grace and humour, making only minor suggestions for changes. He will spend the next two days tidying up the rewrites. His lack of fight is partly due to being in the middle of writing an eight-hour mini-series on *The Odyssey*. He has somehow managed to incorporate *The Iliad* and *The Oresteia*. He has also banished the gods, and invented huge swathes of missing chronology.

I spoke to Edgar. David Norris now says that the tax-shelter deals on *Dream One* and *The Emerald Forest*, from which I was to benefit, have all collapsed. The deal I made with Jake was that I would take substantially less money in salary in return for a share in the tax savings. I have now worked eighteen months for Goldcrest without earning a penny.

---

6 JANUARY 1984

Last two days in Melissa's windowless, airless Burbank office in casting sessions. The special smell of Burbank: hard-baked, refried smog.

I saw a lot of boys, a better bunch this time. The most impressive (although strange and quirky, and therefore not quite right) was Donald Sutherland's son, Kiefer. He and his twin sister used to play with Charley and Daisy when they were 3 or 4-year-olds. Two sets of boy–girl twins. Donald and I used to watch them with mordant fascination, these Midwich cuckoos, involved utterly in each other, excluding the world beyond. Kiefer is as strange and special as Daisy and Charley. Before we left London, Daisy said, 'I am so lucky being a twin. It must be awful to be alone in the world.'

Having problems casting Jean, the mother. One learns a lot about the characters during casting. Several actresses have turned down the role after reading it: Jo Beth Williams, Tess Harper of *Tender Mercies*, Susan Anspach, etc. I suspect this is partly to do with current notions of how a modern woman should be. Jean is a wife and mother, not a popular role today; also, the part is small. But overriding these considerations, the characterization is ill conceived and unrealized. Now we have rewritten it along the lines discussed with Jeff Young, I am hoping it will prove more enticing.

Sunday lunch with Bob Chartoff at his beach house. During *Point Blank* and *Hell in the Pacific*, Christel and I rented a house in Malibu colony. It belonged to Rod Steiger. I used to start each day by plunging into those big Pacific breakers. I am shocked at the devastation along the coast. Rocks and whole cliff sides are subsiding, and the beach has shrunk alarmingly. The sea laps right up to the beach houses. The owners have so much invested that they conspire to pretend nothing is wrong. When I express my shock, they say it is the time of year for high tides. I lived a whole year through on the beach and never saw anything like this. Most of these people are in the entertainment industry so their capacity for self-deception is unlimited. Bob's ex-partner, Irwin Winkler, once made a memorable statement about a colleague. He said, 'We're friends. We lie to each other.'

Bob Chartoff came to London in January. While he was away, another storm struck Malibu Beach, wrecking hundreds of million-dollar homes, including the front of his fourteen-bathroom place. When he got back, Vanessa, his wife, had gone, taking their son. Since then, she has refused to speak to him or explain why. Divorce is pending. He must cut everything down the middle. She gets *Rocky I*, he *Rocky II*, and so on. Next to his house, on a complete lot, Bob has a tennis court. I asked him what the land it stood on was worth.

'At least one million dollars.'

'How often do you use it?'

We figure an average of two sets a week. A hundred per year. Interest on $1 million would be at least $100,000, so it costs him $1,000 a set. We played today. I was 3–1 down in the first set when Vanessa called. He was surprised. He went off to take the call. When he came back he said that he had thought it inhuman that she refused to talk to him for six months. Now she was speaking again, he wished she wouldn't. I went on to win 6–3, 6–1. Two thousand dollars worth.

10 JANUARY 1984

Still trying to cast Jean but, more important, Tommy. Tomorrow I will shoot tests on five boys. Working intensively each morning on the third draft script and making solid advances.

15 JANUARY 1984

Leave for Rio tomorrow. The rewrite of the script is finished. Yesterday I did a reading with three actresses, my short-list for Jean. Meg Foster was wondrous. She has a bruised look, yet her pale blue eyes seem to light up an interior world with a clarity that makes it almost painful to watch. She is so exposed. She read the new scene where Jean tries to make contact with Tommy. It wrenched the heart. She has a dark, sonorous voice, which she plays like a saxophone. She found sudden, high notes that I would never have expected. I was always concerned that the scenes in the apartment would seem merely naturalistic and therefore out of kilter with the mythic scale of the rest of the film. But Meg is epic. She will bring power as well as truth to those scenes.

All week meeting more boys and shooting tests for Tommy. Reviewing the tests with Melissa and Rospo, we all agreed that none of them made it. It is very difficult. The boy must be on the verge of manhood, yet capable of maturing to become chief, fall in love, kill, suffer. I have now asked Melissa to go to New York to continue the search. Meanwhile, if no boy jumps out of the pack, I will go with Charley. He has a touching vulnerability and the eyes of innocence. He was accomplished in *Dream One*. He is 17, the right age.

There is one boy I met, C. Thomas Howell, an experienced actor and quite marvellous in Coppola's *The Outsiders*, who could possibly play the role, but he is tied to a TV series and would not be free until a month after we begin. The boy who plays the part must have at least six weeks' intensive training, which means starting almost immediately.

Crisis. Bags packed ready to leave for Rio. Call from Terry
Clegg. Goldcrest just had a board meeting and resolved that
they would not go ahead with the picture unless we cut
three-quarters of a million dollars from the budget. Michael
Dryhurst is in London, but out of contact at a funeral. I said
I considered the demand completely abitrary, and that they
should approve the budget as it stood. I would make whatever
savings I could later on. I told him that to delay approving
the budget was unreasonable since it is well within the limits
($15–17 million) upon which we had agreed from the outset.
Delays now will serve only to increase future costs, disrupt
preparation and damage the morale of the unit. Then they
sprang a new surprise. Approval to go ahead would also be
subject to getting an outside completion bond. Our deal, hith-
erto, was that Goldcrest would take a fee of $4\frac{1}{2}$ per cent of the
budget and guarantee completion themselves. Terry said it
was a board decision and could not be changed.

Goldcrest was adventurous, bold, tough, decisive. Without
Jake it is lurching alarmingly. They demanded that I go to
London to discuss the budget. I said if I went to London it
would not be to see them, it would be because I was not going
to make the picture.

I had a war council with Edgar Gross. We agree that our
position is strong. It would be financially disastrous for them
to pull out at this stage. We tried to reach David Norris with
whom we are trying to renegotiate the deal after the collapse
of the tax shelter. He is in New York, but does not answer our
calls.

I am in a state of shock. We try to speculate about what
happened at the Goldcrest board meeting. We know David
Norris is on our side. I am sure Bill Gavin, Head of Sales,
would not want the film to founder since he has done the hard
work of selling it to so many distributors around the world.
He would have to go back to them all and give them their
money back. That means that David Puttnam and Dickie
Attenborough must have voted with James Lee against me.

I resolve to go to Rio and continue my preparations. As a

precautionary measure, Ed will discreetly shop around town for alternative finance. We know MGM would like the picture, but could a deal be made in time?

---

17 JANUARY 1984 *BRAZIL*

Arrive 8 am in Rio. Meetings all day with Flavio on casting, a planning session with Possi on tribe training and, finally, dinner with the admirable but hectoring Maureen. Fell into bed at 1 am after only two hours' sleep on the plane last night.

---

18 JANUARY 1984

My birthday today, 51. Drove to Paraty, three-and-a-half hours from Rio down the coast, with Christel and Simon. Stayed at the enchanting, lovingly restored hotel, Pousada del Oro. Paraty is a seventeenth-century town that lies in a magical bay. It was built by freemasons to ferry gold to Portugal in defiance of the Church. The masonic signs are carved on to every cornerstone. When the gold trade collapsed, the town was abandoned, and so accidentally preserved. Arrived at 10, had a late dinner with Christel, Simon, Peter Tors, my animal trainer, and Fernanda, his well-connected Brazilian assistant. Convivial.

---

19 JANUARY 1984

The hinterland of Paraty has the quality found in the foothills of the Andes. Waterfalls, rapids, streams cutting through ravines overhung by majestic trees, with lianas and tree roots twisted around rocks. It is accessible and saves dragging a unit into the jungle 3,000 miles away. There are good hotels and it is close to Rio. Simon and I explored the jungle, probing its hidden places and finding some wonderful spots.

There is a small private zoo here and Peter Tors, an American who has been working on a wild-life drama series down here for American TV, suggests that we house and train our animals here. He will now set out to buy the creatures we need, which include twenty howler monkeys, two or three jaguars, an anaconda, an ant-eater, a sloth and so on. The trained eagles will have to come from the US or Europe. There are none in Brazil. I am bringing Joe Camp from LA to train the jaguars. Peter's task will be to acquire the animals, house and care for them at the zoo, and eventually move them to Belém. It turns out that Brazil has laws forbidding its citizens to trap or tame wild animals and it is an offence to transport them over state lines. However, with Fernanda's connections and a few strategic bribes, these things can be worked out. The zoo in Paraty has a licence to keep wild animals, so once they are here we are legal again.

Peter sounds very plausible and I find myself handing over $10,000 in cash since he claims all transactions must be done in US dollars and there will be no receipts. We agree the shopping list and off he goes. I give him some ground rules. I want only animals that are already in captivity. They must be treated with extreme care. After we have used them we will pass them into the enlightened hands of the São Paulo zoo. I have resolved that in the cause of making this film no tree will be cut down, no animal harmed or killed, and no human life lost. Please God, as we say in Ireland.

---

24 JANUARY 1984 *BELEM*

Simon and I have come back to Belém to continue preparations. Marcos is already here organizing the art department. Possi has the training in full swing and will take the Belém Indians to Rio to link up with the rest. We moved into a spacious rented apartment today. After most of last year in the cramped confines of rue St Honoré, it is good to have space.

Gerry Levy, my highly organized location manager, suddenly confronted me with the news that the construction company building the dam at Tucuruí has refused permission for us to use various facilities – vehicles, cranes, lights, etc. – painstakingly extracted during three separate visits to the site by the careful cultivation of the people there. So we chartered a plane and set off with Simon, Marcos, Gerry, Roberto and Ian Whittaker, the set dresser, who first worked for me nineteen years ago on *Catch Us If You Can*. It is the rainy season. We hit a terrifying storm and for eighty minutes the Comanche was tossed about the skies. For much of the time the windows were lashed with ferocious rain as though we were flying through a waterfall. Only a thin grey light penetrated the cloud. Suddenly we would lurch into a patch of open sky and glimpse the majestic scene as all around – above, below, on all sides – great thunderbolts and forks of lightning snaked across from one range of clouds to another. Then the view would be snatched away again. Faces turned to grey, to green, and ran with cold sweat. The seatbelt cut into my groin as the plane dropped into sickening air pockets. We had to brace ourselves against the roof with one hand, clenching the seat with the other. Simon called for a sick bag, and held it before him on the verge of vomiting. Finally, he could hold out no longer, but just as he was about to throw up, Marcos snatched the bag away from him and filled it in one violent heave. I shall always treasure that moment, the look on Simon's face – panic, astonishment, helplessness. He called back to the pilot for another. The pilot turned and rummaged in a drawer behind him.

'Get back to your controls,' I cried, as the plane lurched again. I gave Simon my copy of *O Liberal*, the Belém newspaper, and his breakfast fell into it.

Tucuruí was submerged by the storm. We nosed about, the pilot hoping to catch a glimpse of the airport through a break in the cloud. Finally he did and we gratefully descended, kissing the earth. We vowed never to enter a plane again. We decided to return by riverboat, but evidently it takes three days. They told us it was the worst storm they could remember. It had been raining continuously for six days. As always life is up to its old tricks of imitating art. This is straight out of the script. At the end of the story Markham tells Tommy that the dam will bring industry and settlers who will cut down more forest and make it impossible for the Invisible People to live as they always have done. Tommy and his people perform a rain ritual, creating a huge storm in an attempt to sweep the dam away. Markham goes to the dam in a plane such as ours to be greeted by the same words. 'There has never been such a storm.' Tucuruí airport has been closed all day. We are the only plane to have come in or out.

The weather was too bad to go back, so we spent the night in the company hostel. The trouble arose over a letter Gerry wrote to the head office of Electronorte asking them to confirm in writing that these facilities would be made available to us. Since they are millions of dollars and many months behind schedule they cannot be seen to be doing anything that might cause delays. We have given the men on the site two video recorders and arranged for Caito to send them up a regular supply of film videos. They reassured us of their help. There will be no problem. Crisis over. A day of panic, fear, pain. Gerry has not yet learned the way things are done here in Brazil.

---

26 JANUARY 1984 7 am

Up at 5 am for 6 am take-off. The storm has subsided. At the airport they greeted us with the news of fog in Belém. We kicked our heels and at 6.30 am we decided to risk it and divert to Cametá if necessary. I had spent a night there before on an earlier trip and met the wonderful Mr Calixto. Ten minutes out of Tucuruí the starboard engine faltered and failed and we turned back. As the plane lost altitude we once again caught each other's eyes. Only hours ago we had vowed never to fly again and here we were. The plane juddered alarmingly as it crabbed and yawed on one engine. We limped on to the runway. The battering the plane got in yesterday's storm had apparently shaken something loose.

---

28 JANUARY 1984

We got back to Belém in a replacement plane, drained by the experience. A late call from Michael in London. He had come from a budget meeting at Goldcrest. Although I had taken a strong line with Goldcrest, Michael and I had nevertheless agreed on the phone that he should make some conciliatory cuts in the budget as a co-operative gesture.

He said the meeting was very rough. Terry Clegg's attitude had undergone a marked change and James Lee was very hostile. They were still insisting that we obtain a completion bond, which is terribly difficult at this late stage and contrary to our agreement. The completion-bond representative would have to go out to Brazil, visit all the locations and study the budget. This would take at least three weeks. During that time, the production would come to a halt. Michael tells me Goldcrest have instructed us not to enter into any further commitments until a bond is in place. It is a disaster. I called Ed Gross and Jake. Jake felt the only solution would be for Embassy to take over the financing of the picture. He would put this proposition to Jerry Perenchio. It makes a lot of sense for them. They are already committed to $9 million for US distribution. When the foreign sales are taken into account, they will have to put up only another $2 million and they own the whole thing.

I went out with Simon and Marcos to finalize the exact positions for the sets we are building in an area called Embrapa. This is a swathe of jungle near Belém that is preserved by the University for research. I found an enormous tree with a flat, spreading canopy 80 feet in diameter. I decided to build the *shabona* under it so that the central open section will receive the dappled light from the feathery canopy of this wonderful tree.

Simon and I have spent the afternoon revising the schedule to spread the sets over a longer period so that they are not all required at the same time. This will reduce the size and cost of his labour force.

A call from David Norris saying how badly he felt about the way Goldcrest were treating me. He was on the point of resigning, and so was Bill Gavin, the sales chief. Then Jake called to say that Perenchio will take the picture over and he had made an offer to Goldcrest. James Lee had jumped at it. He is convinced we will go over budget, and is dying to unload the film. Embassy are driving a hard bargain. They will compensate Goldcrest for what they have spent, but refuse to pay interest on the money, nor will they allow Goldcrest to take sales commissions on the substantial foreign sales they have already made. Goldcrest will lose money on the deal. No overhead, no commissions, no interest. Nothing to show for their efforts. Not an honourable withdrawal, a total capitulation.

Spoke to Edgar. The financial implications for us are not good. Jake had said Embassy would give me the same deal I had with Goldcrest, not a comma would be changed. In fact, they are offering the standard Hollywood contract, the one that screws me to the floor and makes profits a miasma. They intend to impose a 15 per cent overhead, which will amount to $2 million (easily the biggest budget item), for a picture they have not developed and which is being made independently. It is a scandal.

I regret that Goldcrest got off the hook so easily. They have spent or committed $4 million up to now, and would have to take that loss to cancel the picture. Jake has given them an easy way out. I can't be hard-nosed with Jake because his motive is to save the film. Needless to say, no one from Goldcrest has informed me of their decision. I have worked the last two years for Goldcrest without any fees making two pictures as a partner, as a gesture to the values they claim to support. It was a crusade; I joined with belief and conviction. Of course, once Jake left it was no longer Goldcrest. But can Jake be the same man, now he is in thrall to Jerry Perenchio? I am in no position to negotiate. Embassy are the bailiffs. They will simply take possession and I will be a hired hand on my own film.

29 JANUARY 1984

Took the crew for a picnic on an island across from Belém yesterday. We ate fish, turtle, crab from the river. We swam in the muddy waters, so warm and brown that it was like bathing in soup. Caito, Charley and I probed the surrounding jungle. Caito found several fruits of delicate and exotic flavours. One is constantly experiencing new tastes in Amazonia. The waterfront market is a cornucopia of strange fruits, wild herbs and arcane vegetables. It brings home to me how narrow are the choices offered by industrial farming and how bland the tastes. Here, everything has the tang and sharp aroma that recalls childhood. It confirms that memory is not remiss. Things did taste better then.

When we returned for a meeting at my apartment with Possi, the square below, with its *belle-époque* theatre where Caruso sang in the high rubber days, was swarming with people, fireworks and a dozen bands beating out the samba rhythms. This is the day when the keys of the city are handed over to the carnival king. The rhythm and sheer volume of percussion breaks down all resistance. Christel, Charley, Possi, Joao and I joined in. You don't have to dance, the music sets up vibrations in your body, *it* dances *you*. This is part of the build-up to carnival. It is also a naturalization process. It is how one becomes Brazilian. You begin by shedding 2,000 years of inhibitions. I wonder what James Lee and Jerry Perenchio would think if they could have seen me carousing in the streets while they wrestle to own and disown me.

30 JANUARY 1984

Michael Dryhurst arrived this morning from London. A war council. I showed him the revised schedule and we reviewed the budget cuts. Jake needs an accurate figure for his negotiations with Goldcrest. The real cost of the picture, when we have taken credit for tax shelter, cruzeiro savings, etc., will be not $17 million but closer to $14 million. However, Embassy will tack on their $2 million overhead. Since it is their own money they are taking, this overhead business is just a device to allow them to take the first $2 million profits without sharing it with me and my colleagues.

By lunchtime we had the final figures and I called Jake. He was thrilled at how low the true cost is. It is a very good deal for Embassy.

---

31 JANUARY 1984

Jake called again. They are still trying to conclude the deal. Goldcrest are demanding to be paid interest on their money. Embassy are being very tough. The negotiations are conducted by phone and telex and Jake feels it will not be settled until the parties sit down face to face. Embassy will have to take over our Brazilian corporation, Goldcrest Filmes Limitada, and Embassy want Goldcrest to indemnify them against any losses or law suits that might arise out of the way that company was set up. In other words, Embassy are aware that Limitada is a fiscal trick to circumvent the stringent Brazilian currency controls and if there are repercussions they want Goldcrest to be responsible.

Meanwhile, we are in limbo. Goldcrest are still funding our day-to-day costs, but have forbidden us to make further commitments until the matter is settled. Embassy are sending out their production controller, Mike Glick, together with Jeff Young to survey the locations and examine our arrangements. We now have to go through the same time-consuming exercises that we did with Terry Clegg. I also understand Embassy are seeking a completion bond. Apparently they have a blanket deal with a bond company for all their pictures.

---

3 FEBRUARY 1984 *EN ROUTE: BELEM–RIO*

Left the apartment at 5.30 am this morning to find the elevators switched off for the night, and no lights on the stairs. Descended gingerly by candlelight. No driver – he must have overslept. Prowled the still-dark streets for a taxi. Plenty of people about making that early start so typical of the tropics, where serious work is done early, tails off in the middle of the day and picks up again in the late afternoon.

Monty, the new unit manager, arrived 5 am in Belém from London, to be met with the news that he would be continuing with us to Paraty, where he will take charge of the production office there. Simon and I are taking Alan, our construction manager, down to Paraty to instruct him on what we require in these locations.

James Lee telephoned last night to tell me that Goldcrest were baling out – the first word I have had from them. He said Goldcrest would continue to finance the film until the contracts were settled and that he was anxious to cause me as little disruption as possible. While all this was going on, Terry Clegg was in a plane on his way to Rio. He was coming to keep an eye on us for Goldcrest. He arrived to find Goldcrest were no longer involved. He stayed a day and turned around and went back mumbling darkly about his employers and their methods.

All day yesterday in Belém we did make-up and wardrobe tests on the tribes. We solved the Fierce People totally. They looked magnificent, but the Invisible make-up still is not right. It looks contrived. We began to move towards softer colours, blending one into another, and that seemed a good direction. In the evening I shot video tests with some of the outstanding extras who emerged from the tribe training sessions. Dira Paes is 15 with dazzling looks and an enchanting charm. I had decided to test her for the part of Kachiri's young cousin, but she was so good that, on impulse, I asked her to learn a scene in English for Kachiri, the girl who falls in love with Tommy. She speaks only a little English, but she learned the lines in ten minutes. Her test was breathtaking! Simon, Possi, Marcos, Caito were watching. I turned and saw their faces – they were enraptured. Every glance, gesture, move was electric. She has natural timing. There is a potent blend of innocence and sexual provocation. A star!

I had been trying to cast Claudia Ohana, who is lovely, but at 21 a little old. She is also not quite Indian enough, but a very accomplished actress. Her agent in Paris is the redoubt-able Marjorie Israel who was asking a huge fee for Claudia. I refused, and decided to look elsewhere. I feel sorry for Clau-dia who would have had the part if her agent had been more reasonable. Dira is much more suited to the role, so I suppose I have to thank Marjorie Israel.

---

6 FEBRUARY 1984 *COPACABANA PALACE, RIO*

Back in Rio with the tribe training in full swing. Next week we move the whole circus down to Paraty where our rehearsals and first four weeks' shooting will take place. The last two days in Paraty were brutally hot. Simon and I traipsed deep into the forest with Monty and Alan, showing them where paths must be cut and the construction of the *shabonas* commenced. Last night I felt exhausted from the heat and sun and travelling.

The Embassy men, Mike Glick and Jeff Young, have ar-rived in Rio and I dined with them last night. Their job at this late stage is to satisfy themselves that locations, schedule and budget are in order. I submitted to a barrage of questions, all of which were shrewdly directed. Glick is experienced and quick. Both are generous and enthusiastic, which is a relief after Goldcrest's niggardly attitude.

I had the runs all night. Whether from food, sunstroke or what, I don't know. What is sure is that only one subject, one worry, kept turning in my mind: the casting of Tommy. Glick brought a videotape of the tests Melissa made in New York of the boys she found there. There was one who is possible, and I will bring him here to screen test. Watching Charley here I more and more believe he can do it. His innocence is so touching. *Dream One* proved his skill as an actor and he has the looks. His body has developed well in the last months. Yet I have doubts. He lacks voice control and timing. Does he have the maturity for the later scenes? Jake, I suspect, will resist it. It could be very damaging for Charley if he failed in the part. If only this New York boy turns out to be marvellous, everything will be solved and I will not have to confront the Charley problem.

9 FEBRUARY 1984

The Embassy people are swarming all over us. Jake calls every day as he negotiates with Goldcrest. Everyone is nervous. I told Jake I was thinking of using Charley. I wanted him to know this before Embassy conclude their deal with Goldcrest.

Meanwhile the New York boy arrives today and I will test him tomorrow along with Charley. Jake said to show the tapes to Jeff Young who is here in Belém and get his view. After the tests I must make a decision. Earlier today Charley said, 'I don't want to do it, Dad. It's too much responsibility. I think it would be bad for you and for me. I want to go home.' He has always touched my heart, and touched others too. I would hate him to be hurt by it. But if he did this part, he would have to grow up as fast and hard as Tommy does in the story. Caito took Charley out in the speedboat and talked him out of going home. Caito somehow manages to turn up just when he is needed.

Christel has conjunctivitis. It is epidemic here. I dread the actors getting infected. It could wipe us out because it tends to go from one to another, each bout lasting a week.

11 FEBRUARY 1984

The boy is here from New York. Philippe also came in from Paris, and I met him at the airport at 5 am. I was so happy to have him with me. Instead of going to the hotel to rest he came back with me to the apartment and we ate breakfast and talked for two hours. Then I took him and Caito to an island by boat to make the crucial tests with Charley and the New York boy. It helped Charley to have Philippe behind the camera, knowing that he is a fan of Charley's acting, and that they had worked together on *Dream One* for four months. Charley and Dira together were dazzling. My heart sang when I saw them through the viewfinder. The New York boy took his turn. I had rehearsed him thoroughly the previous day, and now did everything I could to make it work because part of me still desperately wanted to find an alternative to Charley.

Came back. Ran the tests for Michael and Philippe. Long discussions but there was only one choice. The New York boy was very disappointing, and his 22 years showed.

Mike Glick says he is impressed with our planning and preparations. It is a massive film. We have armies of men constructing sets and manufacturing props. His view is that it is a complex picture but that we have it in hand. He says he will recommend it unreservedly. After our meeting I spent the evening with Jeff Young at my apartment. I finally broached the Tommy problem, and showed him the tests. I explained the dilemma. He loved Charley's test. He left at 1.30, taking the tests with him to LA. I drank too much. But I had won him over. The day had begun at 5 am, but I lay in bed, my mind racing, happy to have it resolved.

---

12 FEBRUARY 1984

Got up early. Told Michael to call Charley's agent and make a deal. I arranged for Charley to go to Rio with Christel to join the training with Possi and the tribe. Dira and her mother will go too. Charley took the news quietly. He was pleased, but scared. He misses his girlfriend. He knows it is a long haul.

---

13 FEBRUARY 1984 *RIO*

One calendar month to shooting. Philippe and I came in today to supervise the tribe training, which the actors join today. Charley was in good spirits. We talked a lot about acting. He has that mysterious quality of being able to assume another character yet remain himself. Philippe and I worked on the plane, defining camera and lighting.

Glick has phoned and telexed his report to Embassy and we await their decision. Goldcrest are becoming more and more alarmed as it appears Embassy still feel they have the right to back down if all is not to their satisfaction.

14 FEBRUARY 1984

A tumultuous day yesterday with the tribe. Made tests for the part of Mapi, Tommy's friend, but did not find him. Further tests for make-up, hair, etc. In the evening dinner with Philippe, Flavio, Dira and her mother. Everyone is fascinated by Charley and Dira. Sitting across from each other, they make a study in contrast. Woke up with a gnawing anxiety. I had no word yesterday on Embassy's decision, not even from Edgar. Ominous silence.

Rospo called last night casting doubts on my decision to use Charley.

Philippe and I snatch time to work on the script whenever we can. Last night we discussed the problem of lighting the night battle between the Invisible People and the Fierce People. It is the old problem of how to shoot a scene in the dark! There must be a light source. Simulated moonlight always looks false. My first approach to the construction of a set or choosing a location is the light – the direction of the sun, the position of the windows, whatever. I design my shots in relation to that light. We finally decide to use a kind of strobe light, suggesting that it is the murderous flashes from the machine-guns of Jacareh and the Fierce People that not only massacre the Invisibles but make them visible as well. Although this is hardly a realistic solution, it is emotionally satisfying and in such a tumultuous scene, I don't think the audience will question the dubious optical reality.

17 FEBRUARY 1984 *BELEM*

The first day of the major recce when I take the key technicians on a tour of sets and locations and brief them. Today we covered the whorehouse complex, the *shabona*, the village of the Fierce People and the exterior/interior of the Markham apartment. All these are under construction.

All my team are now assembled. Gale Tattersall arrived breathless from his last-minute equipment dramas. My assistant director is Barry Langley, a very experienced man in his forties, who is frustrated at not having progressed to director or producer. His scepticism irritates me but I recognize its value. He always points out what could go wrong. Continuity is being done by Pat Rambaut, a good Irish convent girl, now a widow with two sons to support. She is brave and full of adventure. She is entranced by the rain forest and clambers after us into the toughest spots, oohing and ahing at all she sees.

Gerry Levy, the location manager, scribbles notes and makes diagrams. His natural ally is the English caterer who is touring with us to ferret out suppliers and arrange facilities. Wherever we shoot, the first question is how and where do we feed the crew. A film unit works long hours and they demand and expect an endless flow of food and drink. The amounts they consume are quite prodigious. Tea on arrival (usually 7.30 am, sometimes earlier) is accompanied by biscuits. At 10 o'clock, there is a break of fifteen minutes for 'breakfast', bacon and egg inside a roll is the favoured dish, but sausages, beans and fried bread must be present in ample quantities. Lunch must offer a choice, but include roast meat, boiled and baked potatoes, cooked vegetables, a sweet pudding as well as fresh fruit and salads. In the afternoon tea must flow continuously and at 4 o'clock large slabs of cake are consumed. If the shooting day goes past 6.30, a hot supper is provided to be eaten on the hoof. The caterers have their kitchen inside a container that fits on to a truck or folds down and slots into the hold of a 747. At each location space must be found to erect a marquee where chairs and tables can be set out. One of the less pleasant aspects of film-making with a British crew is that when you address them the answers are usually muffled by mouthfuls of food.

Then there is the little knot of Frenchmen. Philippe has his gaffer (chief electrician) over from France, and Raph Salis, who is doing special effects. He has spent the last three months in his workshop in Paris preparing the various devices we will need. One of the most difficult of these is effectively to give the illusion of an arrow entering the body of a naked Indian. If the victim is wearing clothes it is easier: we can conceal a plate under his clothes, then fire an arrow down a thin wire which is attached to the plate. The wire is painted to blend with the background in such a way that the camera cannot see it. The audience sees the arrow fly through the air and enter a body. To overcome the bare-body problems, Raph plans to make chest casts of our intended victims and fit them with a false torso which will conceal the essential metal plate. The body paint will help to blend it in. We took on one member of our tribe because he has a deep indentation in his ribcage. We can put the plate in that and just cover it with plastic skin and make-up. Then even other special-effects men will be unable to see how we did it. Raph is using a crossbow on a tripod to fire the special arrows. Gale and Barry shake their heads at the crossbow and the little Frenchman. 'You'd think they'd learnt their lesson at Agincourt,' says Gale.

It was a good, constructive, technical day. The logistical problems are enormous, but not overwhelming because we have been systematically dealing with them for many months. It is, nevertheless, exhausting to explain one's ideas, lay out scenes, design shots, for twelve hours at a stretch. The crew struggles to take it all in. At this stage, they just have to absorb it all and there is not much they can contribute until they know my intentions. It got more relaxed as the day went on, with some good suggestions coming from Philippe, Gale and Barry. Ian Whittaker, the set-dresser, is with us too. He comes up with a lot of simple, practical solutions to complex problems.

Got back to the office to find a message: 'Call Rospo – extremely urgent!' He opened the conversation by saying, 'This is probably the last time we shall ever speak.' He had seen the video tests of Charley and the New York boy. He said I was making a disastrous mistake, that it was absurd to use Charley and that if I could not see it, I was either a fool or a psychotic. He said Charley had no sex-appeal, that he was a self-involved adolescent, without charm or acting skill. In order to save me from myself, from being the laughing stock of Hollywood, he intended to communicate these views to Jerry Perenchio tomorrow, and strongly advise him not to make the picture if I insisted on using Charley. He then hung up.

Called Edgar and told him. He was devastated. He said,
'We have to stop Rospo. The deal is at a critical point. If
Embassy have doubts now, it could all collapse.'

He spoke to Rospo and called me back. Rospo told him
that in years to come I would thank him for this, even if it
seemed an act of treachery now. He felt he was in the same
position as the general who tried to assassinate Hitler. Edgar
was so shaken he began to question Charley himself, not his
competence, but for the effect on the boy that such conflict
could have.

'If we don't head him off from Embassy, this picture is
dead,' said Edgar.

I said, 'No. There is nothing we can do, and nothing we
should do.'

Let Rospo do his worst. I have reached the point where I
am ready to go home and forget the whole thing. I will do it
as I see it, or not at all.

Tomorrow we set off in two Lear jets to continue the recce
in Tucuruí (the dam), Carajás (virgin rain forest), Itatiaia (waterfall) and Paraty (streams, gorges, lagoons). I shall be out
of touch, perhaps I should say 'out of reach' and so I will try
to concentrate on the work in hand rather than worry about
the machinations going on in Hollywood.

---

23 FEBRUARY 1984 *PARATY*

The recce is finished. Everyone knows now what I hope to
shoot and can all set about trying to see that as much of it is
achieved as possible.

Back in the Pousada de Oro hotel. We have offices set up
and Monty is in charge, but there is no telephone at present.
Accommodation is very difficult because Paraty is booked
solid until after carnival. We are renting houses and barns.
The tribe is here and we have found an area of jungle for the
training. The local sheriff, Gabriel, comes straight out of a
Western. He has murderous eyes and is much feared around
here. Whenever a fugitive from justice takes to the jungle,
Gabriel goes in and hunts him down. He usually brings him

back dead rather than alive. He wants to play a part in the film, and I have just the role for him. He is therefore full of charm and very helpful. He runs the town. He had undertaken to erect thatched huts for our tribe camp and provide the other facilities we need. He is as good as his word. It is almost ready. Possi is already planning to move the tribes in.

Back in reach of a phone, and the calls have started. Jeff Young took the tests back to LA and showed them to Perenchio, Alan Horn and the other executives. He did not tell them Charley was my son. They all favoured Charley, and there were no objections. Now Jeff is alarmed. Rospo has called him and implies that I did not search hard enough because I had always intended to use Charley.

Since Jeff had backed my choice of Charley he felt his own position was exposed. He called Melissa and got copies of her notes and schedules, which recorded all the boys we had seen and tested. He then took these to two important casting agencies and asked them to examine the notes. Were there boys we had not seen whom we should have seen? They both agreed that we had turned over every stone. Jeff was relieved and passed this report on to his bosses, who are now aware of Rospo's extraordinary action. They are predictably nervous. They demanded to take another look at the test tapes, which Edgar had already shipped back to me. They are somewhere in transit. I pointed out that the tests would not have altered since they last saw them.

A later call from Jeff Young. He knew I had been interested in C. Thomas Howell and, on his own initiative or more likely on instructions from his bosses, had pressurized the TV company Howell is working for and got them to agree to release him earlier. If I will agree to delay the start of shooting by one week, he would be able to do it.

I said, 'Wait a minute, Jeff. I have cast Charley, made a deal with his agent. We all agreed he was the best available choice. He is already being trained. He must learn how to move, gesture, harden the soles of his feet to walk barefoot in the jungle, learn the dances that he must perform, the weapons he must use, and generally be integrated into the tribe. The last two weeks before shooting are devoted largely to rehearsing the actors. Without Tommy, this would be impossible. The body make-up must be refined and finalized for each actor. It would be out of the question for him to turn up on the first day of shooting. Also C. Thomas Howell is very dark and there would be very little contrast between him and the Indians. Besides which, all these arguments are secondary, since I have made my decision and I am sticking to it.'

Edgar called. Jeff has been working on him and he was getting nervous. Maybe I should reconsider. Why not test C. Thomas Howell? Then decide. I told him I had already decided.

---

28 FEBRUARY 1984

All the actors playing Indian parts are living with the tribes we are creating in the training camp. I spend most nights there too. We all sleep in hammocks under the stars. Each day starts with calisthenics – everyone naked. How quickly they all become used to nudity, men and women. It is important that they look and feel at home without clothes or shoes. The pale patches made by bikinis are darkening in the sun.

Each day we have training sessions in body painting, and as the feathers and ornaments begin to arrive from our workshops in Belém, where we are copying the authentic originals, we gradually assign them to each character. Our anthropologist, Dr Eduardo, advises us on customs, behavioural patterns. We have a specialist training the men in weapons. The women are learning to carry baskets on their heads and the mysteries of making manioc.

Marc Boyle, my English stunt co-ordinator, is training the men in how to do death falls, and other tricks they have to perform.

Possi teaches them the dances and every night there is music by Junior Homrich around the camp fire. Charley felt very lost at first but now he loves it, and is doing well.

---

29 FEBRUARY 1984

We are having terrible problems getting the equipment out of customs. Roberto Bakker, our production manager, is spending all his time in Rio trying to get things released. As a result, other areas of the production are being neglected. We are very strung out, with so much going on in Belém 1,500 miles away – set construction, manufacture of props, etc. – and the training and preparations here. Transport is a nightmare. We have one phone in the office and it is continually jammed. In this last week before carnival, Brazil goes crazy. The whole country is preparing their costumes and floats and parties.

Powers Boothe, Meg Foster and the other actors have assembled and we are fitting their costumes. The clothes fail to turn up more often than not. I have a highly recommended Brazilian, Clovis Bueno, as wardrobe master, but he is proving very erratic and communication is difficult. Fortunately he has a lovely girl, Solange, helping him and she is saving the day.

Our transport is in disarray. We have more than forty rented VW combos. The drivers never buy petrol until they run out. Half the vehicles are always out rescuing the other half.

The $42,000 we paid to the film union was to recompense Brazilian technicians for the ones we brought in from abroad. They are being paid to stay at home. Instead, most of them have turned up here in Paraty. We have to find somewhere for them to sleep, then transport them back to Rio.

Michael Dryhurst is swamped. He had taken to writing people memos from his hotel bedroom, always a bad sign.

The deal is still not concluded between Embassy and Goldcrest. Since the crisis over Charley, Embassy have been dragging their feet. Goldcrest are still funding us, insomuch as we are drawing on the £2,500,000 worth of cruzeiros.

Michael greeted me tonight with the news that Goldcrest has instructed us to give two weeks' notice to the crew. Edgar has arrived and so has Jeff Young. They take turns with the telephone trying to reach Embassy and Goldcrest to find a solution. With the telephone tied up, our other business sinks deeper into chaos.

I have tried to keep these problems concealed from the crew and cast, but they are all beginning to suspect that the film is in trouble. Their return tickets are normally held in the production office, but a lot of them are demanding to have them in their own possession. I told Edgar that I refuse to give notice to the crew, since it is just a ploy by Goldcrest to force Embassy to conclude the takeover.

---

2 MARCH 1984

The training and preparations are going wonderfully well. Each day is a joy, watching the tribes take on character and credibility. Possi has been staging the ritual dances. They must not appear to be choreographed and although the movements must be learnt, we have to eliminate any theatrical gestures. Indian dances are all derived from animal movements. Possi and I know from our Xingu experience what is right and wrong.

Today we started actor rehearsals. These will occupy each morning. At present I am working only with the actors in the Indian roles. I have brought Peter Marinker (who helped me with the dubbing of the Tupi) here so that he can coach the Brazilian actors in English and all of them in Tupi.

We start by dividing the tribe into families and defining their relationships. Then we encourage each person to develop a character. We improvise scenes and build up their sense of community. Once this is started, I ask Marinker and Possi to develop it while I work with the principal actors.

Tonight word came that the deal is finally settled. We now belong to Embassy. Jeff Young was in high spirits. We had dinner. When he had drunk a fair bit, he was emboldened enough to warn me that disaster was impending in the production office. Poor Bunny with two supposedly bilingual Brazilian girls who were constantly disappearing, was becoming hysterical as wave upon wave of chaos hit her. We went to see Michael who is aware of the problems but is hamstrung by the absence of Roberto Bakker, which further aggravates things as the Brazilian crew have no one to take their problems to and Dryhurst is frustrated by the language problems. Also our accountant, Fred Harding, is still persistently sick and has left us and returned to London. We have a replacement on the way who will need time to grasp it all.

Much of the camera equipment is still in customs, and Gale and Philippe and Les Bosher, our camera mechanic, are kicking their heels. Jeff has taken it upon himself to try to organize the transport situation.

---

3 MARCH 1984

Did a read-through of the script. It is always difficult for actors to make an initial commitment to their character. I try to ease them into it by instructing them to read their dialogue completely devoid of expression during the first run. I read the directions myself, so that they hear the film described in my voice. It is extraordinary how much comes through the flat delivery of their lines. All the thought and work they have put in privately towards building a character is somehow there, one can sense it. At the end we are all moved by the story. We stop. It is well to let it sink in for a day. The afternoon is spent in general training.

The standby crew is so called because their job is to 'stand by' the camera until needed. There is a carpenter, a painter, a plasterer, a rigger and a stage-hand. Although each has his craft, they work as a team. They build camera rigs, platforms and towers out of scaffolding, tubing and wood. The painter touches up the sets where the paint is scratched. On location a piece of white rock might catch the sun and cause a glare. The painter will spray it with black washable paint. They do a hundred and one jobs.

We brought our team over some weeks ago to work with the construction crew in Belém. The standbys have been very taken with the sexual largesse of the Brazilian girls and some of them found that they could not bear to leave their girl-friends behind in Belém. One of them approached Michael to be allowed to bring his girl to Paraty. Michael Dryhurst said he had no objection providing the standby paid for her air fare and accommodation.

'If I give you the money, will the company get the air ticket for her?' he asked.

'Yes,' said Michael, 'What's her name?'

The standby furrowed his brow. He tried to get his tongue round some Portuguese vowels, but to no avail.

'I'll have to get back to you on that.'

So some of them have their girls here. They find Brazil a paradise. They are a little resentful that I expect them to do some work, having grown used to languid pleasure. I have asked them to set up a workshop for Raph, the special-effects man, and with some reluctance they have started on that.

---

5 MARCH 1984

A wonderful rehearsal this morning. We start to work our way through the script. We covered the opening scenes today, where Jean and Bill are arriving in Brazil, moving into an apartment with their two small children, and their family visit to the site where the rain forest is being cleared for the construction of the dam. They have a picnic and Tommy wanders into the jungle, where he encounters Wanadi and a party of the Invisible People who abduct him.

I describe each location, and give them an idea of how I will shoot the scenes. We explore the relationships. We try out the dialogue. For the most part I do not allow them to get up and act it out. I find it better to save that for the day, and if I do, I ask them to give it to me with only 50 per cent emotional content.

I had intended that Rospo be present for the rehearsals because I like to revise the dialogue quite extensively at this stage, so I am having to do this myself.

So much becomes clear once the actors speak the lines – anything clumsy or jarring or out of character becomes obvious. For the most part, it is a pruning process. To make a script flow and convey the story to the reader, we tend to put in rather more dialogue than eventually gets on to film. At this point I must start to tell the story with the camera, by the actions of the actors, by their reactions and expressions.

Hitchcock always said that dialogue should be there to enhance the atmosphere, not to tell the story.

As we rehearse, a lot of dialogue falls away as we discover more economic ways of developing the narrative. Powers is a very penetrating actor, with great concentration. This is a big break for him, and he means to make the most of it. His wife is with him. They have been together since high school, and only a few months ago they had their first baby, a child of winning beauty that simply charms your heart. Powers is enslaved by the child, otherwise he is quiet, reclusive, saving himself for the role, conserving all energy. We speak of an actor having 'presence', and it means exactly that. What all good film actors have in common is concentration, the ability to focus all their attention, intellectually and emotionally, into the character and scene. Most of us are always partly somewhere else, thinking of what will or what has happened. Being 'self-conscious' is allowing part of oneself to be aware, to stand back and observe the situation instead of being totally in it and off it.

I have seen actors who do everything right in their preparation, are impressive in rehearsals, but once the camera is turning they disappear, disintegrate, while others can focus everything into that moment. Most of the time film actors are waiting; the camera is running only a few moments per day. They get tired and bored, they start thinking of other things, start a love affair, so that when the moment comes they cannot deliver. When I was under pressure from the studio and the producers on *Point Blank*, Lee Marvin said, 'Just remember, when the camera is turning it all belongs to you and me.' Maintaining concentration and commitment over many weeks in trying conditions is not easy, but my intuition is that Powers will do it. Waiting about is the bane of film-making.

A couple of years back the Cannes Festival marked its thirty-fifth anniversary by giving a special award to a number of directors – Antonioni, Bergman, Satyajit Ray, Volker Schlöndorff, Billy Wilder and myself among them. We had to turn up to rehearse the ceremony. Billy Wilder and I were the first to arrive. A flustered organizer asked us if we would mind waiting.

'Do I mind waiting?' Wilder asked rhetorically. 'All my life I am waiting. Making movies is waiting. I am waiting for the finance, waiting for the actors, waiting for the sun to come out, waiting for the lighting, waiting for props. Fifty-three years I am making movies! Do you know how long the camera was running during that time? Maybe two weeks!'

I tell actors that what I expect of them is that they prepare their character and know him or her so well that they know just what he or she would say or do in any given circumstance. They must defend their character. If I ask them to do something that they feel is against the grain, they must fight me.

The Markham family is quite ordinary. Meg and Powers must resist the temptation of making their characters too 'interesting'. We must dare to make them even a little boring at first. What they do must be very simple and unemphatic, but every gesture and choice of word must be designed to give the audience information about the kind of people they are, where they come from.

We need a moment inside the car to suggest the end of a long boring car journey. I recall the games I played with my own kids when they were young and fretful on an outing. I draft in a song and an exchange that came directly from my daughter Telsche who was always fidgety. We decide to pass on Telsche's characteristics to the little girl, Heather. This then suggests the relationship between mother and child. We go on to talk about the boy and the dynamics of the family group. We must not suggest that Tommy's tendency to wander off is because his mother is too involved with Bill or out of jealousy of his sister, because such guilts do not find a place in the later narrative. They would create misleading implications. The boy's abduction must be inexplicable, must have the mystery of myth. The Markhams are optimistic Americans, successful and sure of their values. It is the arbitrariness of their loss that drives them to search on for ten years. They cannot accept what has happened to them. Only at the end does Bill understand – through his experiences with the tribe – that it was his thoughtless blundering into this world with his bulldozers that triggered the tragedy. Just as in *Deliverance*, when the four city men arrive in the Appalachian village and

crassly insult the hillbillies, it is a metaphor for their insensi-
tivity to nature. Another river is being dammed. Nature,
malignantly personified in the mountain men, wreaks its revenge. Here, the Invisible People are the benign manifestations of a savage nature.

Tommy is still innocent enough to enter into harmony with
nature. Bill is drawn into the depths of the forest to find him
and finally comes to understand that he is carrying the guilt
of all his fellows who destroy the natural world. He expiates
his guilt by deciding to destroy the dam he has built.

I do not tell *all* this to Powers. I hint at it, in such a way
that he will grope his way towards it. He must struggle with
the acting problems of making these enormous changes, this
psychic volte-face. For if the audience does not believe this
volte-face, the film will not work.

At present we concentrate on Bill's and Jean's emotional
response to the kidnapping. This is difficult enough, to find a
true response. Powers says the jungle itself will help: hot,
humid and spiteful, he feels he will find the truth of the situation by reacting to that, since the scene requires him to fight
his way through it. I have heard this before from other good
screen actors: react to the circumstance, the location, the
props, the other actors – let them do the work. To respond, to
react, to be there. An actor must carefully prepare, then, when
the moment comes, be open.

Ingmar Bergman was giving a rare lecture at the National
Film Theatre recently. At the end of a marvellous discourse
full of insight and humanity, he was confronted with one of
those inane questions from the audience. 'What are you trying
to do when you direct?' – something he had been illuminating
for the last hour. His answer was much better than the question deserved: 'I try to make each scene – not real – but alive,
alive.'

Human behaviour in extremity is often quite unexpected,
though more often than not these days, people summon up
memories of comparable moments in movies and copy the
responses of actors. Most actors, in turn, draw on what they
have seen other actors do. So the acting out of great emotional
moments has a tendency to become ritualized, but when we

witness on screen a response that is original, surprising yet
true, it is a great marvel.

I was shooting the scene in *Point Blank* where Lee Marvin
lays a trap for his friend who betrayed him and puts a gun to
his head as he makes love. As Lee drags him from the bed the
friend knows he is going to die. How could the actor respond?
The situation was so powerful that a subtle reaction would
have been lost. Since it was a night scene, his face was only
partially lit, giving him even less scope. We tried various
approaches, none of which felt right, or as Bergman would
say, 'alive'. On impulse I told the actor to faint. He objected
that he was playing a tough gangster and I was asking him to
behave like a Victorian spinster. He finally did it. An extraordinary situation becomes more extraordinary. Audiences did
not laugh, as we feared they might. The shock went too deep.
But it worked only because it was archetypally true. Marvin
was sexually betrayed by his friend, the man he loved. That
man, *in flagrante delicto*, faints into Lee's arms.

Although we rehearse and discuss these solutions, I never
know if they will work until I am looking at them through the
lens. The relationship of the actors and settings is not only to
each other but also to the camera.

In *Deliverance* there is a scene where Voight has just shot the
mountain man. He, Ned Beatty and Burt Reynolds are hanging on to rocks in the turbulent river. The experience has
violently changed Voight's character. They are trying to
decide what they should do. I said to Voight, 'When you say
that line, look over your left shoulder.'

'Why would I do that?' said Jon.

I improvised. 'You hear something. You are alert to everything.'

In fact, the turn of his head gave the composition a tremendous power, the eye went to Voight and the power was transferred to him. Jon's acting was brilliant, but the composition
gave it a sudden, electrifying charge. Sam Fuller calls it 'the
one thing'. It is the extra ingredient that transforms photography into cinema.

The acting process is finally mysterious. It has to do with
the nature of reality, and the concept of identity. An actor's

hold on this is as fragile as it is for the rest of us, perhaps more so. Yet from time to time he can focus these things in a way that breathes life into life itself.

---

7 MARCH 1984

Yesterday was carnival. Everyone turned out for the procession. Christel and I went to join them. By 11.30 pm there was still no sign of anything happening. We went to bed and slept right through it. I just hope that now it is over, things will settle down.

Peter Tors keeps promising that the animals he has bought will be arriving, but there is no sign of them. Joe Camp and his assistants have come from Los Angeles and have started working with the one jaguar Peter Tors has acquired. They pronounce it totally unsuited to training since it has been maltreated at some stage. They cast doubts on Peter Tors's judgement and experience with animals.

I need tracking shots of a jaguar running through the jungle. It will last only a few seconds on screen, but is elaborate to set up. The jaguar is one of the most merciless killers in nature. There is always the chance that he will turn on his trainer and he kills with devastating speed. I recall that night at Mr Calixto's house. His jaguar stared at me with eyes of absolute aggression. I felt I was looking at the source of all hatred.

We are building a 10-foot-high chain-link fence to enclose the chosen area of jungle and contain the jaguar. We must then level out a track so that a pick-up can run smoothly along it. The jaguar is released in the jungle parallel with the track and lured with meat by his trainer. The pick-up is driven alongside him. This will need to be done every day for two hours for three weeks before we can put a camera in the pick-up and shoot it. In choosing the piece of jungle, I have to face in a direction where the animal will be backlit and the sun penetrate since the scene requires a misty forest. We lay down smoke for this but it needs backlight if it is to look like mist. The jaguar must be trained to become accustomed to the truck, the noise, the smoke, the terrain, and the idea of running to retrieve the meat. The present jaguar refuses to have anything to do with any of this.

We found a wonderful French falconer and he has just arrived from Paris with two beautiful eagles. His first shot is of an eagle swooping down on to a pool of frogs. It is part of the sequence in which Tommy summons the rain to break the dam. His familiar – the eagle – is sent out to arouse the frogs, whose cries in turn whistle up a storm. We build a 70-foot tower hidden by trees from which the eagle can be launched and swoop down to the pool of frogs below where the falconer waits with a lure right next to the camera. Ten days' training required for this one shot.

8 MARCH 1984

Our preparations are falling behind schedule. We have taken on more people to catch up. Every department is stretched and crying out for more help. This, in turn, means more transport and accommodation, and more money. Costs are escalating in an alarming way. It seems out of control. Roberto Bakker has arrived from Rio to be met with a revolt from the tribes. They claim that their contracts do not reflect the agreements we made with them.

Goldcrest and Embassy have still not finalized their arrangements and although Embassy has agreed to make certain dollar payments direct in Los Angeles, they have been very slow to do so. Joe Camp and his assistants are hopping mad that their wives have not received the money due to them. I called Edgar and told him to send money to them by messenger from my personal account. Goldcrest were contracted to pay the first instalment of my fee ten weeks ago. Needless to say, they have not.

12 MARCH 1984

The production is still in chaos: most of our camera and grip equipment is still held by customs; Concine have yet to give final permission, and Peter Tors's animals never turned up and the $10,000 is spent. Yet, despite all the problems, I feel perversely happy about the film. The last few days of rehearsals have been encouraging and inspiring.

Many of the actors are either inexperienced, like Charley, or have never acted, like Dira, like the boy who plays Mapi, like Claudio Moreno who plays Jacareh. These rehearsals have been acting classes to a large extent. Possi is superb, demanding discipline and commitment. Peter Marinker has been very helpful with the Brazilian actors, and Powers has helped Charley a lot.

The part of Werner is played by Eduardo Conde, a Brazilian pop singer, a quirky eccentric character. It was meeting him that gave me the idea of how to change this character, and it is largely written for him. Rui Polonah has developed great authority as Wanadi, the chief of the Invisible People.

The body make-up is working well now and the tribes look thoroughly at ease with it. The tough physical training has given their bodies a hard but supple look. Charley looks strong and fit, his muscles well defined.

Christel has taken over the non-Indian wardrobe design and has dressed Meg Foster, Powers and Werner. She is also designing the clothes that the Indian girls are forced to wear when they are captured and pressed into service at a whorehouse.

Of course, no one is ready, but I insist on starting the film tomorrow on schedule. Today we went to the first location and rehearsed the scenes for the first week's shooting. I defined the camera set-ups and everyone knows what is expected of him.

After a month of hot cloudless weather, it has started to rain. More is forecast for tomorrow. There is a lesson here for any country suffering from drought. All that is necessary for rain is to invite a film unit.

In an ideal world, the first week's work should always be reshot. It takes that long for crew and cast to settle down. Then the movie begins to find its song, others pick up the melody and soon they can all sing it. Let us pray it happens soon.

PRE-PRODUCTION

			EXT. WITHIN JUNGLE	EXT. WITHIN JUNGLE EXT. STREAM (in enclosure)	EXT. STREAM	EXT. WITHIN JUNGLE (Thatched House) EXT. WITHIN JUNGLE	EXT. Mountain Slope EXT. STREAM (in view of Stream)	EXT. STREAM (in view of Cathedral)	EXT. WITHIN JUNGLE	EXT. WITHIN JUNGLE EXT. STREAM in view of Cathedral	EXT. WITHIN JUNGLE	EXT. WITHIN JUNGLE
BREAKDOWN SHEET No.												
LOCATION OR STUDIO												
DAY OR NIGHT			D	D	D	D	D	D		D	D	D	D
SCRIPT PAGES													
PROD. No.													
TITLE *THE EMERALD FOREST*													
PRODUCER *John Boorman / Michael Dryhurst*													
DIRECTOR *John Boorman*													
ASST. DIRECTOR *Barry Langley*			REST DAY						REST DAY				
COST CHARACTER PLAYER	**No.**												
MARKHAM	1			1	1								
TOMME	2		2	2	2	2	2	2		2	2	2	2
WANADI	3		3	3	3	3	3	3		3	3	3	3
KACHIRI	4		4	4	4		4	4		4	4		
MAPI	5			5		3	5	5		4	5		5
SAMANPO	6			6	6	6	6	6			6	6	6
ULURU	7			7			7	7					
CAYA	8			8	8						8		
PEQUI	9			9	9								
KACHIRI'S COUSIN	10		10				10	10			10		
KACHIRI'S YOUNGER COUSIN	11		11				11	11			11		
KACHIRI'S FATHER	12												
PERRERA	13												
COSTA	14												
PROGRAMMER	15												
WERNER	16												
PADRE LEDUC	17												
JEAN	18												
TOMMY	19												
HEATHER YOUNG HEATHER 20A	20												
PILOT	21												
TRADER	22												
BABY Sc. 121-147	23												
CARLOS (JABUTI)	24										24		
PAULO (WISNAH)	25										25		
RICO (GNARU)	26										26		
WOMAN Sc. 66	27		27										
ANOTHER BOY Sc. 48	28						28	28			28		
FIERCE WOMEN Sc. 66	29												
CHILD Sc. 102	30												
THUG 1 Sc. 134	31												
THUG 2 Sc. 134	32												
OLD MAN Sc. 139	33												
WOMAN Sc. 139	34												
YOUNG WARRIOR Sc. 140 "MONKEY"	35			35	35	35							35
DRUNK 1 Sc. 160	36												
DRUNK 2 Sc. 160	37												
JACAREH	38												
BORDELLO MADAM	39												
			17		17	17	17	17			17	17	17	17
			46.	101	108	112	5	48		101	225	50	51
			62	108 Shut	333		To Comp			44 103	213	128 DAY

Film strip board. ▽

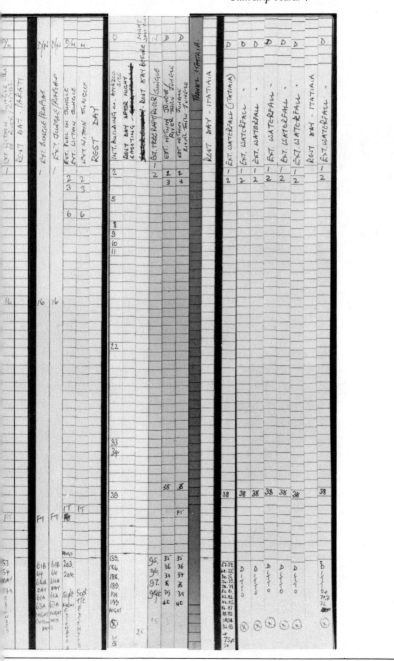

△ *Simon Holland's sketch for the dwelling place of the Invisible People.*

▽ *The first attempts to find a make-up for the tribe.*

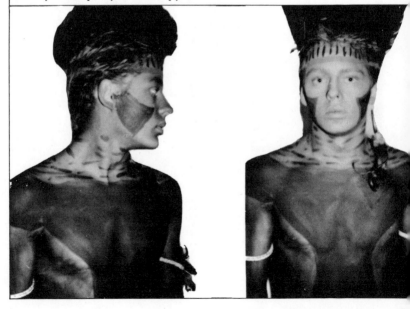

◁ *Training sessions to create the tribes.* ▽

▽ *Image from the story board.*

MARKHAM WALKS WITH EXPLOSIVES INTO TURBINE TUBE

Image from the storyboard. ▽

CUT TO TOMME IN A TRANCE

These first two weeks' shooting have been horrendous. It has rained every day, sometimes without respite. We just try to keep shooting, but it is miserable. We are way behind schedule, and we just cannot seem to stem the haemorrhaging budget. All Goldcrest's predictions appear to be coming to pass. Jerry Perenchio is seriously considering abandoning the film. He lost millions when Ridley Scott's *Blade Runner* went way over budget. He is terrified of runaway costs and I can't blame him. Jeff Young has been marvellous, never losing faith with the film and pleading with Jerry to hang on.

The crew's morale is low. Apart from spending each day wet through, there is a species of mosquito here in Paraty that is excruciating. The body does not seem to be able to deal with it. The bites become hard white lumps sitting on huge welts. Everyone is losing sleep from the unbearable irritation. There is constant anxiety about snakes and biting spiders; tarantulas abound.

The key grip simply walked out this week. He left for London without a word. I suspect others would walk out too if they weren't so attached to their Brazilian girls. The standbys are sluggish and mutinous. I drive the crew on by sheer willpower, cajoling, insulting, threatening. Most of our equipment is still in the customs. I cannot do tracking shots. I have no crab dolly. We are using the Steadicam to get movement and so far it has been a disaster. The electronics are much too delicate to withstand the rain and tropical conditions.

My editor, John Merritt, who has done several films with me and goes back twenty years to my BBC days, has been sick since he arrived and just cannot take the climate. He is going home. There are no good editors available. I shall have to do it myself with the help of Ian Crafford, John's assistant.

Powers has done only one scene and is fretting at the hotel. It is the important scene where Markham, after recovering from fever, confronts Wanadi, angrily demanding the return of his son. The scene did not work. It is hopelessly complex with far too many ideas in it. Markham's powerful emotion, resonating against a spectacular waterfall setting, made the subsidiary ideas simply irritating. Also the paint on Charley's face gave him a clown-like look. I had to change it and the scene needed to be reshot. A frantic telex from Embassy arrived forbidding me to reshoot the scene until they had seen and assessed it. I ignored it, and did it over after some radical rewriting.

On the positive side, Possi has kept the tribe in good heart, and they have been magnificent. Philippe, Gale and Simon are a great support, and Michael Dryhurst still manages to keep calm and controlled in the face of enormous difficulties. Charley is working very hard. He is anxious, and feels the pressure. Now and then he blows up and screams at me. We have a shouting match and the crew look away, suddenly finding it necessary to polish the camera or go off for supplies. But he looks good. He is absolutely real. The training has paid off. He is part of the tribe, completely integrated.

One night I got back to the hotel, wet and exhausted. There was a call from Embassy. They wanted to know what I was going to do about the rain. I was reminded of a Hitchcock story. He was shooting on location and bad weather had got him behind schedule. 'What the hell are you going to do about it?' the studio trouble-shooter demanded.

'I shall do whatever is necessary', said Hitchcock in his measured tones, 'to complete what, in the course of time, you will come to refer to as "our film".'

---

8 APRIL 1984 *ITATIAIA*

After four weeks, I am two weeks behind. I have decided to leave the unshot scenes and pick them up in the Belém area later. It is essential that we get to Tucuruí on schedule otherwise we might lose it altogether. We have made some good scenes. The dark pools with their mossy boulders overhung with vines and lianas provided perfect settings for the ritual initiation of Tommy, the death of Wanadi and the scenes around the *shabona* where the Invisibles bathe and play. We have some vivid material.

Now we have moved high into the mountains where,

thankfully, it is too cold for mosquitoes. Unfortunately it is also too cold for the actors and crew. We are shooting a big action sequence where Tommy and Markham are pursued by the Fierce People. Powers has a wet suit under his costume, but Charley, of course, cannot. It is still raining most of the time. Of course, the locals say they have never seen anything like it for forty years.

More crew have left, and morale is still low, but around the camera is gathering a group which takes pride in surviving this misery. Barry's sheer professionalism won't allow him to falter. Pat, the continuity girl, is incredibly tough. Gale is giving everything, but it is a struggle for him. He has been sick on and off all the time, but has never missed a day. His camera assistants are having tremendous problems adjusting to these conditions and continue to act as if they are making a commercial at Pinewood. I have a great prop man, Bernie Hearn. He is young and quiet, yet has emerged as one of the great strengths of the unit. He loves the jungle, thrives on adventure. He is always ready for anything. His quick intelligence and ability to improvise have saved the day on many occasions.

Philippe has a wonderful attitude. He always reminds us how lucky we are to be doing this kind of work, to come to such places. He is tireless, moving across the rocks with elegant grace, humming Mozart, shaming a lot of people by his attitude, me included. I get depressed and angry. All my work and careful planning, the terrific story waiting to be released on to film, all frustrated by weather, a recalcitrant crew and what seems like a succession of disasters.

---

21 APRIL 1984

An awful thing has just happened. Paul Engelen and Peter Frampton, my two make-up men, have worked as a team on several pictures. They have been magnificent, working inhuman hours to get forty or fifty people ready each day, supervising the tribal paint, as well as simulating wounds and general make-up.

Paul's wife and two little girls have come out from England

to visit him. A car was bringing them here from Rio. On the way they had a terrible accident and are in hospital in critical condition.

It is bitterly ironic. I am continually afraid that someone will get hurt falling on slippery rocks, or snake-bitten, or drowned, or catch malaria – all the hazards of shooting in the jungle.

My films have had a lot of dangerous action sequences but no one has ever been killed or seriously injured. A broken finger, cuts and bruises, nothing more. I have always had a horror of this: it is absolutely immoral to risk life for the sake of entertainment, and yet an expedition like this is continually hazardous. I am very cautious and safety conscious.

The other day, Powers Boothe suddenly seized up in a scene under a waterfall. He was supposed to be injured and almost drowning. Tommy was helping him. We were shooting some distance away. Charley was desperately trying to keep him afloat and calling to us for help. We could not hear his cries against the roar of the waterfall, and kept on shooting, thinking how convincing their acting was. Powers could not move a muscle. Only Charley kept him afloat. Finally we realized and Harry, the standby, a trained diver, and Bernie the prop man quickly followed by Marc Boyle the stunt co-ordinator, went in and pulled him out. Charley had swallowed a lot of water and vomited it up. Powers needed oxygen and it was a couple of hours before he could get on his feet.

It recalled a similar incident in *Deliverance*. Ned Beatty was sucked into a whirlpool. He went under and it was forty-five seconds before he re-emerged downstream. We all dived for him. It was terrifying.

Afterwards we asked him what his thoughts were when he believed he was drowning. He replied like a true actor: 'I thought, how the hell will John be able to finish the film without me? Then I realized that the crafty bastard would somehow find a way. It made me so angry I was determined not to drown.'

The standbys have been terrific in these river sequences, and they are, all of a sudden, pulling for the movie.

Apart from the lack of time, I find I have no stomach or heart for this journal. The problems so dominate my thoughts that it is hard to think of anything else.

We finished up at Itatiaia. It was horrendously tough, but the stuff is good. The suffering is there on the faces of Powers and Charley. It worked for the scenes. I sent Powers right back into the river after his accident. He came through. The Engelen family are still in hospital, and although they are badly smashed up, they will live. We got the best help for them. The Brazilian doctors and surgeons are terrific. It has been very hard on Peter Frampton, since Paul is his best friend. Paul has left the picture and Peter is now in charge of make-up. Fortunately, Michael Dryhurst's wife, Anna, is with us. She is a highly skilled make-up artist and she has stepped into the breach.

The rain keeps on coming. It is sleeting down here outside my window. Below I can see the dam between squalls. We are kicking our heels. We have shot no film for four days.

We chartered two 737s to take us to Tucuruí, one a freighter with all the equipment aboard. At Rio airport six of us were arrested because our work permits had not been extended through a bureaucratic error. We were taken into custody and held for four hours while Roberto, Michael Dryhurst and our lawyers tried to have us released. Meanwhile, our charter plane sat on the runway, every extra hour costing a fortune. I felt the sheer dead weight of an authoritarian bureaucracy, the helpless frustration.

They finally let us go. By now the weather had clamped down at Tucuruí and we were forced to divert to Brasilia. As we arrived there we discovered that a state of emergency had been declared. It was under military rule and there was a total information blackout – nobody was allowed in or out of the city.

There has been smouldering unrest and riots throughout the country as the populace demands direct elections for the new president. The present system is that the outgoing president, always a general, nominates his successor and it is ratified by parliament. The President Designate is so unpopular that the deputies are afraid to vote for him for fear of the anger in their constituencies. The President has therefore banned all press from the proceedings so no one will know who did the voting.

We finally reached Tucuruí to discover that the freight plane carrying our equipment had broken down in Rio and could not fly until some spare parts were found. We are still waiting for it to arrive. Philippe and his gaffer and electricians are able to use this time because they have to set hundreds of lights on the dam. These lamps have been sent here separately for this purpose. It is a huge undertaking as the dam is more than a mile across.

There is quite a comfortable hotel here but we have been able to get only a limited number of rooms. Half the crew have been put into the workers' hostels, and there is a revolt. A dozen of them, including the standbys, Bernie, my prop man, and a few others, left for the airport, quitting the picture. Luckily, the 30-seater plane that plies daily between here and Belém is always full. It gave me time to go down to the airport and talk them out of it. They poured out their grievances. They claimed that the production office did not care about their welfare and they were being treated like animals.

Michael Dryhurst had gone back to Belém to prepare things there, so is not with us. I called a meeting of all departments to hear complaints. Some were simply misunderstandings, others genuine. I promised to try to put things right. I called Michael Dryhurst and asked him to come to Tucuruí to sort these things out.

When he arrived there was an open meeting that I chaired, where the crew repeated their grievances. Michael just sat there and said nothing by way of justifying his decisions with regard to the way the production was run. Afterwards, Bunny announced her intention of resigning and Michael offered to leave if I was dissatisfied with his performance. We were all terribly tired. Some had undergone the trauma of arrest and incarceration over the work permits. There was the appalling journey from Rio to Tucuruí with the delay at Brasilia, the poor accommodation at Tucuruí, etc. It was the low point for all of us.

However, most of the problems evaporated when it was explained why things were done in a particular way. Roberto Bakker, after a bad start, has never got a grip on his duties as production manager. He has had several bouts of sickness, and often simply disappears. Bunny has taken the full brunt of it, and is on the point of collapse.

Jake arrived here and sat in on one of the meetings when the departments catalogued their grievances. They claimed that they had carried on this far only out of respect for me. They have been through a lot. These talks have cleared the air, and there is a better spirit abroad. We have never recovered from our bad start, and nerves and muscles are frayed.

---

23 APRIL 1984 *CARAJÁS*

The location plan devised by Michael and myself was Paraty-Itatiaia-Tucuruí-Carajás-Belém. (There is an old film adage, 'Always start at your furthest location and work back to base.') Although by now the rainy season was supposedly over – and the rainfall at Carajás is never high – the gods heard there was a camera on its way and deluged Carajás, to such an extent that it would have been madness to proceed there from Tucuruí, so Michael and I decided to go straight from Tucuruí to Belém. Although this increased our costs (cancelled charter aircraft, hotels, holding over cast to last week of schedule), the carrot of Belém loomed large to the crew who had not seen a proper town now for four weeks.

---

26 APRIL 1984 *BELEM*

When the equipment finally arrived in Tucuruí the shooting of the dam sequences and the scenes on the edge of the clearing where the Invisible People discover the dam and the vast area of scalped land all went extremely well. There was a new energy. Belém beckoned. The girls were waiting. Everyone worked well and quickly. We caught up the time lost by the equipment delay.

Today we shipped back here, and it feels like a turning point. We start on the scenes in the apartment, which should give everyone a breathing space. I am spending the rest day touring the sets and locations with Simon to see how everything has progressed in my absence.

I am still two weeks behind schedule after the Paraty disaster. I have cut two scenes from the script and simplified some others. We are running a bit longer than intended, so I have room to manoeuvre.

We have a cutting room set up at our offices and I have reviewed everything shot so far with Ian Crafford.

Most directors shoot a master shot of a scene and then film it in closer shots from various angles and decide later how to put it together. This allows a lot of scope for controlling pace and means that the director can decide in the tranquillity of the cutting room what angle to use at any given moment.

I have a different method. I cut the scene before it is shot. I project it in my head, working out all the shots, the camera movements and pace. Every night, I project the whole picture through so that I can see the scene to be shot next day in context; I know then what its rhythm should be. Once on the set, it is often necessary or desirable to adjust and change, but I still shoot only the bits I need. I never make a master. I find I can sustain energy and vitality if the actors and technicians believe that every shot we make will be in the final picture. For the same reason, I shoot very few takes of each shot. I prefer to spend the time on preparations and rehearsing so that when the camera turns everyone knows that *this* is *it*. I like to build concentration and tension to that one point in time. Consequently, I use much less film than most directors. I often curse myself in the cutting room for not having shot more 'cover', but generally it is a method that works for me. It is a better use of resources. Kubrick likes to do many takes. Jack Nicholson told me that on *The Shining*, Stanley sometimes did seventy or eighty takes on a set-up. He said he was so exhausted he used to fall asleep on his feet between takes. When I saw the film I could see what Kubrick had been up to. He was trying to get performances that came out of extremity, exhaustion.

Film, as Sam Fuller told me in my master class, is whatever works. Skin the cat the best way you know how.

Some directors use tricks to get performances: insulting the actor, shouting at him, all manner of things. I prefer to take them into my confidence, to tell them almost everything, to work as collaborators. At the end of a take I tell them right away if it is good or bad and why. Only occasionally, if the actor is having trouble with a line or a movement, I pretend the take was spoilt for some technical reason. I never forget that the actors have to stand there alone and actually do it. However much work I have put into a scene, when the camera is turning, all I can do is stand and watch.

I give my cutting notes to the editor and he assembles the scene precisely as I have intended. Only later do we try other ways. Because there is so little film printed, I can cut as I go along and can see how the film is shaping up. As sequences are cut together I include them in my nightly 'cinema of the mind', going from what is actually there to what is yet to come. The actuality is never quite as good as the film in my head. Each day we fall short, each day is a little death.

There are moments that surprise and delight, but the shooting part of a film is mostly a grind, mostly a series of problems and disappointments as this diary bears witness. The compensations are mainly the pleasures of working with my colleagues and on this film those are many.

I think the film is beginning to work. The variety of camera movements and our care with foreground textures make it very visceral and fluid. We are achieving the sense of being inside the jungle, part of it, and sharing the experiences of the Invisible tribe.

---

4 MAY 1984

Markham makes the painful decision to leave Tommy with the Invisible People. He goes back to Belém. He is a changed man. How does he explain his decision to Jean? Meanwhile, the village of the Invisible People has been sacked by the Fierce People, who have now acquired guns. They massacre the tribe and abduct the young girls, including Tommy's wife, Kachiri. In trying to rescue them, Wanadi and most of the warriors are killed. Tommy sets out to track Markham back to the city and seek his help. The climax of this journey finds Tommy standing before the modern highrise where the Markhams live. It is dawn. He must climb the outside face of the building to get to Bill and Jean; he knows no other way to reach them. The climb must be epic, yet credible.

When Marc Boyle, my stunt co-ordinator, inspected the building I had chosen, he pronounced it impossible to climb. 'There is no stunt man in the world who could go up that.' Tiers of projecting balconies were separated by sheer marbled columns. These were 3 feet wide, rising up thirty floors without a grip or a handhold.

I remembered a half-Indian boy on one of the islands across from Belém whom I had seen climbing palm trees by making a loop of a palm frond and fitting it between his feet. We brought the boy over and he found it was possible to straddle the column. Charley tried it and discovered he could do it too. He is double-jointed and was able to turn the soles of his feet inwards at 90 degrees to grip the sides of the column.

A stunt sequence of this nature must be carefully planned, safety being the first consideration. Although the insurance company insists that we use stunt doubles, I like the actors to do their own stunts if possible. I decided in this case that Charley could do it himself. He is very sure-footed and a good climber. There would be a sequence of shots, each one achieved in a different way. When cut together they would, I hoped, add up to total conviction.

In the first shot I began on Charley's face then tilted and tracked the camera as he climbed the first three storeys in continuous action. The audience would see the palm loop working and because there was no cut there could be no fakery involved. The danger was that Charley might lose his balance and fall backwards. It was not a great height and we were ready below to catch him and break his fall. He did it with ease, although the rehearsals scraped the soles of his feet which were becoming quite sore. The purpose of tilting the camera was to look up and see how far he must climb, and the tracking gave a vertiginous sensation.

The second shot was a closer side-angle with Charley climbing up through it. Beyond and below him lay the city. For this we reproduced a section of the column and set it up on the roof of the building. Although he appears to be high up the building with a long drop below, the floor of the roof was only a few feet below him. In order not to see the roof we had to place this structure close to the edge, so there remained an element of danger.

The third shot of the sequence is the one that we hope makes the audience say, 'You win, I believe it.' This is a long shot looking at the face of the building. Here we see the tiny figure of Tommy, square on, going up that column. No fudging, no tricks. There he is. This is the easiest shot of all. We got access to an apartment some two-thirds up the building, and put Tommy in a harness and lowered him down three floors by cable. Marc and a couple of his assistants then take up the slack as he climbs. At that distance the camera cannot see the cable, which has been painted to match the colour of the column.

Finally, the camera looks down from the Markham building as Tommy hauls himself up and over the rail. We look straight down over Tommy to the street thirty storeys below. His head and shoulders obscure his feet, so the standbys had built a narrow wooden ledge for a toehold. He climbs up over the wrought-iron rail, and if he should fall at this point he would plunge thirty storeys. The only real danger is if he lost his nerve, but Charley relished it and it went off well.

The biggest problem was the huge crowd that built up to watch Charley's climb. They cheered and urged him on. The excitement drew people out on to the balconies of the apartment block and we had to beg and plead with them to go back inside. The scene was supposed to be happening at dawn when the city stood silent, but people just could not restrain themselves from popping out to see what was going on. At one stage I thought it would prove impossible. In these cases it is better simply to wait for people to get bored. Finally they did.

In *The Heretic* I shot a giddy rooftop sequence in

Manhattan. I wore a harness with a safety rope. This gave me great confidence in leaning out over the precipitous edge and climbing on and off the camera, which was jutting out into space. It was not until we had finished that I discovered the safety rope was not connected to anything. Perhaps you could define film directors as people who behave as if there is a safety net when there is none.

---

12 MAY 1984

In order to shoot the several night scenes inside the *shabona*, we covered the open central area with black plastic sheeting. In this way the scenes could be shot during normal daylight hours.

The weather pattern in Belém is a daily torrential downpour that lasts about an hour and usually occurs around 4 o'clock each afternoon. Last night it rained for seven hours. This morning we arrived to find the *shabona* had collapsed. The weight of water lying in the plastic sheeting had buckled and torn down the structure. It was a ruin. We tried to replace the sheeting to keep out the rain, but to no avail. We struggled all day, soaked through, and at 4 o'clock Barry Langley said, 'You might as well wrap it up. There is no way we can shoot today.' Bernie Hearn, the prop man, who had wrestled all day with the damage, said, 'I think we could prop up the roof in one corner.' I weighed it up. Even if he could do it, I could shoot only one angle towards the outer wall, since the reverse shot involved looking across the *shabona*, which was a shambles. The only scene I could shoot was the very demanding one where Wanadi and Markham discuss Tommy and the chief gives Bill their hallucinogenic drug. It is a solemn scene, with many subtle nuances and a tranquil late-night atmosphere.

I spoke to Powers and Rui to see if they felt prepared enough to shoot it at such short notice. Rui shrugged. One time for him was as good as another. Powers had waited all day without working. He was frustrated and aching to do something. He agreed.

Before offering him the drug, Wanadi tells Bill that he cannot receive it in a naked state. He hands him a bowl of paint and Bill smears it on his face. This scene arose out of my experience with the Xingu. I mentioned earlier that when they came to cut the trees for the *quarup* ceremony, they said I could not witness this ritual 'naked'. They painted my face and I was allowed to watch. I told Powers this story and it was his own idea that he should understand what is meant when Wanadi says, 'You cannot enter "the world" naked', and put the paint on himself. It becomes a gesture symbolizing Markham's acceptance of their culture and his readiness to enter its inner reality. The scene must be calm and intense.

Bernie and the standbys propped up a corner of the *shabona*, and set up plastic sheeting against it, to keep out the light and the rain. As we shot, wind rattled the plastic sheets, rain hammered on the roof. All around us men struggled and cursed trying to hold it all from being swept away. Powers and Rui were magnificent. They put the distractions out of their minds and played the scene beautifully. It was exhilarating. All the work and preparation we had done was now coming to our aid. They knew what they had to do. The soundtrack, of course, was full of extraneous noises. That will be rectified when we loop the scene back in London. It was one of the best things we have done. It came out of extremity. The purest hope, born of despair.

---

20 MAY 1984

We are all exhausted, but the end is in sight. The scenes in the *shabona*, the rituals, and the daily life of the Indians look magnificent. The apartment scenes were destroyed in the Brazilian laboratory and have to be done over. It is heartbreaking. This was so emotionally taxing for Meg, and now she must do it again. The only consolation is that the cost can be claimed from our insurers.

There is a certain routine emerging here in Belém. I get up at 6 am and arrive at the set by 7.30. We start shooting at 8 and go on to 5.30, when it gets dark.

The heat and humidity in the middle of the day saps energy but most people have adjusted fairly well by now. After shooting I go back to the office and work with Michael Dryhurst on production matters. I arrive home at 8 and eat dinner. I then spend an hour organizing the next day's shooting. There are usually one or two calls to make to London or Los Angeles. Then I prepare for bed and run the film through in my mind.

The schedule is simply flipped on its head for night shooting. We are about to begin two weeks of night shooting, staging the scenes around the whorehouse.

Since I sent a telex to Alan Horn asking him to stop the continuous harassment from Embassy, things have been quieter. I suppose it was because we got off on such bad footing. Embassy took over the film so close to shooting, the wretched Rospo business started them doubting, then we got so far behind schedule. The people running Embassy come out of television with little experience of feature film-making. Although Mike Glick has supervised a lot of films and he is always reasonable in his dealings with us, he suffers hysterical pressure from above and is obliged to hand it down to us.

The Embassy people are so gloomy and pessimistic. Every action and decision Michael Dryhurst and I make they interpret in the worst possible way. They treat us as adversaries, and assume that we are irresponsible wastrels. Throughout all our struggles and difficulties, there has been not a single word of encouragement. They have made no positive comment on the rushes they have seen.

Jeff has now left to be a producer and I miss his wonderful enthusiasms. Jake gives unflagging support, but he does not seem to have the ear of Alan Horn or Jerry Perenchio. It is quite mystifying. After wooing Jake so assiduously and paying him a large salary, they ignore his views. They wanted him because of his brilliant track record at Goldcrest of picking good projects and nurturing them to success. Yet every subject he puts up they turn down. Certainly he is not allowed to take decisions. He is helpful with advice, as a friend, but if I need a decision I have to go to Alan Horn and he in turn goes to Perenchio who discusses it with Norman Lear and an edict is passed down.

Embassy has an overseer with us all the time. He represents both them and the completion-bond company.

At the end of each day's shooting we fill out a progress report. It shows all the details of the day's shooting – scenes shot, amount of film stock used, how many set-ups, which actors worked, the amount of screen time achieved. This information is telexed back to Embassy each night with comments from their representatives. They hold a copy of our schedule in LA, so they can judge from this if we have slipped behind or deviated from our intentions.

Each week our new accountant, Kevin O'Driscoll, produces a cost statement. It follows the same lines as the budget, divided up into various categories: film stock, actors' salaries, construction, transportation, etc. Each week shows bumps and dips as some items exceed the budgeted allowance and others fall below it.

We are trying to claw back some of our early losses and reverses. The cuts in the script have helped. The crew is moving at a good pace now and we are not getting any further behind. If anything, we are catching up. Citibank invested our cruzeiros very well and the interest keeps well ahead of inflation. This has helped offset our still burgeoning Brazilian costs.

The dollar continues to rise in value. This reduces the sterling costs of the picture to Embassy. Some things are turning in our favour.

The brunt of the battle with Embassy falls on Edgar. He is in daily contact with Embassy executives, particularly the legal and business affairs people. He is distraught. The simplest matters assume inflated proportions. It does not augur well when we get to the distribution stage.

---

9 JULY 1984 *BELEM*

I have neglected this journal for the last seven weeks, too tired to turn my mind to it. Today is a time for rejoicing. Yesterday was our last day of shooting. Two days to clear up and then on Thursday, 11 July, we all fly home.

We have come out bang on schedule. We caught up the

lost time and it looks as though we are well under budget. Certainly we have not touched the 10 per cent contingency, which is well over $1 million. It is quite an achievement. It even elicited a telex of congratulation from Embassy. They are surely very relieved. Goldcrest, on the other hand, must be feeling pretty foolish. Given our budget savings and the pre-sales, they would have been $2 million in profit right now, with the potential of making many millions more.

The Engelen family is back in England and on the mend after many surgical operations. Apart from this we came through without any major mishap. Most people had days out with fever or diarrhoea, but we avoided hepatitis and malaria. Quite a few have picked up skin funguses and there are some cases of hookworm. Pat Rambaut has a very painful swollen foot from a sting ray, but she remains one of the ever smaller club of people who never missed a day's work: Philippe, Barry and myself being among the total of eight that remain. I sent Bernie Hearn home one afternoon suffering from a raging fever. He agreed to go only if he was not thrown out of the 100 per cent Club. He had, after all, turned up in the morning, and he dragged himself in the following day, so he stays in. Gale was out for a week with a debilitating fever, and Philippe and I shared the operating. Gale has done a terrific job, toting the Steadicam as well as his other duties. It has taken a heavy toll. My constant demand for fluid camera movements in jungle conditions has kept the crew laying tracks, carrying the heavy crane over rocks and through rivers. These movements are not contrived, but integrated into the narrative and despite the complexity of so many of the shots, the film is shaping up to look very simple and unforced.

Powers has gone home a week before the rest of us. He was totally drained by his sustained act of concentration. He had never endured a schedule of this length before. His performance has given a focus to the film. It is through him that the audience relates to the other elements and characters. He has carried it well. His professionalism and seriousness set standards for the others, particularly Charley whom he helped enormously.

Charley, on the other hand, got stronger and stronger as time went on. He was learning all the time and his confidence grew. At the outset I was leading him through every move and gesture and intonation. Latterly, he has made suggestions, had good ideas and brought a lot of colour and shading to his role. He instinctively knows what is true and right. His directness and simplicity have been the anchor of the film. He is always real and always present.

Peter Benoit, our publicity man, has been interviewing us with a video camera. Charley told him that we started out as father and son and ended up as friends, which touched me deeply. Meg made some very perceptive comments. She said Charley had two fathers, Powers and me, to guide and teach him. We watched Charley growing up, as Tommy does in the story. In the end we learnt as much from him, she said, as he from us. Finally, we were all teachers and taught, fathers and sons. Rui was yet another father. He remained gentle and patient, bringing a goodness to the film that expressed the essential quality of the Invisible People. In a way I don't quite understand, I feel Takuma is responsible for Rui's wonderful performance as the chief. Not just in terms of what I was able to pass on to Rui, but in a more mysterious way Takuma's spirit seemed to be present in Rui.

Bunny and Michael Dryhurst came through their crises and got ever stronger. She held it all together, and he fought the battle to keep down costs. For all the things that were flying apart, he made the centre hold. His loyalty and dedication have got me through this ordeal.

Because we were always behind, always trying to catch up, the pressure was relentless. Barry Langley organized and husbanded our resources to get the most out of each day.

Half the crew have set up homes with their Brazilian 'wives', buying furniture and settling down to the very domestic routine they were trying to escape from in England. Many of the girls here have children from earlier liaisons and I often see my men wheeling pushchairs in the Belém streets.

The tribespeople have gone back to their lives. Possi came to dinner last night to bid farewell. He told us how many of them had saved their money and bought homes and businesses. The farewells have been very touching. It has been an experience that has changed us all, marked us all, and bonded us all together. I have never encountered such warmth and affection. Charley is completely Brazilian, and would love to stay here for the rest of his life.

For most people, this is the end of the picture. I still have six months of post-production ahead, but that is a time to relish. The pressure will be off and I can function like a normal human being.

---

11 JULY 1984 *EN ROUTE: BELEM–LONDON*

The scenes at the airport were astonishing. I expected the girls to weep, but it was unnerving to see all these hard men shedding tears.

One of our fellows, I'll call him W., has led a life of dedicated debauchery, not just here in Brazil, but all over the world, and we know the sun never sets on British film crews.

For W., Brazil was a Mecca. The fulfilment, the revelation, the ecstasy he had sought in vain in the brothels of the world, he finally found here. Every night W. got drunk and headed for the whorehouse. Despite carousing half the night, he somehow managed to do his work the next day. The whorehouses of Belém, I am told, are charming places, with dancing and cabarets. The girls are affectionate and very pretty. W., after a lifetime's wanderings, had found his spiritual home. The projects at Carajás and Tucuruí, with their thousands of male workers, have spawned shanty towns with huge populations of whores. After the first day in Tucuruí he came to work and described in hushed, awed tones, a street with a hundred houses, forty-eight of them whorehouses – most of the others were bars. In one or two you could get a haircut.

W. was the last to arrive at the airport. He was very drunk and had come straight from his favourite dive. He checked his luggage, but at the last moment could not wrench himself away. He leapt over the counter, grabbed his bags from the conveyor and disappeared into the night. One of his friends told me a terrible thing had happened to W. For the first time in his life he had fallen in love – with a whore.

Kevin O'Driscoll is staying on in Belém and it will take several months to conclude all our affairs there, including auditing the books of Goldcrest Filmes Limitada.

Meanwhile, it is a great relief to the rest of us to be airborne and finally going home.

---

14 JULY 1984 *TWICKENHAM STUDIOS, LONDON*

Watched all the accumulated rushes, some two hours of material. Everything came out fine. I am spending a couple of days with Ian in the cutting room and then home to Ireland for a week's rest.

Ron Davis is a brilliant sound editor and has worked with me for many years. I took him out to Brazil to record stereo sound effects in the rain forest. I had a long session with him today about which effects I need in each sequence. While we are editing he will organize and assemble his sound effects.

Spoke to David Norris. He was delighted with the outcome: on schedule and $1½ million under budget. He then told me that Goldcrest is planning to shoot a David Puttnam production, *The Mission*, in Colombia. I was astonished. Colombia was one of the countries our advisers warned us against as dangerous and unstable. The budget is considerably more than mine. Goldcrest seem to be compounding their folly.

---

18 JULY 1984

My fellow governors at the British Film Institute were taken aback to see me turn up for a meeting after all these months. Surprise, surprise, they were still debating the demise of the British film industry, a requiem I have attended for twenty years. The Government is now planning to withdraw the niggardly support it gives and rescind the tax-shelter arrangements that have so stimulated investment. There must be a record number of nails in this coffin, and yet the corpse is still screaming to be let out.

There is a curious anomaly. All the British film studios are doing bumper business. Technicians are earning more money, more regularly than ever before, yet cinema attendance is collapsing. This is not just the effects of TV and video hire. In France and the US cinema attendances are up and the number of screens is increasing. Our cinemas, like so much else in this country, are dirty, decaying, uncomfortable places.

Coming from the exuberance of Brazil, I get a fresh insight into our national malaise. All our actions are punitive. We are intent on punishing one another, exacting penance. Certainly cinema managers fall into this category. This is the only country in the world where you cannot discover what time a film starts. It is always the 'programme', which includes forty-five minutes of junk before the movie begins. They are 'clamping' cars now in London, with great relish, and I notice that they also stick a large notice over the windscreens. They use a glue that makes it painfully difficult to remove. This is the Punitive Mentality.

One is allowed the odd sweeping generalization after a long absence abroad, and here is another, nearly the obverse of the last.

Institutions like the British Film Institute are the best things we have. They are run with great dedication. They draw on the resources of selfless public service that redeem us from grasping materialism.

The National Film Theatre has been an important part of my life for thirty-five years. It is the only way to be in touch with world cinema. Since movies are like psychic vacuum cleaners, sucking up the spirit of their time and place, they afford a way of being in touch with other countries and cultures. At many levels movies are a unique form of communication, making a future universal consciousness possible. The BFI's archive stores up and preserves the history of film. It is a memory for the world.

Overleaf is the text of an advertisement that the completion bond company took out in *Variety*.

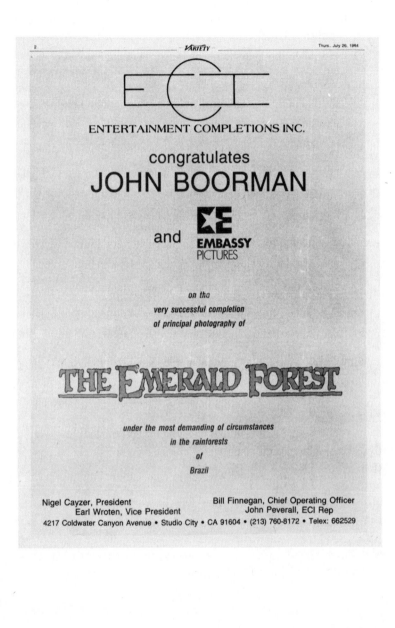

24 JULY 1984 *ANNAMOE, IRELAND*

Finally home. A balmy summer, hotter than anyone remembers. We were dreaming of soft Irish rain, heavy skies, but this will do. The evening light etches long shadows giving every object a plinth on which it stands out from all other things. The equatorial sun, shadowless, solders everything together into a single mass. How vivid are familiar objects after long absence: the patterns on the carpet, the cracks in the ceiling, the curve of an old chair. They normally go unnoticed, but now they trigger memories of themselves and *leap* at one anew. But stronger than new. They carry history. My deep weariness falls away.

The horses keep their distance, watch warily. They are wild, unridden, and hope to remain so.

Glad to see the pair of grey herons still gliding under the tunnel of trees that enfolds our little river where the water has warmed itself, flowing over the sun-baked rocks that turn the river wild with white water in winter. I stripped off and entered the peat-brown water. A benediction. A pair of ducks scuttled away. The Wicklow hills recede in soft folds, dissolving in heat haze. Back in Middle Earth.

I dried off in the sun and walked over to the oak grove. Two hundred and fifty years the oaks have stood there and I have watched them slowly dying the last fourteen years. I missed them, old friends. In the rain forest the growth is violent, palpable. It is urgent, thrusting, and death is sudden. Trees crash down, limbs snapping like firecrackers. This is the old world, its time is gone and there is a melancholy about it that I find to my taste.

The children arrive tomorrow. Meanwhile, Christel and I speak in hushed voices as we cock ears to the silence. In Brazil, the jungle rattles, croaks and screams; music blares; people shout; cars drive on their horns; even the sky cracks and thunders with the daily downpour of rain.

Here the peace and quiet is a balm.

Home.

SHOOTING

Stills photography by Roberto Faissal Jnr.

The first assembly of *The Emerald Forest* runs 2 hours 35 minutes. We estimated the script at about 2 hours 10 minutes. The present version is very loosely cut, and trimming and tightening will lose some 20 minutes. Eventually some scenes will be shortened and some excised altogether. Screening the rough-cut for the first time is a nerve-racking occasion. However imperfect it is, however many shots and optical effects are missing, with, as yet, no music or sound effects and a ragged dialogue track, you still know if it is going to 'play' or not. I am putting off the fateful hour. The film is arranged on fourteen reels, each in length between 750 and 1,000 feet, or 8–10 minutes.

Ian and I run them one by one on a Steenbeck editing machine. We keep refining them, and I try to get some pace and rhythm going. Some of the action sequences were shot without sound at all. We hand them to Ron Davis and he puts in some temporary sound effects so that the track does not go completely dead.

I love this phase. The slow mechanical editing processes give time for reflection: cutting and joining, adjusting the soundtracks, looking at offcuts, hanging the strips of film in bins, rearranging them. All around us, on shelves, cans of film cover the walls. Every shot is numbered, each can labelled. The continuity girl writes into the script a description of every shot. We can pull out any one of the thousand or more set-ups and take a look at it. She also describes each take. We may shoot four, five or ten takes and more but only one or two of them will be printed. The unprinted takes have descriptions against them saying what was wrong – a camera fault, an acting problem, the light not right. I can call up and consider everything we made in those seventeen weeks. I am happy to have the film all around me – all its volatile fragments finally trapped in cans and awaiting my bidding. Later on I will call on them, juxtaposing, trying different solutions, fine tuning. Right now, Ian and I are working in broader strokes. In a day or two we will take it over to the preview theatre and see if we have a movie.

19 AUGUST 1984

We screened the rough-cut today. There were just four of us: Ian Crafford (editor), Ron Davis (sound editor), Michael Dryhurst and myself. The film is full of gaps and gaping holes. In particular, the great storm culminating in the dam bursting is largely missing. Next week we will shoot the model shots of the dam. Then we will build a section of the dam: a site hut overlooking the construction. Powers will come over to London to do the scenes where he attempts to blow up the dam. All this will be shot against a 'blue screen' background. The model shots will then be 'matted' in by a process that replaces the blue screen with the background shots or 'plates'.

When the lights came up, I saw the relief on all faces, and felt it in my heart. The film works. It is very powerful and moving. It creates a world of its own. All the agony of making those jungle shots paid off. We have caught the sense of what it is like to be in the rain forest. It looks very fluid, seamless. Those complex camera movements look effortless and unforced. It has a pleasing simplicity. It is harder to judge the performances at this stage, but they seem fine. Charley is terrific. I am sure there will be a credibility problem for some people. The story will seem remote and far-fetched, but I hope the sounds, the images and the characters will seduce and disarm the audience.

One or two things are evident. The sequence of scenes mapping the progress of Markham's and Werner's expedition up river is too long. I will cut one or two of them.

Although there is so much missing from the dam sequence, the emotional forces that drive towards it are so strong that once the dam is destroyed, the picture has to end rather quickly. At present we have several scenes that tie up the loose ends: there is an enquiry into the dam disaster and a scene where the remnants of the Invisible tribe are rebuilding the *shabona* in which the dying Jacareh arrives seeking absolution.

Both scenes have important content, the first lends technical credibility to the destruction of the dam, and establishes that Markham will not be blamed; the second provides a pleasing reconciliation and a sense of redemption. When Tommy allows Jacareh to die among them, we see in him a new maturity. However, the tumultuous events and powerful emotions that come before make them seem schematic and redundant. They will have to go.

---

21 AUGUST 1984 *SPILSBY, LINCOLNSHIRE*

Only a few weeks since we finished shooting and here we are again. Philippe, Gale, Michael Dryhurst, Simon. The crew of 120 is now reduced to eight of us. Phil Stokes has been building the model dam since February. I sat down with him last December and showed him the storyboards Simon and I had made and the detailed photographs. He went off to think about it and came back with a scheme that he described to me. He worked out a cost figure that was less than we had in the budget and one-third of what Gilles Lacombe was asking. Michael and I checked him out with people for whom he has worked in the past and got nothing but glowing testimonials. We gave him the job.

He has dammed a river, built a system of sluice gates, rented a factory and manufactured all the miniature cranes, trucks, scaffolding, buildings, ladders required. Now the great dam of Tucuruí stands in a Lincolnshire field. Last night was the climax of seven months' work for him. A series of exhaustive tests on video and film have indicated the speed we should shoot at (96 frames per second or four times normal speed); the whole structure is wired with tiny lights, a fine water vapour extruded from the high jets to give the illusion of distant rain. The dammed river takes twenty-four hours to rise to the required level. Seven months' work all compressed into forty-nine seconds of screen time. We rehearsed the lights, the lightning, the rain. At last Phil gave the order to release the water, but forgot to cue the lights and rain. In vain we yelled. The dam broke. Finally he heard us, but too late. Now it must be rebuilt and tried again.

22 AUGUST 1984

We just saw the rushes. Apart from the absence of lights and
rain it looks magnificent. The scale is good. The concrete – a
mixture Phil arrived at after long trials – breaks in appropriately small pieces. The cranes buckle and crash into the tor-
rent.

Tonight we attempt a flash flood on the Amazon. Simon
has been planting a miniature plastic rain forest along the
gentle English stream.

24 AUGUST 1984

The Lincolnshire wolds stretch away from Spilsby to the sea,
some twelve miles to the east. A breeze from the North Sea
fans the baked clay of a burning summer. A hot silver line
streaks the horizon, announcing the sea.

We shoot at night. In the day we explore this neglected
flank of England. On its coast can be found the seaside resort
of Skegness. Like Orwell on the road to Wigan Pier, Philippe
and I venture into this 'other' England. Blackpool is vulgar,
ornate, overblown, excessive. 'Skeggy' is bleak, windblown. It
is garish and sad. Favoured by industrial workers and coal
miners from the North and Nottinghamshire, it is a place of
surpassing ugliness. All this I half expected, given its reputation. Nothing prepared me for its denizens. These holiday-
makers look like the undernourished slum dwellers of the early
Industrial Revolution. Skinny girls, runt-like boys, fat wad-
dling women, worn-out men. They must be the remnants, the
last leftovers. They wander the streets consuming fish and
chips, candy-floss, ice-cream. Joyless children clamour for
money to spend in dolorous amusement arcades. The wind is
whipping the fine sand into flurries on the promenade and
only a brave few lean against it, squinting against the grit.

The mean hills surrounding the town are covered in
caravans. Symbols of desert journeys, they lie permanently
dumped here, rented by the week. On the beach pale skins
are raw pink and blistered from the wind and sun. I never

POST-PRODUCTION

Photography by Roberto Faissal Jnr.

△ *The dam at Tucuruí.*

The model of the dam being prepared for shooting.▽

Photography by Michael Dryhurst.

△ *The dam being prepared for shooting.*

Water rushing through the broken dam.▽

thought I would see in 1984 scenes I remember as a child, but here they are. Old men with knotted hankies over bald heads paddle in the sea, their trousers rolled up. Philippe is quite bemused by it, but I am deeply depressed. The wounds of the Industrial Revolution cut deep. It takes more than thirty years of welfare state to heal them.

I looked at my fellow countrymen and felt alien. I could find nothing in D. H. Lawrence, nor even in J. B. Priestley, to help link me to them. Twenty years ago I probed England for stories, burrowed into its by-ways making documentary films. I knew it then. I have been away too long, and I am a stranger in my own land.

There is no grace nor dignity in these people, no harmony in their dress, no art in their play. Here is a tribe gone sadly wrong, mutated. Worst of all, they seem to have lost the knowledge of what they have lost. I can imagine Takuma's distasteful look if he were to gaze upon these people. This thought prompted another; it flashed into my mind with the certain force of revelation. When Takuma looked at me, he must have seen what I see now. I was Skegness to him, with my pale face and silly clothes and awkward manner.

A few miles away Lincoln Cathedral crests a tor that commands the county. I have pilgrimmed here before, as I have to the other great English cathedrals: Salisbury, Canterbury, Worcester, Wells. The mystery of how they came to be intrigues me; why at that time a powerful urge possessed people to send stone surging to the heavens? I try to imagine those churches brightly painted, the carved figures with blue eyes and red lips, garish as Skegness.

Inside the cathedral we inspect one of the only original copies of Magna Carta. These copies were sent out to be displayed in all the great cathedrals of the land, sent out from Runnymede where I once bathed in the mystic waters. England was mostly covered in forest then. Tribal life had disintegrated into the feudal. Written rights were granted. The concept of individual freedom was kindled. The person was liberated from the tribe. Henceforth all things were possible, and the price was aloneness.

Brazil still has hold of me, the Xingu experience has set me apart. Everything about my homeland is disjointed, at one remove. I see faint and faded pictures. I hear diminished echoes.

Back at Spilsby, our lights prick the night. Phil Stokes gives the signal and the dam bursts with magnificent, consuming power. Three cameras, going at four times normal speed, record it.

---

13 OCTOBER 1984

The actors have come in from the US and Brazil, and the looping is finished. It took seven weeks in all. It was very laborious, particularly the Tupi, but it has sharpened and improved the performances.

We have shot the 'blue screen' material of the dam bursting and these shots are currently being 'married up' with the model backgrounds we shot in Lincolnshire.

The mechanical eagle is proving a disaster. Although Oxford Scientific Films have cleverly animated its movements, it is not convincing. A soaring eagle makes constant minute wing adjustments as it flies and we just cannot achieve the right degree of subtlety. Fortunately, we were able to get better and closer shots of the real eagle in flight than we had ever anticipated, so there are only two or three scenes where the mechanical eagle is now required. We are moving to a different technique: rotoscope. We take one of our real eagle shots and, frame by frame, paint out the background. Then a new and appropriate landscape can be 'matted' into its place, thus transposing the eagle to another place and situation. It is a slow, painstaking and costly process, but after many attempts the mechanical-eagle solution has been abandoned.

The film is now running at 2 hours 10 minutes. It is tighter and moves faster but, having cut away a lot of underbrush, some other problems reveal themselves more clearly. After the kidnapping, we jump ahead ten years and the story effectively has to begin again. Since we are then telling the two parallel stories – Markham's search and Tommy's life with the Invisible People – it is hard to get it moving and flowing. I am finding it difficult to hit the right balance between the two strands. Once Markham and Tommy meet it is fine.

The next problem comes when Tommy returns to the apartment seeking his father's help. The scene with his mother does rather bring the picture to a grinding halt.

Lastly, after Markham has helped Tommy rescue the girls and they have their touching farewell scene, it feels like the end of the film. However, the final chapter of the destruction of the dam is yet to come. I have still to get this right, although I believe the emotional flow is sound. I continue to make changes and alterations, but I will do nothing radical until the previews. I need the perspective that will come from setting it before an audience.

---

5 DECEMBER 1984

The musical score is the last element. Only when the film is in its final form can the composer fit his music exactly to each sequence. Very often he will be involved much earlier than this and can prepare themes and musical ideas, but he cannot write until the 'fine' cut is ready. He usually gets about six to eight weeks for scoring and copying.

The director sits down with the composer at the editing machine and tells him where music is required, what function he wants it to perform and precisely where it should begin and end. However closely you work with the composer, the day a hundred musicians arrive on the music stage to record it is always a rude shock. It is never quite what you expected or hoped for, and at that stage it is very difficult to change. This method is antithetical to the film process, which, in all respects, from scripting to editing, proceeds on a push–pull, try it–change it kind of basis.

Music and film have always been in love, but never happily married. Movies can scarcely survive without music and today, for most composers, the only opportunity to write and perform orchestral music is for film.

In the silent days, music was undisturbed by dialogue or sound effects; these films, with their montage editing, had the rhythm and pace that related well to music. D. W. Griffith was the first man to accompany a film with an orchestra. It was for *The Birth of a Nation*. The music was largely a medley of popular classics, with, of course, 'Dixie' weaving in and out. It was all applied very instinctively and owed a lot to the musical traditions of the circus: a roll of drums to heighten a dramatic moment, etc. Eisenstein and Prokofiev intellectualized it; Prokofiev's theory and practice of music was the model followed for many years, and it remains the dominant tradition today.

Although there were some great and original composers in Hollywood like Bernard Herrmann, there was a pervasive tendency in the factory-made film to have what we call a 'Mickey Mouse' score – in the cartoons, every movement and action is matched to a musical chord or accent. In drama films this was applied to every emotion of the characters. The score told us exactly what to feel at each moment – sympathy, triumph, fear, tension. It usurped acting, made it redundant. It certainly helped a lot of bad actors and directors.

There was, inevitably, a reaction against this kind of music. Many directors rejected scored music altogether in favour of pop songs, jazz, and sometimes no music at all. Composers began to provide music that suggested a general atmosphere, rather than specifically coinciding with the action. Carol Reed startled everyone by using nothing but a zither in *The Third Man*. It provided a haunting, repetitive motif evoking Vienna and mystery. He used sound effects very dramatically to fill in gaps that would traditionally have been underscored by an orchestra.

I did something similar in *Deliverance*. Warners insisted I cut the budget before they would go ahead with the film. Slashing my fee was not enough. I had wanted to use Appalachian music as an element, but the nature of the film seemed to call for a dramatic orchestral score. This fiscal pressure forced me into a decision. I had $65,000 in the budget for orchestra and composer. I decided to do the whole score with a banjo and guitar playing variations on a single traditional folk piece called 'Duelling Banjos'. We recorded it with two musicians in an afternoon. There were no royalties to pay since there was no known composer. The total cost was $1,500. The $63,500 savings brought the budget down to the figure Warners were demanding. Against their better judgement I forced Warner Records to release the music. It became a number one hit and Warner's royalties for the record paid for the whole cost of making the movie.

Kubrick, who questions every convention, decided that if scores no longer fitted the action, then why do you need specially composed music, when you can have your pick of the great composers. This brought us back full circle to D. W. Griffith.

Then along came George Lucas and Steven Spielberg and their favoured composer, John Williams. We were back to 'Mickey Mouse'. Williams's command of the orchestra is awesome. The coming of *Jaws*, *Star Wars*, *Close Encounters*, and *Raiders of the Lost Ark* coincided with improved stereo systems in cinemas. Williams provided overwhelming, sweeping scores that start on the opening titles and never stop until the movie is over. These films are total musical experiences. Not since the silent movies had anyone done that. Audiences are told exactly what to feel and how to react at every moment; this allows the movies to hurtle along with kinetic fury, the music providing a rapid interpretive shorthand, fusing all the elements into a single wash of excitement.

Although such a score would serve to weld together the disparate elements of *The Emerald Forest* and guide the audience through this unfamiliar territory, it would also blunt their sensibilities and distance them from the raw experience of the rain forest and the Indians.

Junior Homrich, with his range of flutes and percussion instruments, was with us all through the shooting. He provided a beat, a mood for whatever we were doing. It proved a marvellous way of getting the Brazilians into the right frame of mind.

I finally decided to ask him to do the whole score. I brought him over from Brazil. We transferred the film on to videotape and have spent weeks going back and forth finding what works by trial and error. Not a note has been written down. He tries out his varied instruments for each section, until we discover the right tempo and sound. We edit and alter as we go along. A typical score would have ten half-day sessions, a week's recording in other words. We have spent seven weeks in a small studio with Junior recording on twenty-four tracks. He overdubs, using a different instrument on each track. We are carefully integrating his music into the sound effects. We try to get his music to grow out of the sounds of the forest. The only additional element is provided by Brian Gascoigne who is an expert in electronic music and a consummate composer in his own right. He has used his Fairlite synthesizer to simulate a version of the Indian bass flutes, *samponas*, which provide a musical theme for the eagle.

Junior is a superb musician. He can play most musical instruments, keyboards, guitar, bass, as well as his extraordinary range of percussion items. He uses earthenware pots, silver goblets, and even his own body. He finger-taps his chest, head, throat, mouth, to produce a medley of notes. His Indian instruments include a rain stick – seeds inside a bamboo tube. As the seeds tip from end to end they produce the sound of rain falling on trees. Gourds are used as resonators for stringed instruments. There is a bass drum made from a hollowed log.

It has been a very rewarding time. Modern technology allows us to synchronize a videotape of the film to a twenty-four-track music recorder. A computer is programmed to find each preordained section and rock back and forth over it as we lay down each of the twenty-four tracks. Altering and editing as we go along, it is a revolutionary way to make a score. The system is so fast and time-saving that it took us only seven times longer than normal to complete the score.

---

20 DECEMBER 1984

Because of the way I make films – looping all the dialogue, building a soundtrack – the total effect is not apparent until all the tracks have been mixed and dubbed. This process will begin after Christmas and takes five weeks. Each of the fourteen reels of the film will have some fifty tracks – dialogue, effects, music – which will be mixed down to a six-track magnetic stereo, then to a four-track optical stereo and finally to a mono-optical track, for the various projection systems on which it must play.

At present the work copy of the film is scratched and stressed from the editing process; the soundtrack is a very rough approximation of what it will finally be. For these reasons I have resisted Embassy's clamouring demands to see the film. Only Jake has seen it. He was overcome and wept. Tears streamed down his face.

Jake's enthusiastic reports to his Embassy colleagues further whetted their appetites. Succumbing to pressure and anxious to give them some chance to comment before finalizing the film, I sent it out to LA with Ian Crafford to let them take a look. Although I warned them that the soufflé was still in the batter stage, the comments that came back were effectively saying, 'Why is this batter, not soufflé?'

They said the Indian rituals were too long and looked like a National Geographic documentary, a film within a film. The music, one executive commented, was too ethnic. They did not like any of the scenes involving Jean, especially the major one when she finally meets Tommy. They liked Charley's and Powers's performances and the action sequences.

Jake attended the screening and was given the task of communicating their thoughts to me. Their comments may or may not be just. The real blow is that if they are not enthusiastic, they will not get behind the film, and certainly not give it the big advertising budget that it will need to compete with the other big summer films.

After I recovered from these wounding comments, I saw that in some specifics their strictures were justified. I made a number of changes. However, I will make no major alterations until after the previews.

Past experience at least helps one to deal with these setbacks. I took the rough cut of *Deliverance* to Burbank Studios to show Warners. It was only a week after the end of shooting. I was exhausted from a tough schedule. I flew into LA carrying the film as baggage. There was a strike of porters and no trolleys. I had to carry the twenty-four heavy cans myself. The Warners' car did not show up. I took one of LA's ramshackle taxis. The driver was high on something. He zig-zagged the freeway. I arrived a nervous wreck. After the screening, Ted Ashley, John Calley and the other executives retired without a word. I was told to join them in Ashley's office in half an hour. My heart sank when I saw their long faces.

'So you didn't like it much,' I said.

'We like it fine,' said Ted. 'But someone has just pointed out that no picture without a woman in it has ever been a box-office success.'

I told him it was a bit late in the day to discover that little nugget.

Bob Chartoff and I screened *Point Blank* for Bob O'Brien and the other MGM executives in 1967. This was the time that Hollywood was just waking up to the fact that the audience consisted largely of teenagers. It became fashionable for executives to bring their sons or nieces to screenings and all our fates were put into the hands of some pimply 16-year-old. Two such youths were present in the MGM screening room. They laughed, talked and jeered all through the picture. It was agonizing. At the meeting afterwards O'Brien was thunderously angry.

Chartoff said, 'I guess you didn't like it.'

'It's not the picture,' O'Brien said. 'I'm furious with you for bringing those two punk kids with you.'

'We thought they were with you,' said Bob.

It turned out they were a couple of junkies who had walked in off the street. They just followed us into the screening room.

---

21 DECEMBER 1984

Dream One finally opened in Paris. Several very good reviews, a rave in *Libération*, the others were mild and kind. Claude had very little money for advertising. The business is very poor. Everyone is disappointed.

1 FEBRUARY 1985

The dubbing theatre at Twickenham has an excellent reputation. The two sound mixers, Gerry Humphreys and Robin
O'Donoghue are very quick and sensitive. Ron Davis's soundtrack is subtle and evocative. All those nights he spent in the
jungle recording stereo atmospheres have paid off. It is at this
stage that the picture finally emerges. It is very exciting. The
soundtrack heightens the visual textures and the looped dialogue dramatically improves the performances. The film has
a visceral, sensual quality, and is very intense. The music
seems to grow out of the sounds of the forest and subside back
into them, just as we had hoped.

3 FEBRUARY 1985

In between dubbing I drive down to Technicolor's lab, near
London Airport. Philippe has been over from Paris several
times for the 'grading' or 'timing' of the film. This involves
setting the exact colour balance and light density of each of
the 1,000 shots in the movie.

Film is composed of three separate layers of emulsion, each
one sensitive to one of three primary colours. By combining
these in different degrees it is possible to achieve any hue or
colour shading. It always requires three or four printings over
several weeks to reach a satisfactory result. When this is
achieved, the colour and density information for each shot is
recorded on a punch tape that subsequently runs with the
negative to produce the same results for each print. In practice
the prints never come out exactly the same, because any var-
iation in the chemical bath will alter the outcome.

We have not yet got it right, but it is close enough for the
previews.

24 FEBRUARY 1985 *EN ROUTE: DALLAS–LOS ANGELES*

With two prints fresh from Technicolor, I arrived in Washington for the first sneak previews. We are testing three

different language versions. Even at this stage, the problem is still unresolved. We showed a version where the Indians speak English, and an experimental one that has them speaking in Tupi, with an English translation 'shadowing' it. The 'shadow' is delivered in the actor's own voice. A third, subtitled version, was delayed by technical failures at Technicolor. Michael Dryhurst will bring that out in time for the San Diego sneaks next weekend.

Ed Gross came in, as did a phalanx of Embassy people: Alan Horn, the President, Norman Lear, the co-owner of the company, David Weitzner, the Head of Marketing, Jake Eberts, Joe Sugar, Head of Distribution, and six or seven others. Jerry Perenchio is in bed with back trouble. They were at best cool, at worst hostile. They are extremely nervous about the picture. Despite my conciliatory meeting with Alan Horn, a cautious, mutual suspicion hovers in the air. They are hardly on speaking terms with Jake, whom they consider in my camp rather than theirs.

We played the two versions side by side in a multi-complex theatre in Sweetwater, a suburban shopping centre outside Washington. The previews were organized by a marketing expert called Alan Freeman. He is sharp, clever, and very experienced. His researchers have been out in shopping malls, schools, and other public places, offering invitations to a selection of people that represent, by age, sex, income and education, the average movie audience.

After all this time, the moment finally comes when I must set the film before an audience. The anxiety level was almost unendurable. I paced up and down at the back. I felt wired to every member of the audience. I could sense every thought and feeling. It was agony. Every time someone left to go to the toilet or buy popcorn, my heart sank, thinking they were walking out.

Alan Freeman collated the cards afterwards and we convened for a post mortem. The 'shadow' version proved too much of a strain. They could not understand Rui, who has so many important lines. They missed a lot of Eduardo Conde's (Werner) too. On the other hand, they found the English version damaging to the credibility of the story.

They loved everything to do with the Indian lore and life. They described the film as a unique experience, they enjoyed being taken into another world. They loved Charley. They totally rejected the scene where Tommy returns and meets his mother. They resented it as holding up what they perceived to be the narrative: Tommy getting Markham's help in freeing Kachiri and the girls. Altogether the scene just asks too much of the audience. Coming so close to the end, it has a disastrous effect on their appreciation of the film. The card scores came out a little below average. The audience taught me a lot. There are all kinds of changes I want to make, ways I can make the film sharper and clearer.

The North suburbs of Dallas, where we made the second test, is a vast tract of flat farmland that has been brutally transformed into a new city. It is just a huge, concrete car park connected by freeways and interrupted by tower office blocks in bold, daring shapes, mostly of glass. The heart of this new town is a ten-acre covered shopping centre. All these shopping malls have modern, multiplex film theatres.

These centres are built speculatively and their presence encourages houses and condominiums to mushroom around them. It is extraordinary, bringing my Amazonian Indians to such a place. The office towers bestride the landscape, going on and on for miles and miles, hundreds of them. They gleam, sending off sun flares – blinding, beautiful, arrogant. It is like driving through the tombstones of a doomed race, the kings of capitalism, perhaps. They are surely finer than any pyramids, sepulchres, monuments of the past.

---

3 MARCH 1985 *EN ROUTE: SAN DIEGO–LONDON*

In San Diego we played the subtitled version with the offending apartment scene heavily edited. To our surprise, there was no resistance or adverse comment about the subtitles. There has never been a major US release of a picture in this form. It was so successful that Embassy are wholly in favour of it.

We tested in two different locations, Friday and Saturday. The reception was very heartening. The audience at last understood everything. The humour emerged. The cards showed a significant improvement in the score ratings, taking us way above average. The combination of subtitles and the editing of the apartment scene have transformed our results. Alan Freeman regards the cards as only a crude guide and puts more credence on the telephone interviews his researchers make the following day to a sample of 100 people from each audience. They quiz each person for twenty minutes or so, and get a more considered and natural response. In the cards, they are asked to rate the film: excellent; extremely good; very good; good; fair; poor.

The more discriminating and educated people are loath to score, 'excellent', which they might consider should apply only to Shakespeare and Mozart. At the other end of the scale, the cruder types, if they like it at all, probably just plump for 'excellent'.

We have had the report from the telephone interviews in Dallas and Washington. They indicate strongly that people respond favourably to the Indian culture, to the environment of the rain forest, and to the mystery and the underlying themes.

Embassy's view up to then had been to underplay the Indian element in the advertising since they believed it would not attract an audience. They wanted to sell the film on action. This made me nervous. Although we have plenty of action, it is not out-and-out action like *Raiders of the Lost Ark*. It is fatal to promise audiences something you cannot deliver, yet it is done all the time.

In Los Angeles we had a series of meetings on marketing, distribution, advertising, publicity. The poster ideas David Weitzner presented were mostly on the action theme, and, based on the preview results, there was no resistance to discarding them.

Over all the meetings hung the shadow of Weitzner's departure. There was a lot of furtive comings and goings to and from the meetings. Finally, they announced David's resignation and named his successor, Martin Rabinovitz.

He came in from New York and met us in San Diego. I liked him right away. He is a Canadian. He was surprisingly confident and relaxed for someone entering such a fraught and volatile situation. He was genuinely overwhelmed by the film and, of course, had the benefit of seeing it for the first time in its most acceptable form with an appreciative audience.

The final meeting last night after the 'sneak' was quite extraordinary. All the Embassy people are immensely encouraged by the reception the film is getting. Alan Horn has fallen in love with the picture. Joe Sugar has become a believer. Suddenly they are getting behind it. Rabinovitz's arrival and appreciation of the film has been a focus for the others. We laid plans for the opening of the film. It will be July with 1,000 prints. For the first time we are working in harmony. There is a new spirit.

The Embassy people were right about the apartment scene, which I had completely misjudged. Seeing it with an audience made that clear to me. I had always regarded it as the heart of the movie – Tommy's reconciliation with his mother and her finally being able to release him. I was wrong. Its failure lies partly in the way the scene is executed, but mostly in its structural position in the film. The audience is so caught up in the urgent dilemma of the tribe at this point that they can spare no sympathy for Jean. I have thought out a much simpler way of achieving that reconciliation and I will recut it in London.

I am relieved it is all over. Our hopes are high now.

While we were in Los Angeles, Jerry Perenchio summoned Jake to his home, where he is prostrate with disc trouble. He told Jake he wanted to terminate their relationship. They are settling his three-year contract and he is no longer with Embassy. I fear the battles he fought on my behalf created his rift with Embassy. Without Jake, *The Emerald Forest* would probably not exist. As we travelled the country we saw *The Killing Fields* playing everywhere, garlanded with Oscar nominations, another picture initiated by Jake in his Goldcrest days.

7 MARCH 1985

I have made all the alterations to the picture. It now runs under two hours. I had a call from Alan Freeman with the results of the telephone interviews from San Diego. He was very excited. Many people revised their rating of the film upwards. This is very unusual, he says, and augurs well for word-of-mouth recommendations.

13 MARCH 1985

I have just reread this diary. Today I must deliver it to the publisher. What strikes me most strongly is how the movie-making process touches the modern world at so many points, this film particularly so. We deal with money and imagination, technology and relationships. We link different parts of the world, several nationalities. We use carpenters with their hammers and saws, as well as electronics experts. The script stage is private and contemplative. Shooting is public and extrovert.

Everything gets into the movie. Films are witnesses and testaments to their times. All the anger and love, the pain, the ambition – everything felt during the making – seeps into the celluloid.

When I started out making movies I used to feel guilty that craftsmen were using good timber to construct my fantasies when they could be building homes. There is a terrible arrogance about taking these resources and converting them into shadows, into nothing.

The Indians, with their music, dance and ritual, are constantly striving to escape their material lives into the spirit world. In making a movie we take the material elements of our society and transmute them into a stream of light flowing on to a wall, hoping that it will contain something of *our* spirit.

As Takuma said, he and I do much the same work.

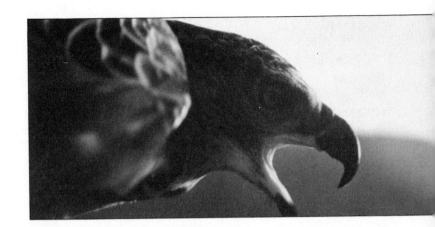